European Review of Service Economics and Management

2020 – 2, n° 10

European Review of Service Economics and Management

Revue européenne d'économie et management des services

PARIS
CLASSIQUES GARNIER
2020

The *European Review of Service Economics and Management (ERSEM)* is an international pluridisciplinary Journal devoted to services studies in the field of economics and management. Papers can be submitted in English or in French. The journal is led by an editorial board bringing together economists and management scientists who were involved in the thematic series "Économie et Gestion des Services" (EGS) of the Journal "Économies et Sociétés". Keeping the editorial policy unchanged, it continues EGS which ceased publication in September 2015.

The *European Review of Service Economics and Management* is devoted to those activities that constitute the main sources of employment and wealth in contemporary economies. ERSEM publishes original high-quality contributions that aim at improving our knowledge of service activities, on the theoretical and empirical as well as on the managerial and public policy viewpoint. It also publishes, in a "Debate and Viewpoints" section, shorter articles which develop personal viewpoints addressing specific economic, policy or management issues regarding services. The Journal covers any type of service activity: market and non-market but also services within manufacturing firms. It has no thematic boundary.

ERSEM is simultaneously published in paper format and in an electronic version available through the website of Classiques Garnier.

Papers should not exceed 70,000 characters (including notes and spaces). Author's name, affiliation and full contact details (postal address, telephone, Email) should be provided. Submitted articles should include a title, an abstract (maximum 900 characters including spaces), and main keywords.

Papers should be submitted by Email (in Word format) to:
ersem@univ-Lille.fr

See the editorial guidelines on the journal's website:
http://ersem.univ-lille1.fr

La *Revue européenne d'économie et management des services* est une revue internationale pluridisciplinaire, qui publie en français ou en anglais des articles d'économie et de gestion sur le thème des services. Elle est portée par un comité éditorial constitué d'économistes et de gestionnaires issus de l'ancienne série « Économie et Gestion des Services » (EGS) de la revue « Économies et Sociétés ». En maintenant une ligne éditoriale inchangée, elle prend la suite de EGS qui a cessé de paraître en septembre 2015.

La *Revue européenne d'économie et management des services* est une revue dédiée aux activités qui constituent les sources principales de richesse et d'emplois dans les économies contemporaines. *La REEMS* accueille toute contribution originale de qualité qui permet d'améliorer nos connaissances des services, sur le plan théorique et empirique, mais aussi managérial et en termes de politique publique. Elle publie également, dans une rubrique « Débats et points de vue », des articles courts, qui développent un point de vue personnel sur une question d'économie, de politique économique ou de management des services. La revue couvre l'ensemble des activités de services : qu'il s'agisse de services marchands ou non marchands ou de services internes aux firmes industrielles. Elle ne connaît aucune limite thématique.

REEMS est publiée sous forme papier et électronique. Elle est mise en ligne sur le site des Classiques Garnier.

Les propositions d'articles ne devront pas excéder 70 000 signes (notes et espaces compris). Outre une identification des auteurs (adresse postale, téléphone, Email), elles devront comprendre : un titre, un résumé inférieur à 900 signes (espaces compris) et quelques mots clés.

Les projets doivent être adressés par courrier électronique
(en format Word) à l'adresse Email suivante :
ersem@univ-Lille.fr

Voir les consignes éditoriales sur le site web de la revue :
http://ersem.univ-lille1.fr

ISBN 978-2-406-11027-9
ISSN 2497-0107

CONTENTS

ARTICLES

DEBATES AND VIEWPOINTS

SOMMAIRE

ARTICLES

DÉBATS ET POINTS DE VUE

ARTICLES

RE-DESIGN OF SERVICE SYSTEMS BASED ON EMPLOYEE SATISFACTION, CUSTOMER SATISFACTION AND LABOUR PRODUCTIVITY

Takeshi Takenaka[a],
Hiroshi Nishikoori[b],
Nariaki Nishino[c],
Kentaro Watanabe[a]
[a]National Institute of Advanced
Industrial Science and Technology
(AIST)
[b]MS & Consulting, Co. Ltd,
[c]The University of Tokyo

INTRODUCTION

Improved productivity of the service sector, which employs many workers and which accounts for a great part of GDP, has been a crucially important objective for over a decade in many mature economies undergoing rapid change in economic structures. Earlier studies of Japan have revealed lower labour productivity and lower total factor productivity of the service sector than those of other countries such as the United States (Morikawa, 2007). Additionally, some service sector difficulties, such as lower investment in information and technology (Fukao, 2015) and long working hours (Morikawa, 2010), have been indicated as factors contributing to low productivity. Based on results of those earlier economic studies, the Japanese government has cast productivity improvement of service sectors as the most important issue from the mid-2000s to the present. Nevertheless, it remains difficult for service industries to adopt or even identify the most effective modes of operation for their businesses. Productivity improvement is often discussed as a positive change in output (value or profit) per unit of input (cost and labour). Roughly speaking, along with growth of chain-store operation systems, the scale of retail and restaurant companies has developed in the 1970s and 1980s in developed countries. High productivity was achieved through improvement of input efficiency based on scale merits. Additionally, well-standardized and efficient service provision systems and low prices for customers have been sources of competitiveness. However, in subsequent decades, severe worldwide price competition depressed company profitability. What is worse, such competition often depressed labour productivity and quality of services. Specifically in the case of Japan, restaurant industries have been adversely affected during this decade by severe labour shortages. It has become increasingly difficult to maintain service quality. Moreover, workers of younger generations tend to dislike working for service industries such as the restaurant industry because of their bad reputations of job conditions and high employee turnover rates. Accordingly, major Japanese restaurant chains have recently become interested in introducing new technologies including robotics, food-processing machines, or self-check-out systems to maintain their levels of service with fewer employees. Although automation might be desirable for jobs that should not necessarily be done by humans, employee skills and motivation to work are expected to constitute the basis of high service quality and high customer satisfaction. Additionally, increasing costs of labour and natural resources compel restaurant companies to shift to high-value-added business models. Therefore, strategies of service productivity improvement should be reconsidered from pursuing efficiency to enhancing the value of services provided by employees. Nevertheless, it is often difficult for service companies to predict how a change in the business model will affect customer and employee satisfaction and how productivity will be changed.

Given that background, we have tackled various difficulties related to service productivity improvement to support service industries from a service engineering viewpoint. Service engineering, an inter-disciplinary research field developed especially in Japan from the early 2000s, aims to realize service ecosystems to create value (Watanabe et al., 2016;

Watanabe, Mochimaru, 2017; Ueda *et al.*, 2017) through observation, analysis, design, and application of services. Analysis of service systems using quantitative and computational approaches is done widely in service engineering. Service value should be evaluated in terms of social aspects and multiple perspectives such as customer satisfaction, employee satisfaction, efficiency, and profitability (Takenaka, Nishino, 2017).

Figure 1 presents value aspects from important stakeholders (customer, employee, company (management) and society) and their representative key performance indicators. Although this figure might be an oversimplification, this representation has often been examined in service studies exploring the *services triangle* or the *service marketing triangle* (Kotler, 1994, 2008). Moreover, the *service–profit chain* proposed by Heskett *et al.* (1997, 2008) is a well-known model showing that increased employee satisfaction (ES) positively affects consumer satisfaction (CS), and eventually improves company profitability. Many researchers have tried to verify the service–profit chain theory using quantitative data (Chi, Gursoy, 2009; Hogreve *et al.*, 2017). In addition, the value of services should be evaluated from the perspective of sustainable development goals (SDGs) such as gender equality (goal 5), decent work, economic growth (goal 8) and responsible consumption and production (goal 12) (World Health Organization, 2015). Recently, many companies have begun to realize that addressing SDGs can be expected to improve customer and employee engagement.

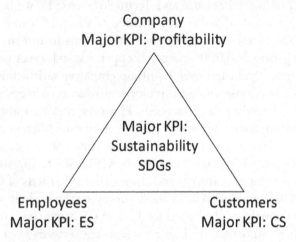

FIG. 1 – Services triangle and representative key performance indicators (KPI).

Nevertheless, establishing common and standardized numerical indicators to evaluate various aspects of services is often difficult. Additionally, building a computational model based on analysis of relationships among different indicators requires collection of data on a large scale across companies or industries. For this purpose, we have developed indicators of CS and ES in collaboration with a research company.

Given that background, this paper presents efforts at standardizing ES and CS indicators. Results of analyses of company performance using those indicators and management indexes are presented. Then, a theoretical service model is constructed from a game theoretic viewpoint considering employee, customer and company players. Finally, simulation results are shown. They illustrate the effects of human resource strategies considering the pay structure for service management.

1. DEVELOPMENT OF STANDARDIZED EVALUATION INDICATORS FOR SERVICES

Through more than four years of collaboration in a research project involving MS & Consulting Co. Ltd. and the National institute of Advanced Industrial Science and Technology (AIST), we have strived to develop a standardized survey method of ES and CS and evaluation criteria. The former is a major marketing consulting firm in Japan, conducting over 200,000 mystery shopper research cases per year. In all, they have conducted over 1 million employee satisfaction surveys. Mystery shopper programs and employee satisfaction surveys are usually customized according to client needs. However, they have also designed some questions for evaluating performance among different companies in the same business categories or among different service industries. Through research collaboration with AIST, MS & Consulting Co. Ltd. have developed common and standardized methods of CS and ES surveys. This paper introduces those survey methods along with some examples of analyses conducted for ES and CS using those indicators.

Another important indicator to evaluate services is profitability or productivity from a management viewpoint. We have collected management data such as sales, profitability, labour cost, and labour productivity, along with further collaboration with restaurant and retail companies. Using those data, we have also examined relations among ES, CS, and profitability. Nevertheless, it is often difficult to compare those management indicators among companies with different business models. This paper presents a case of a Japanese apparel company that shows a positive relation between the ES level of apparel shops and year-on-year sales (Nishikoori *et al.*, 2018).

1.1. EMPLOYEE SATISFACTION SURVEY AND STANDARDIZED INDICATORS

This section introduces the ES survey method, based on earlier studies (Nishikoori *et al.*, 2018), which we developed using data of 96,600 employees. Questionnaire items for ES surveys were designed originally by MS & Consulting Co. Ltd. based on some earlier studies of employees' job satisfaction, including "servant leadership theory" originally proposed by Greenleaf (Greenleaf, 2002; Parris, Peachey, 2013), Herzberg's two-factor theory of work motivation (Herzberg *et al.*,1959), and psychological ownership theories (Heskett, 2008). They used about 45 questionnaire items as common items with some items added depending on the survey. However, it was necessary to reconstruct questionnaire items to standardize ES survey methods from statistical viewpoints and from universality of questionnaire items. Although ES survey methods of many types exist, they sometimes ask about different aspects of employee satisfaction. For example, in a single survey, employees might evaluate their satisfaction on different aspects such as satisfaction with leaders, teamwork, team members, job conditions, or the perceived worth of their own jobs. Therefore, authors have tested questionnaire items statistically based on a psychological scale development method. Through trial-and-error adjustment, we reduced the number of questionnaire items so that they could be categorized into some important and different categories with good universality. At present, we use 36 questionnaire items as common questions. For this method, we categorized questions into two groups in advance related to the satisfaction with the work environment and satisfaction with work itself (Tables 1 and 2). Then those questions were categorized into five groups related to Leadership, Team hospitality, Team capability, Job autonomy, and Job Satisfaction.

TAB. 1 – Results of factor analysis using questions for work environment evaluation: n = 96 600, 128 companies, factorization (ML, Kaiser, Promax).

Factor	Questions	Factor 1	Factor 2	Factor 3	α
Factor 1 (Leadership)	Trust	0.907	0	-0.072	0.945
	Clear vision	0.853	-0.051	0.03	
	Empathy for vision	0.833	0.009	-0.015	
	Effective advice	0.833	0.032	-0.043	
	Consistency of words and action	0.823	-0.051	0.052	
	Careful listening	0.794	0.064	-0.083	
	Clear plans	0.786	-0.048	0.102	
	Interest in members	0.71	0.116	-0.067	
	Communication	0.662	-0.051	0.15	
Factor 2 (Team hospitality)	Mutual care for co-workers	-0.069	0.963	-0.15	0.872
	Awareness of co-workers' growth	-0.064	0.738	0.14	
	Hospitality for customers	-0.043	0.719	0.071	
	Personal relationships	0.116	0.671	-0.073	
	Sharing vision	0.145	0.514	0.21	
Factor 3 (Team capability)	Capability of performance	-0.051	-0.01	0.896	0.879
	Ability to accomplish	-0.062	0.003	0.889	
	Proactive expression	0.12	0.267	0.399	
	Benchmarking	0.186	0.162	0.393	
	Frequency of meetings	0.219	0.077	0.375	
	Environment to enhance good points	0.172	0.304	0.322	

TAB. 2 – Results of factor analysis using questions for job satisfaction evaluation: n = 96 600, 128 companies, factorization (ML, Kaiser, Promax).

Factor		Factor 1	Factor 2	α
Factor 1 (Job satisfaction)	Working is worthwhile	0.839	0.036	0.906
	Sense of belonging	0.807	-0.08	
	Intention of recommendation	0.737	-0.029	
	Physical and mental health	0.725	-0.073	
	Sense of achievement	0.648	0.181	
	Appropriate assessment	0.506	0.166	
	Sense of growth	0.438	0.34	
	Pride in one's own job	0.424	0.408	
	Motivation for improvement	0.389	0.255	
Factor 2 (Job autonomy)	Sense of influence	-0.035	0.78	0.853
	Sense of meaningfulness	0.046	0.743	
	Sense of responsibility	0.035	0.71	
	Sense of decision-making	0	0.649	
	Proposals for improvement	-0.052	0.533	
	Sense of customer satisfaction	0.188	0.53	
	Clear division of roles	0.106	0.495	

Figure 2 shows normalized scores (Z score) of Bartlett scores of five factors according to some business categories. The score is calculated using 96 600 employee data. Comparison among industries reveals overall tendencies in ES indicators. In this case, restaurant-chain companies, for example, have high scores in all five aspects of ES. Actually, this result was helpful for the Japanese restaurant industry group, which had been concerned about unwarranted rumours related to working conditions. We were specifically concerned about low ES levels of drugstores, supermarkets, hair salons, and business hotels because those industries were fundamentally appreciated by consumers in Japan for convenience. Although details are not presented herein, the results of mystery shopper programs for the same companies of retail companies sometimes show high CS levels. Those gaps between higher CS and lower ES might reflect long-term instability of service systems.

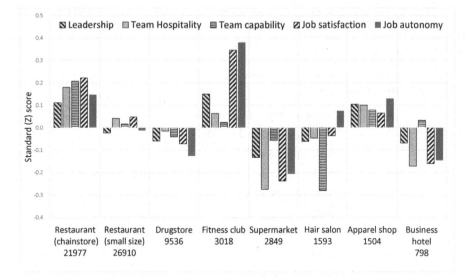

FIG. 2 – Employee satisfaction with service industries
shown by number of employees.

1.2. CUSTOMER SATISFACTION INDICATORS ACQUIRED
THROUGH MYSTERY SHOPPER PROGRAMS

Customer satisfaction has been investigated intensively in consumer
and marketing studies (Hennig-Thurau, Klee, 1997). Some indicators
are already used as standards in many countries. The Swedish Customer
Satisfaction barometer, for example, is the first common indicator
to measure more than 30 industries in Sweden (Fornell, 1992). The
American Customer Satisfaction Index might be the most well-known
index (Fornell, 1996). The method has been applied to many countries
for large-scale surveys of customer satisfaction, even in Asian countries
such as Japan, Korea and Singapore. Although the definition and relation between satisfaction and loyalty still presents difficulties (Dick
and Basu, 1994), some key questionnaire items are commonly used to
evaluate customer loyalty. For example, intentions for repeat purchase
or intentions of recommendation to others are widely used indexes that
represent customer loyalty to services.

Apart from questionnaire survey methods of customer satisfaction targeting general consumers, mystery shopping (or mystery shopper programs) has also become popular in marketing research to assess service quality and some aspects of customer satisfaction (Wilson, 2001). In Japan, mystery shopper programs are popular as marketing research to improve service quality in many service industries including restaurants, retail outlets, beauty salons, amusement parks, and gas stations. By mystery shopping, well-trained mystery guests visit a shop and report details of services using a pre-designed checklist that includes required items to keep service qualities that the company specified. Additionally, mystery guests are often asked about their satisfaction using some questionnaire items including satisfaction with food quality, atmosphere, hospitality, price and intention of a repeat purchase or recommendation to others.

As described above, MS & Consulting Co. Ltd. conducts over 200,000 mystery shopper research cases per year in Japan. We have strived to standardize CS and have calculated the average and standard deviation of results for all results of mystery shopping. Through those efforts to normalize scores of CS using some different indicators, one can compare performance among different shops of a single company or among companies in the same industry.

Figure 3 presents an example comparing performances of three restaurant companies of CS using mystery shopping. The mystery shopping surveys are conducted 69, 342, and 77 times, respectively, for the shops of restaurant companies A, B, and C. The averaged scores were used to denote companies' performance. The Z score is calculated using all mystery shopping results on restaurants for a certain period. Through such comparisons, companies were able to ascertain their strong and weak points in business.

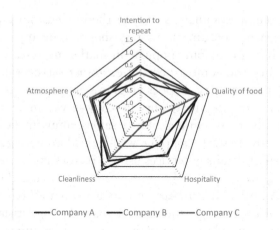

FIG. 3 – Comparison of CS using Z scores for three restaurant stores.

1.3. RELATION BETWEEN CS AND ES

Some companies that have conducted mystery shopping surveys also conduct ES surveys for their employees. Table 3 shows relations between CS and ES for 48 restaurant companies from October 2016 through September 2017. Although the numbers of mystery shopping surveys and employee satisfaction surveys vary among companies, an average of 832 employees were surveyed for employee satisfaction and 588 mystery shopping surveys were conducted for each company. Table 3 shows some CS items that are correlated significantly with ES factors. Especially, "Job autonomy" correlates significantly with three CS items: "Intention to recommend", "Satisfaction with food", and "Satisfaction with hospitality". This result suggests that autonomous and confident employees could enhance CS. This also supports the service-profit chain theory (Heskett, 2008). Furthermore, "Satisfaction with hospitality" correlates with three factors: "Job satisfaction", "Team hospitality", and "Job autonomy". Especially, "Job satisfaction" which is strongly related to employee loyalty to the company as shown in Table 2 could be enhanced by CS. These results suggest not only that high ES enhances CS, but also that high CS enhances ES. Based on those findings, we propose a theoretical service model constructed from a game theoretic viewpoint, in which an employee player can acquire some sort of satisfaction from CS in addition to salary as described in the next section.

Figure 4 shows a plot of the normalized score of Job satisfaction (ES) and Satisfaction with hospitality by company (CS). Overall, significant correlation was found between these two indicators, as shown in Table 3, but some outliers are also observed. Results might show that ES is not connected to CS and vice versa. Through such analyses, individual companies can also learn about their service models.

TAB. 3 – Correlation coefficient matrix showing ES and CS
in 48 restaurant companies (*, p<0.05; **, p<0.01).

	Leadership	Team capability	Team hospitality	Job autonomy	Job satisfaction
Intention to repeat	0.26	0.06	0.27	0.28	0.22
Intention to recommend	0.30*	0.11	0.28	0.34*	0.26
Satisfaction with food	0.34*	0.24	0.15	0.32*	0.19
Satisfaction with hospitality	0.28	0.07	0.39**	0.37*	0.40**

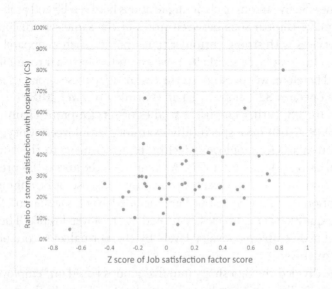

FIG. 4 – Plot of Z score of job satisfaction and ratio of strong satisfaction by company.

1.4. RELATION BETWEEN ES AND PROFITABILITY

As Heskett *et al.* (1997, 2008) pointed out for service–profit chain theory, many service companies that provide customer service such as restaurants or retail shops have clear awareness that ES engenders higher CS, which in turn engenders higher profits. Many studies have examined how increasing customer satisfaction can stimulate future consumption or increase willing-to-pay premium prices, which in turn can increase the profitability of service firms (Mittal, Kamakura, 2001; Andersen *et al.*, 1994). However, it is often difficult to find a direct relation between the level of employee satisfaction and profitability among different companies because business models vary according to companies, even in the same business category. For, example, Yee *et al.* (2008) used data of 206 service shops in Hong Kong to present empirical evidence that ES plays a significant role in enhancing the operational performance of organizations in the high-contact service sector. In the study, they asked the shop persons to assess their shop's profitability relative to industry norms using subjective evaluation. Although that is one effective means of comparing profitability among companies, more quantitative means of assessing the relation between ES and profitability are desired from a management perspective.

One effective means of clarifying relations between ES and profitability is to make comparisons between stores of the same service company. For services with strong customer touch points, such as apparel shops, the level of employee satisfaction was found to have a strong effect on sales. Therefore, we investigated the case of a Japanese apparel company which operates 825 shops in Japan (Nishikoori *et al.*, 2018).

As for ES, earlier empirical studies of service-profit chain (Yee *et al.*, 2008, 2010) have specifically examined employee loyalty, which refers to a service employee's feeling of attachment to the employer organization (McCarthy, 1997). Among the indicators of ES presented in section 1.1, "worthwhileness of working", "sense of belonging" and "intention of recommendation" are included as job satisfaction factors. These questions are also closely related to employee loyalty. Therefore, we defined "employee loyalty level" by the normalized score of those three questions.

We divided the 825 shops into five groups based on "employee loyalty level": Top 10% employee loyalty level as Rank-S; the next 20%

as Rank-A; the next 40% as Rank-B; the next 20% as Rank-C; and the bottom 10% as Rank-D. Table 4 presents an example of results reflecting the relation between the employee loyalty rank of apparel shops and year-on-year sales. Results show that sales of rank S shops increased the most among all ranks. We also found that sales of rank D shops did not increase compared to those of other groups. Certainly, the apparel shop sales are influenced by product popularity, but all shops of the same company sell almost identical goods. For that reason, the relationships with customers and skills to recommend attractive clothes are important points related to improved sales.

Whereas analyses using year-over-year sales per store are insufficient, we are interested in identifying how increasing an individual's ES can contribute to enhancement of labour productivity. In future studies, we would like to clarify details of the relation between productivity or value added by each employee and CS and ES using more detailed data. Through such analyses, we aim to build a computable model of the service system. The next section proposes a generalized service system considering CS, ES, and profitability based on the empirical findings presented above.

TAB. 4 – Year-on-year sales at an apparel company for respective loyalty ranks.

Employee loyalty Rank	Year-on-year sales (2018/03)
Rank S	+13.6%
Rank A	+8.6%
Rank B	+9.1%
Rank C	+9.4%
Rank D	+4.1%

2. MODEL FORMULATION
AS A GENERALIZED SERVICE SYSTEM

This section presents a proposal of a theoretical service model constructed from a game theoretic viewpoint according to empirical data of CS, ES, and profitability. As described in the previous section, employees and customers share mutual relations. For that reason, we use the idea of game theory, treating interdependent decision-making situations mathematically. Then, based on findings presented in the previous section, we construct a simplified model formulated within the game theory framework comprising players of three kinds: managers, employees, and customers. Details of the model are explained in the following subsections.

2.1. FORMULATION OF A SERVICE

To formulate a service, we make the fundamental assumption that a service is defined by some key factors which can dictate its quality and customer satisfaction. For example, in the restaurant industry, factors such as food quality, server hospitality, and restaurant atmosphere can strongly affect the entire service quality and customer satisfaction related to consumption of the service. According to this idea, we express one service as a tuple of some factors such as $(r_1, r_2, \ldots)$, wherein we designate r_i as a "resource" as a generalized notion. In the model, the resources are supposed to be decision variables determined by a manager player or an employee player.

Now, we generally formulate a service S as

$$s = (r_1, r_2, \cdots r_k) \in R_1 \times R_2 \times \cdots \times R_k \equiv R,$$

where R represents a Cartesian product of each resource set R_i. Herein k denotes the number of resources. Additionally, to express the same service, we occasionally use another form as well: $s = (s_M, s_E)$. It signifies, for instance, that resources are separated into the manager's side and employee's side as $s_M = (r_1, \cdots, r_i) \in S_M$ and $s_E = (r_{i+1}, \cdots r_k) \in S_E$.

2.2. MANAGER PLAYER (COMPANY PLAYER)

The model has multiple manager players who independently run a business supplying some service to the market. The set of manager players is M. For convenience, a service business that a manager player $m \in M$ runs is simply called service business m. Each manager player makes decisions about managerial issues to maximize profit. For simplicity, we assume that each decides a service price $p \in \mathbb{R}$ and employee pay $w \in \mathbb{R}$ and the resources of service $s_M \in S_M$. Then the manager m payoff function is defined as

$$\pi_m(p, w, s_M) = p\, Q_m(s_M, s_E, p) - c_m(w, s_M)_,$$

where $Q_m(\cdot)$ and $c_m(\cdot)$ respectively signify the number of service users and the total cost for running the service business. Therein, $Q_m(s_M, s_E, p)$ represents a demand function under which a service (s_M, s_E) is provided at price p, which is the aggregation of respective customer player's decisions. As described later (subsection 2.4), a customer is defined as a player who makes a decision of whether to consume a service, or not. Therefore, $Q_m(\cdot)$ represents the sum of customers who decide to consume the service.

2.3. EMPLOYEE PLAYER

The model has multiple employee players, each of whom works in a service business. An employee player provides a service directly to a customer. The set of employee players in service business m is defined as E_m. Each employee player makes decisions about the resources of service s_E to maximize the employee's own benefit. This decision of selecting $s_E \in S_E$ can represent an effort to acquire skill and knowledge through employee education or by other means. That effort incurs some sort of cost.

The payoff function of an employee player $e \in E_m$ in service business $m \in M$ is

$$\pi_e^m(s_E) = ES_e^m(w^m, CS_e^m(s_M, s_E)) - c_e^m(s_E)_,$$

where $ES_e^m(\cdot)$ stands for the employee satisfaction of employee e, w^m expresses the pay that manager m has decided to give the employee, and c_e^M represents the cost. Also, $CS_e^m(\cdot)$ stands for the total customer satisfaction felt by customers to whom employee e has provided a service. As one might infer, $CS_e^m(\cdot)$ is a function of $s = (s_M, s_E)$.

The most characteristic point of this model is that an employee can acquire some sort of satisfaction from CS in addition to salary. Based on empirical analysis of ES as introduced in the previous section, a feeling of job meaningfulness or a sense of customer satisfaction can enhance an important point of ES: job autonomy. Although service–profit chain theory emphasizes the influence of ES on CS, the model explicitly includes the fact that CS can also enhance ES.

2.4. CUSTOMER PLAYER

Multiple customer players exist in the model. The set of customer players is C. The role of customer players is simply to enjoy a service by paying a service price. However, because of "heterogeneity" as a characteristic of services, customer satisfaction varies depending on the service context. To address that feature, we formulate customer satisfaction of a customer player $c \in C$ as a sort of real-valued function.

$$CS_c: R \times E \to \mathbb{R}$$

Therein, E stands for the set of all employee players. That is, $E \equiv \bigcup_{m \in M} E_m$. Accordingly, CS_c above can represent a service context, meaning that even if the same service is provided, a different employee can alter its context. Therefore, the satisfaction can differ. Furthermore, this mapping of CS_c differs depending on customers, so that subscript $c \in C$ is assigned. This differentiation also represents an aspect of heterogeneity.

For the model, we assume that each player chooses a service business m from its set M, or that a player does not consume any service. Or rather, for some situations, each player might directly choose an employee $e \in E_m$ in service business m as a service provider. Thereby, we define the payoff function of a customer player $c \in C$ as shown below.

$$\pi_c(e) = \begin{cases} CS_c(s, e) - p, & \text{(if consuming a service)} \\ 0, & \text{(if no consumption)} \end{cases}$$

Formally, when choosing a service business m without provider designation, its service provider e would be determined on a service operation basis. In that case, $\pi_c(c)$ is replaced by $\pi_c(c(m))$, wherein $c(m)$ represents a mapping of $c: M \to E$. To maximize the payoff function, a customer player $c \in C$ chooses a service business m, or an employee e directly.

A model structure overview is presented in Figure 5. Our study addresses this triangle diagram as a service system.

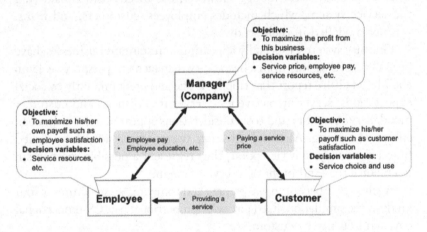

FIG. 5 – Model overview.

3. COMPUTER SIMULATION OF SERVICE SYSTEMS: REDESIGNING THE PAY STRUCTURE

This section presents description of our conduct of a numerical simulation with our model, specifically setting up parameters to replicate an empirical situation of the restaurant service business. Particularly, this simulation addresses issues of re-designing a pay structure for employees. In the retail industry, various pay structures aside from fixed wage systems such as incentive compensation or bonus programs have been introduced to motivate sales personnel to provide enhanced customer services. Incentive compensation has been studied in economics and management accounting in terms of agency theory (Basu, 1985). However, earlier studies mainly examined the structure of compensation contracts for top executives. Banker *et al.* (1996) specifically examine frontline workers of a retail company, and report on a field test of the multi-period incentive effects of a performance-based compensation plan for sales. They reported that the plan implementation is associated with increases in sales that persist and increase over time with a statistical model. However, the mechanism considering the service system, which includes employees, customers, and firms, was not modelled in their study.

Gratuity systems, especially appearing in restaurant businesses, have been discussed mainly from a hospitality management perspective. Lynn and McCal (2016) report that tipping is affected predominantly by social expectations, server attractiveness, server friendliness, and customer mood. Service quality and cost considerations appear to exert only weak effects on tipping. Although gratuity systems have not been studied from a service system viewpoint, they represent a possible mechanism to enhance the total profit of a service system.

Against that backdrop, we prepare and compare pay structures of four kinds in the simulation: fixed pay, sales-proportional pay, CS-proportional pay, and gratuity by customers.

3.1. PARAMETER SETTING

This subsection explains parameters used in the simulation, which are arranged to reflect a situation of restaurant service business.

3.1.1. Resources

In the simulation, we selected representative resources of three kinds, as shown in Table 5, which can represent fundamental factors in a restaurant service business. Therefore, a service is expressed by $s = (r_1, r_2, r_3)$. Herein, r_1 and r_2 are determined by a manager player and r_3 by an employee player.

TAB. 5 – Explanation of resources.

Variable	Meaning	Who decides?	Explanation
r_1	Food quality	Manager	Represents a level of food quality, defined as a real number $R_1 \in [50,200]$. If high, a customer is likely to obtain a high CS.
r_2	In-store atmosphere	Manager	Represents a level of in-store atmosphere, which is affected by interiors, etc. It is defined as a real number $R_2 \in [50,200]$. If high, a customer is likely to obtain a high CS.
r_3	Hospitality	Employee	Represents a level of hospitality that an employee player provides to a customer. It is defined as a real number $R_3 \in [50,200]$. If high, a customer is likely to obtain a high CS.

3.1.2. Restaurant player (manager player)

We herein designate a manager player as a "restaurant player". For the simulation, we assume that two restaurant players exist. When a restaurant player chooses (w, r_1, r_2), as a cost function, the player incurs its cost as

$$c_m(w, r_1, r_2) = f + w^m + \alpha_1 r_1 Y_m + \alpha_2 r_2,$$

where f signifies the fixed cost, Y_m represents the sales, and α_1 and α_2 respectively denote the coefficients. Employee pay w^m, which we assume with pay structures of four kinds, is explained in section 3.2. Fixed cost at the first term includes basic expenditures such as electricity and gas. The third term represents variable costs such as ingredient expenditures. The last term is also a sort of cost depending on r_2, which stands for investment expenditures for equipment, in-store interiors, etc.

Parameters related to the cost function are set as shown in Table 6. Those values are set with consideration of empirical data in chain restaurant stores provided by a company collaborating with our study.

TAB. 6 – Parameters related to restaurant players.

# of restaurants	$|M| = 2$
Fixed cost	$f = 10{,}000$
Cost coefficient for r_1	$\alpha_1 = 0.3$
Cost coefficient for r_2	$\alpha_2 = 0.2$

3.1.3. Employee player

For this simulation, we assume for simplicity that only two employee players exist at each restaurant. Then, as shown in section 2.3, each employee player has its own $ES_e^m(w^m, CS_e^m)$, which is a function of pay and customer satisfaction. Here, for a case in which service s is provided, the function is set as

$$ES_e^m(w^m, CS_e^m \mid s) = \beta_1 w^m + \beta_2 \sum_{c \in C(e)} CS_c(s, e)_,$$

where w^m represents the pay for employee e and $C(e)$ denotes the subset of the customer set $C(e) \subset C$ to whom employee player e provides a service. In addition, β_1 and β_2 are coefficients. Here, we assume employee players of two types, for whom the coefficients differ. The parameters are presented in Table 7. Type 1 signifies an employee who feels satisfaction evenly from pay and CS. A Type 2 employee does not feel satisfaction from CS. Especially for Type 2, it expresses the situation of kitchen staff because, generally in chain restaurant shops, they have no chance to have direct contact with customers. this simulation has one employee player for each type in each restaurant.

Next, the employee cost is simply set up as a linear function $c_c^m(r_3) = \beta_3 r_3$, where β_3 signifies a coefficient. This cost function means that an employee player requires some effort at service hospitality to customers. That is to say, greater effort is necessary as the hospitality level increases.

TAB. 7 – Parameters related to employee players.

	Type 1	Type 2
Coefficient for pay	$\beta_1^{T1} = 1.0$	$\beta_1^{T2} = 1.0$
Coefficient for CS	$\beta_2^{T1} = 1.0$	$\beta_2^{T2} = 0.0$
Cost coefficient	$\beta_3 = 1.0$	
# of employees in restaurants 1 and 2	$|E_1| = |E_2| = 2$	

3.1.4. Customer player

We set up 200 customer players in the simulation. As explained already in section 2.4, the customer players respectively have different $CS_c(s, e)$. For simplicity, we assume that the difference of serving employees does not affect customer satisfaction, but that the difference of service resources does affect it. Then, in a case where restaurant and employee players choose $s = (r_1, r_2, r_3)$ as resources, the customer player's CS is assumed as

$$CS_c(r_1, r_2, r_3) = \gamma_1 r_1 + \gamma_2 r_2 + \gamma_3 r_3,$$

where γ_1, γ_2, and γ_3 respectively represent coefficients. For customers of different types, these coefficients vary similarly to employee satisfaction types. Table 8 presents relevant details.

TAB. 8 – Parameters related to customer players.

	Type A	Type B	Type C
Coefficient for resource r_1	$\gamma_1^{TA} = 1.0$	$\gamma_1^{TB} = 0.0$	$\gamma_1^{TC} = 0.0$
Coefficient for resource r_2	$\gamma_2^{TA} = 0.7$	$\gamma_2^{TB} = 0.2$	$\gamma_2^{TC} = 0.1$
Coefficient for resource r_3	$\gamma_3^{TA} = 0.5$	$\gamma_3^{TB} = 0.1$	$\gamma_3^{TC} = 0.4$

3.2. PAY STRUCTURES OF FOUR KINDS

In most cases today, Japanese chain restaurants adopt a fixed pay system for employees and part-time workers: the pay amount is constant and is unaffected by employee performance. However, a trend toward reconsideration of such a fixed pay structure exists in the restaurant industry of Japan. Although it might not be realistic in some cases, the following four structures are used for the simulation.

3.2.1. Pay structure 1: Fixed pay (current)

Pay for an employee is fixed. Therefore, each employee obtains the same amount of money no matter how many customers to whom they provide a service. Thereby, the pay that an employee player e in service business m receives is described simply as shown below.

$$w_e^m = w_f^m$$

In the simulation, the restaurant players choose the constant value independently.

3.2.2. Pay structure 2: Sales-proportional pay

The amount of pay for an employee is determined as proportional to the restaurant sales. Formally, the sales goal is set. The pay increases only if the restaurant player's sales exceed the goal value. Its formula is

$$w_e^m = \begin{cases} w_f^m + a_s(Y_m - G), & (Y_m > G) \\ w_f, & (Y_m \leq G) \end{cases},$$

where Y_m signifies restaurant m sales, G represents the goal, and a_s is a coefficient. If the sale is less than the goal, then the pay is equal to that given in the case of fixed pay.

3.2.3. Pay structure 3: CS-proportional pay

The pay amount is proportional to customer satisfaction. We define its formula as

$$w_e^m = w_f^m + a_{cs}CS_e^m,$$

where CS_e^m represents the total amount of customer satisfaction that the employee player e can bring about. In addition, a_{cs} is a coefficient.

In fact, this pay structure might be unrealistic in practice because it is generally difficult to quantify the magnitude of customer satisfaction that each employee induces. In this pay structure, however, employees are expected to be motivated to behave in a manner that increases customer satisfaction.

3.2.4. Pay structure 4: Gratuity

Gratuities are used in no industry in Japan. Nevertheless, we consider this pay structure as an alternative. According to this pay structure, in addition to fixed pay, an employee can obtain additional pay directly from customers as a gratuity. The formula of employee payoff function can be described as shown below.

$$\pi_e^m = \beta_1 w_f + \beta_2 \sum_{c \in C(e)} CS_c(s,e) - \beta_3 r_3 + \sum_{c \in C(e)} t_c$$

Therein, t_c denotes the amount of gratuity that a customer player c pays. The last term is added independently of employee pay. Consequently, we regard pay from gratuity as different from ordinary pay. Comparing the case of CS-proportional pay, this pay structure can motivate employees with no additional restaurant expense.

Because a customer player tips a service provider (employee player), we re-define the customer player's payoff function as shown below.

$$\pi_c' = (1 - a_g)\pi_c$$

Therein, a_g signifies the ratio expressing how much gratuity they pay. As the formula above shows, the amount depends on the customer payoff magnitude.

The parameters are presented in Table 9. We compare the performance of service systems under the following four respective pay structures.

TAB. 9 – Parameters related to pay structure settings.

Coefficient of sales-proportional pay	$a_s = 0.3$
Coefficient of CS-proportional pay	$a_{cs} = 0.1$
Gratuity ratio	$a_g = 0.5$

3.3. DECISION-MAKING FLOW IN SIMULATION

Within the formulation presented in section 2, we run a forward simulation in which each player makes decision in a sequential manner. Figure 6 presents the decision flow of the respective players.

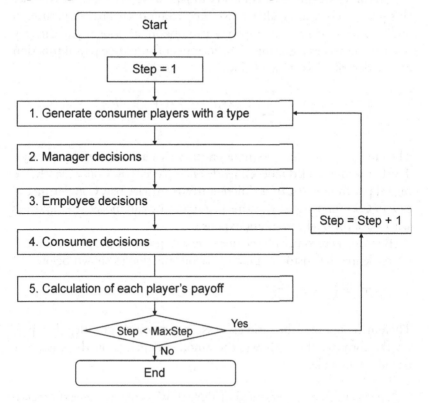

FIG. 6 – Decision flow of players in simulation.

As presented in Figure 6, the respective players choose their decisions on a step-wise and best-response basis: under the assumption that other players keep the same decision in the previous step, each player seeks the best response to maximize the payoff function. Of course, in the same step, players can observe and use information about earlier decisions than self.

However, because it is a forward decision-making process, it is not guaranteed that it always reaches Nash equilibrium. Only for customer players, are their decisions very simple: the task is to choose a service from several service businesses or not, so that rational decisions are possible. Accordingly, in simulation, 200 new customer players are added at the beginning of each step, each of whom is assigned a type A, B, or C with probability 1/3.

3.4. SIMULATION RESULTS

In the simulation, we simply modelled each player game-theoretically as taking a best response given other players' observed decisions. Simulation results are presented in Tables 10a and 10b. Results represented in the tables were averaged by data during 100 periods after convergence to the average. We separate r_3 into two values, r_3^{T1} and t_3^{T2}, for the respective employee types.

The results demonstrate that the gratuity pay system outperforms others, presenting the highest social surplus. In a gratuity case, because customer players give additional payments in addition to the service price, the payoff is presumed to be reduced. However, contrary to expectations, the customer benefit becomes larger. Furthermore, interestingly, except for the fixed-pay case, r_3^{T2} presents high values. Intuitively, because Type 2 employees do not care about customer satisfaction, it is natural to infer that r_3^{T2} is small, as in the case of a fixed pay structure. However, in those three cases, Type 2 employees chose high r_3^{T2} because of incentivized pay structures. Results imply that such pay structures can bring about good effects for employees who do not care about service hospitality.

TAB. 10a – Simulation results: average resource values.

	Fixed	Sales-proportional	CS-proportional	Gratuity
Food quality r_1	120	120	110	124
Atmosphere r_2	54	83	90	99
Type 1 employer's hospitality r_3^{T1}	193	188	191	190
Type 2 employer's hospitality r_3^{T2}	50	182	191	190

TAB. 10b – Simulation results: average payoff.

	Fixed	Sales-proportional	CS-proportional	Gratuity
Restaurant π_m	-11,652	16,222	7,810	24,797
Employee π_e	24,268	30,550	32,982	40,978
Customer π_c	8,012	16,070	12,633	19,555
Social surplus	20,628	62,842	53,426	85,330

3.5. DISCUSSION

Although the simulation model results presented above portray only a simplified perspective of services, they suggest the possibility of improving actual service, spurring companies to rethink their business models using observable indicators acquired in their services. It is often difficult for service company managers to change their business models or internal rules because they worry about whether a new business model will work or not. From an academic viewpoint, although researchers should demonstrate possibilities of enhancing productivity of services with a new service system, it is often difficult to present the probability of a proposed model because many aspects of service systems must be assessed or simulated simultaneously. Computational models of service systems based on game theory and actual data can be useful to elucidate mechanisms of complex service systems and to create new and more sustainable service systems.

CONCLUSIONS

This paper introduces a method of assessing service systems using standardized indicators representing some important aspects of computer simulation and services: CS, ES and profitability. Although our efforts at standardizing indicators related to ES, CS, and profitability are still underway, quantitative and computational approaches to elucidating service systems must be regarded as increasingly important for service research. Service industries are adversely affected by many factors, but they are expected to seek new strategies to enhance productivity considering value for consumers and employees in a sustainable fashion.

As described in this paper, the first data analysis ascertained important factors in CS as well as in ES. Additionally, the correlated relation among CS, ES, and profitability are clarified. Based on those findings, a game-theoretic model that captures a service system structure was constructed. With the model, numerical simulation compared four kinds of employee pay structures. As a result, although operating under a specific parameter set, we found an interesting result, implying that an incentivized pay structure such as that with gratuities can not only increase company profits, but also result in enhancement of the employee's provided degree of hospitality. Even for a Type 2 employee, who is modelled as a player caring little for hospitality, the hospitality level might be enhanced. This is an important implication in face-to-face type service industries such as the restaurant industries because it can invoke some sort of value co-creation situation between customers and employees.

Another interesting implication was identified through numerical simulation. The fixed pay structure case presents negative profit under a specific parameter set that we use. However, under the same parameter set, other pay structures demonstrated positive profit because the amount of pay is determined as proportional to an employee's individual performance. That finding in turns implies that if no employee provides high levels of hospitality, it leads to low demand for the service, which might pose a severe difficulty. The simulation reveals that even under a harsh environment with low demand, an appropriate pay structure might be sufficient to cope with such difficulties.

Recently, digital technologies are changing existing business models of services such as banking, transportation, e-commerce, and other customer services (Vail, 2019). However, traditional and labour-intensive service industries represented by restaurants, hotels, and nursing care services continue to struggle with diverse issues such as labour shortages, high labour costs, and increasing costs of food and natural resources. Those industries are important not only for the economy but also for maintaining the quality of life of local people. Therefore, many service companies are attempting to alter their business models to more value-added or sustainable ones. Accordingly, labour productivity and re-design of services and jobs considering employee and customer satisfaction are drawing considerable attention again.

Future studies must be undertaken through strong partnership with service companies to explore more concrete examples of the redesign of services based on multiple indicators and more realistic methods of using computational models.

REFERENCES

ANDERSON E. W., FORNELL C., LEHMANN D. R. (1994), "Customer satisfaction, market share, and profitability: Findings from Sweden", *Journal of Marketing*, vol. 58, n° 3, p. 53-66.

BANKER R. D., LEE S. Y., POTTER G. (1996), "A field study of the impact of a performance-based incentive plan", *Journal of Accounting and Economics*, vol. 21, n° 2, p. 195-226.

BASU A.K., LAI R., SRINIVASAN B., STAELIN R. (1985), "Salesforce compensation plans: An agency theoretical perspective", *Marketing Science*, vol. 4, n° 4, p. 267-291.

CHI C. G., GURSOY D. (2009), "Employee satisfaction, customer satisfaction, and financial performance: An empirical examination", *International Journal of Hospitality Management*, vol. 28, n° 2, p. 245-253.

DICK A. S., BASU K. (1994), "Customer loyalty: toward an integrated conceptual framework", *Journal of the Academy of Marketing Science*, vol. 22, n° 2, p. 99-113.

FORNELL C. (1992), "A national customer satisfaction barometer: The Swedish experience", *Journal of Marketing*, vol. 56, n° 1, p. 6-21.

FORNELL C., JOHNSON M. D., ANDERSON E. W., CHA J., BRYANT B. E. (1996), "The American customer satisfaction index: nature, purpose, and findings", *Journal of Marketing*, vol. 60, n° 4, p. 7-18.

FUKAO K., IKEUCHI K., KIM Y., HYEOG UG K. (2015), *Why Was Japan Left Behind in the ICT Revolution?*, Discussion papers 15043, Research Institute of Economy, Trade and Industry (RIETI). https://ideas.repec.org/p/eti/dpaper/15043.html (retrieved on March 2020).

GREENLEAF R. K. (2002), *Servant leadership: A journey into the nature of legitimate power and greatness*, USA: Paulist Press.

HENNIG-THURAU T., KLEE A. (1997), "The impact of customer satisfaction and relationship quality on customer retention: A critical reassessment and model development", *Psychology & Marketing*, vol. 14, n° 8, p. 737-764.

HERZBERG F., MAUSNER B., SNYDERMAN B. B. (1959), *The motivation to work*, New York: John Wiley & Sons.

HESKETT J. L., JONES T. O., LOVEMAN G. W., SEASER JR. W. E., SCHLESINGER L. A. (2008), "Putting the service-Profit Chain to Work", *Harvard Business Review*, vol. 72, n° 2, p. 164-174.

HOGREVE J., ISEKE A., DERFUSS K., ELLER T. (2017), "The Service–Profit Chain: A Meta-Analytic Test of a Comprehensive Theoretical Framework", *Journal of Marketing*, vol. 81, n° 3, p. 41-61.

JUDGE T. A., THORESEN C. J., BONO J. E., PATTON G. K. (2001), "The job satisfaction –job performance relationship: A qualitative and quantitative review", *Psychological Bulletin*, vol. 127, n° 3, p. 376-407.

KOTLER P., ARMSTRONG G. (2008), *Principles of Marketing*, 12th ed. Upper Saddle River, NJ: Pearson Education, Inc.

KOTLER P. (1994), *Marketing Management: Analysis, Planning, Implementation, and Control*, Eighth edition., Englewood Cliffs, NJ: Prentice Hall.

LYNN M. M., MCCALL M. (2016), *Beyond Gratitude and Gratuity: A Meta-Analytic Review of the Predictors of Restaurant Tipping*. Retrieved March, 2020, from Cornell University, SHA School site http://scholarship.sha. cornell.edu/workingpapers/21.

MCCARTHY D. G. (1997), *The Loyalty Link, How Loyal Employees Create Loyal Customers*, John Wiley & Sons, New York.

MITTAL V., KAMAKURA W. A. (2001), "Satisfaction, repurchase intent, and repurchase behaviour: Investigating the moderating effect of customer characteristics", *Journal of Marketing Research*, vol. 38, n° 1, p. 131-142.

MORIKAWA M. (2007), *Is productivity in the service industries low? An analysis using firm-level data on the dispersion and the dynamics of productivity*, RIETI Discussion Paper 07-J-048.

MORIKAWA M. (2010), Working Hours of Part-timers and the Measurement of Firm-level Productivity (Japanese). Research Institute of Economy, Trade and Industry (RIETI).

NISHIKOORI H., TAKENAKA T., MAEHARA N., TSUJI H., SHIBUYA U. (2018), "Effective improvement of employee satisfaction and service quality considering maturity levels of employee loyalty", in Proc. of ICServ2018, Taiwan.

PARRIS D. L., PEACHEY J. W. (2013), "A systematic literature review of servant leadership theory in organizational contexts", *Journal of Business Ethics*, vol. 113, n° 3, p. 377-393.

SASSER W. E., SCHLESINGER L. A., HESKETT J. L. (1997), *Service profit chain*, London, Simon and Schuster.

TAKENAKA T., NISHINO N. (2017), "Nature of value and emergent synthesis", Procedia CIRP 62, p. 90-93.

UEDA K., TAKENAKA T., NISHINO N. (2017), "Service as artifact: reconsideration of value cocreation", in SAWATANI Y., SPOHRER J., KWAN S., TAKENAKA T. (eds.), *Serviceology for Smart Service System*, Tokyo, Springer, p. 307-316.

VIAL G. (2019), "Understanding digital transformation: A review and a research agenda", *Journal of Strategic Information Systems*, vol. 28, n° 2, p. 118-144.

WATANABE K., MOCHIMARU M. (2017), "Expanding impacts of technology-assisted service systems through generalization: Case study of the Japanese Service Engineering Research Project", *Service Science*, vol. 9, n° 3, p. 250-262.

WATANABE K., MOCHIMARU M., SHIMOMURA Y. (2016), "Service engineering research in Japan: Towards a sustainable society", in JONES A., STRÖM P., HERMELIN B., RUSTEN G. (eds), *Services and the Green Economy*, London, Palgrave Macmillan, p. 221-244.

WILSON A. M. (2001), "Mystery shopping: Using deception to measure service performance", *Psychology & Marketing*, vol. 18, n° 7, p. 721-734.

WORLD HEALTH ORGANIZATION (2015), *Health in 2015: from MDGs, millennium development goals to SDGs, sustainable development goals*, World Health Organization.

YEE R. W., YEUNG A. C., CHENG T. E. (2008), "The impact of employee satisfaction on quality and profitability in high-contact service industries", *Journal of Operations Management*, vol. 26, n° 5, p. 651-668.

YEE R. W., YEUNG A. C., CHENG T. E. (2010), "An empirical study of employee loyalty, service quality and firm performance in the service industry", *International Journal of Production Economics*, vol. 124, n° 1, p. 109-120.

SERVICE FIRM INNOVATION
Disaggregated sectoral classification analysis for Mexico

Juan Carlos Zagaceta-García[1]
University of Guadalajara

INTRODUCTION

All of the world's most advanced economies are dominated by the service sector. In many, it accounts for more than 70% of their GDP. The service sector is also important for developing and emergent countries (OECD, 2011); for example, it accounts for 52.2% of GDP in China, and 60.1% of GDP in Mexico (World Bank, 2018). Service growth is projected to continue in both groups of countries.

Innovation surveys show that firms invest in innovation in order to gain market share, reduce costs, and increase profits (OECD, 2000). The traditional way of grouping service firms is by industry or by sector (hospitality, banking, telecommunications, transportation, maintenance, etc.). This classification is standardised, to some extent, across countries, so there is data that can be compared across countries, sectors and firms. However, in most developing countries, there is neither any such consensus nor sufficient information available to measure service innovation and its effects.

This paper aims to picture innovation activities in Mexican services firms at a disaggregated level (in this case, at branch level). Most innovation studies in services are made at sector level, regardless of the type

1   jczagaceta@iteso.mx. Doctorado en Estudios Económicos. Universidad de Guadalajara, CUCEA. Periférico Norte 799, Núcleo Universitario Los Belenes, 45100, Zapopan, Jalisco, México.

of classification used. Furthermore, to take into account firms' technological bases in their innovative efforts, we complement this sectoral
study by using Soete and Miozzo's technological trajectory framework
in this study (Soete and Miozzo, 1990). We do this in order to compare
national industry classifications and technological change approaches.
Another motive for this dual perspective is that we consider innovation
a cumulative and specific process, rather than a disembodied outcome
(Gallouj, 2002). We therefore pose the following questions:

- Which sectors and branches of services in Mexico are most
  innovative, using the North American Industry Classification
  System (NAICS)[2]?
- Which sectors and branches of services in Mexico are most innovative,
  using Soete and Miozzo's technological trajectory approach?

Our analysis is based on data from the 2004 and 2009 Economic
Censuses, which include a module of surveys on Innovation and Research
using dichotomous ("yes" or "no") questions. It is important to note that
the two surveys are different: the 2009 survey has more questions than
the 2004 survey, and many of these concern the use of Information and
Communication Technologies (ICTs). Like most innovation studies, the
surveys concentrate mainly on technological innovations. This is because
they were first designed for manufacturing firms, and were just applied
to service firms using the so-called "subordination approach" to service
innovation (Djellal and Gallouj, 1999). However, we think this database
offers certain benefits. First, since the data comes from censuses, it offers
unparalleled coverage of most service firms in Mexico. Second, unlike
traditional questionnaires, the survey's structure covers all types of
innovation, including product and service innovations, process innovations, organisational innovations and external relationship innovations.

The study uses the methodology proposed in Ayyagari *et al.* (2011),
although it has been adapted to the data available in Mexico. Over the
period 2002-2004, these authors addressed innovation in emerging markets using a sample of 19,000 SMEs across 47 developing countries. It
was focused on company level, without distinguishing between sectors.

---

2   NAICS' economic classification from highest to lowest is: sector, sub-sector, branch,
     sub-branch, class.

In addition to individual indicators of innovation activities, they analysed two aggregate indices: "Core Innovation" and "Aggregate Innovation". This article is divided into four sections. The first reviews the relevant service innovation literature, and the second describes the database and methodology. The third section analyses innovation sectors and branches, using both the The North American Industry Classification System (NAICS) and the Soete and Miozzo technological trajectories approach. In the final section, we summarize and discuss the results.

1. SERVICE INNOVATION AND TECHNOLOGICAL TRAJECTORIES TAXONOMY

1.1 SERVICE INNOVATION

Economists see innovation and technological change as crucial elements of economic growth and development (Schumpeter, 1942; Solow, 1957; Griliches, 1986; Fageberg, 1988; Freeman, 1994; Silverberg and Soete, 1994; Freeman and Soete, 1997; Griliches, 1998; Baumol, 2002; Aghion and Durlauf, 2005; Ayyagari et al., 2011). Up until now, services have largely been considered technologically backward, with innovation playing no role in the aggregate performance of these sectors (Cainelli et al., 2006). However, Gallouj (2002) contends that in services, non-technological innovations and innovation trajectories (such as cognitive trajectories) are as important as technological trajectories.

For Gallouj (2002, see also Gallouj and Weinstein, 1997), there are three approaches to literature on innovation in services:

1. The technologist or subordination (or assimilation) approach equates or reduces innovation in services to the introduction of technical systems into services firms and organisations
2. The service-oriented (or demarcation) approach seeks to identify any particularities in the nature and organisation of innovation in services
3. The integrative or synthesis approach favours a similar analytical approach to innovation in goods and services

Compared with the primary and manufacturing sectors, services exhibit certain peculiarities: the product is a process; it is not only intangible and impossible to store, but also "nebulous" and extremely heterogeneous. Furthermore, it is interactive, which means that service customers and providers collaborate in the design, production and delivery of the service, and production and consumption are simultaneous (Gallouj, 2002; Miles, 2005; Castellacci, 2008).

The use of advanced ICTs has enabled the creation of new service delivery mechanisms, reducing the time required to develop and introduce new services. The service sector is a heavy user of these technologies, and the economic impact of such technologies is more visible in this sector (Cainelli *et al.*, 2006)[3].

Although technology is important, other forms of innovation (non-technological product/service and process innovations, organisational innovation, methodological innovations, etc.) are equally important. And if the service company does have an innovation department (which is not the case for most), its actors are seldom alone in the innovation process. They are almost always supplemented by (and in competition with) formalised though non-permanent innovation structures (project groups made up of people from different departments) - particularly in knowledge-intensive activities featuring a high level of informal encounters among its stakeholders (Sundbo, 1998; Fuglsang, 2008; Djellal and Gallouj, 1999, 2001; Gallouj and Djellal 2010).

In conclusion, it can be said that services do innovate significantly, though differently from manufacturing sectors (Miles *et al.*, 1994; Sundbo, 1998; Djellal and Gallouj (1998) and Gallouj, 2002). Taking account of the distinctive features of services requires a multidisciplinary approach that involves organisational behaviour, social networks, marketing, strategy and communication (Tether and Howells, 2007).

1.2 TAXONOMIES OF TECHNOLOGICAL TRAJECTORIES

Many innovation studies have focused on the technologist approach. Surveys originally designed for use by manufacturing firms were thus also used by service firms (Djellal and Gallouj, 1999), despite the fact

---

3   According to Miles (1995), around 80% of IT investment is consumed by the service
     sector in the United Kingdom and the United States.

that they were ill-equipped to accommodate the realities of innovations in services (Gallouj, 2002).

In order to identify the main sources and characteristics of technological change in economic sectors, as well as its economic impacts, various taxonomies have been proposed: Freeman, 1982; Pavitt, 1984; Freeman and Soete, 1987, 1997; Mills, 1986; Lakshmanan, 1987; Pavitt *et al.*, 1989; Soete and Miozzo, 1990; Miozzo and Soete, 2001; Gallouj, 1999).

Pavitt's (1984) seminal work uses a range of criteria and characteristics, including sources of technology, types of user and user needs, innovation appropriation regimes, size of company, degree of technological diversification and others. He divided the economy into four categories, each representing a sectoral model of technical change: supplier dominated firms; scale-intensive firms; specialised suppliers, and science-based firms. Services are included only in the case of "supplier dominated firms" – although non-market services were not taken into account (Gallouj, 2002).

Soete and Miozzo (1990) rejected the hypothesis (supported by some authors) that technological behaviour in the service sector was homogeneous. Their taxonomy uses Pavitt's criteria, yet does not consider services to belong to any single category. Soete and Miozzo's taxonomy includes three types of firms and industries:

1. Firms "dominated by suppliers" of equipment and technical systems. These firms' innovative activities consist of adopting the technologies of industrial suppliers, and can be subdivided into two groups:
   1.1 Personal services: small firms whose customers are sensitive to performance and whose modes of innovation appropriation are non-technological. These modes include professional know-how, aesthetic design, branding and advertising (*e.g.* repair services, cleaning, hotel and catering, retailing, laundry services).
   1.2 Public and social services: large firms and organisations whose customers are conscious of quality, but not in a stringent manner. Moreover, their innovations constitute public goods (*e.g.* education, health and public administration).
2. "Network firms": these follow a trajectory characterised by cost reduction and implementation of a networking strategy. They tend to be sizeable firms, and their main modes of innovation appropriation

are through standards and norms. Their customers are extremely price sensitive. These firms may turn to outside suppliers for their technologies, but always do so from a position of strength. They can be subdivided into two groups by principal means of service delivery:

   2.1. Physical networks: firms whose services are based on tangible resources (e.g. transport, wholesale trade).

   2.2. Informational networks: Codified information is the means of service delivery (e. g. finance, insurance, and communications).

3. "Specialised suppliers and science-based services": These are characterised by small firms whose technological trajectory is based on system design. Their clients are more concerned with technology performance than cost, while the innovation appropriation regime is dominated by R&D know-how, copyright and product differentiation. The source of technology can be in-house, customer or supplier (e.g. service providers having particular relationships to R&D, information technologies and telecommunications).

However, in both of these taxonomies (Pavitt, and Soete and Miozzo), the technological trajectory alone is considered. Yet in services, other (non-technological) trajectories play an important role. These other trajectories may be cognitive (based on the improvement of competences), methodological, data processing, social or organisational (Gallouj, 2002).

2. DATABASE AND ANALYSIS METHODOLOGY

The study is based on 2004 Census[4] data from 13 sectors and 96 branches and 2009 Census[5] data from 12 sectors and 64 branches. The analysis counts the number of affirmative responses linked to innovation

---

4   Sectors 48-49, which correspond to Transportation and Warehousing, are excluded from this census.

5   Sectors 55 and 62, which correspond to Management of Firms and Enterprises and Health care and Social assistance, respectively, are excluded from this census. The number of questions for the 2009 Census was increased and it used the "Open Innovation" approach, defined as "Deliberate use of inputs and outputs of knowledge to accelerate internal innovation, and expanding the use of innovation markets respectively" (Chesbrough, 2006),

activities made by firms (see Table 1 for the 2004 Census, which includes ten questions, and Table 2 for the 2009 Census, which includes 21 questions). Those responses are codified as dichotomous variables (Yes = 1, No = 0). Next, they are grouped at sector and branch levels. The percentages thus obtained are used to construct the indices for the study. It should be noted that these censuses do not include firm level data[6], but they do provide branch level responses. The indices are therefore constructed from the percentages for each sector and branch.

The questions in these tables are classified by innovation type: Product and Service Innovations (PSI), Process Innovations (PI), Organisational Innovations (OI) and External Relationship Innovations (EI). A single activity (question) can encompass several innovation types.

In addition to census questions, we created two aggregate indices of innovation: "Core Innovation" and "Aggregate Innovation" (constructed according to the methodology proposed by Ayyagari, et al., 2011). The "Aggregate Innovation" index measures the total number of responses linked to innovation activities, whereas the "Core Innovation" index counts only those responses linked to activities considered basic or essential to the development of product or service innovations. The "Core Innovation" index includes three questions (1, 2 and 6) from the 2004 Census and two questions (1 and 5) from the 2009 Census. The "Core Innovation" index could express a "technologist view" in which services are seen as unsuited to R&D and innovation (see Gallouj and Djellal (2010) for a critique of this position). For this reason, we consider results for this indicator to be technologically biased. Nevertheless, we use it to contrast results with the "integrative view" of the "Aggregate Innovation" index.

The values for the aggregate indices are constructed by adding up the percentages of affirmative responses for each classification. We find these indices to be useful for indicating which sectors or branches are most innovative. In all cases, high values for these indices reflect high levels of innovation. The maximum values for "Aggregate Innovation" indices in the 2004 and 2009 Censuses are ten and twenty-one, respectively; the maximum values for "Core Innovation" indices in the 2004 and 2009 Censuses are three

---

with an emphasis "on the way to use, manage, apply and also to generate intellectual property" (Herzog, 2008). Besides, this census has more questions on the use of ICTs.

6   Company-level data are not available for reasons of confidentiality, but also for certain variables of some branches and sectors. This is in accordance with the law of the National System of Statistical and Geographical Information, in articles 37, 38, 42 and 47.

and two, respectively. The minimum value for all cases is zero. For all the innovation activities indices, we have created tables for both classification level and census (a detailed description is found in Zagaceta-García, 2016). We also include Soete and Miozzo's classification codes (See Appendix, Tables 1A-4A). However, it is important to note that due to methodological differences, it is difficult to make comparisons between censuses (due to the differing number of questions for each census, confidentiality problems, and the incompatibility of different versions of NAICS).

TAB. 1 – Questions on innovation activity in Mexican firms, 2004 Census.

Code	Question	Innovation type code
1	Had a department dedicated total or partially to the design or creation of new products or processes.	PSI, PI
2	Invested in the creation of new products, materials, devices or components.	PSI
3	Registered products or other works of intellectual creation to intellectual property institutes.	PSI, PI
4	Trained staff in the use of new technologies and work processes.	PI, OI
5	Implemented processes of reorganization in working systems.	PI, OI
6	Adapted their goods or services to changes in the preferences of their customers.	PSI
7	Used computer equipment in administrative processes.	PI
8	Used the internet in their relationships with customers and suppliers.	EI
9	Used computer equipment in technical processes or design.	PI
10	Developed programs or software packages to improve their processes.	PI

Source: based on economic census of Mexico, 2004.

Notes: Each question is classified by the type of innovation: PSI (product and service innovations), PI (process innovations), OI (organizational innovation), EI (external relationship innovations). "Core Innovation" index includes questions 1, 2 and 6.

TAB. 2 – Questions of innovation activity in Mexican firms, 2009 census.

Code	Question	Innovation type code
1	Had specialized areas dedicated to the design and creation of new products or services, production processes or provision of services.	PSI, PI
2	Registered or transacted patents of trademarks, products or processes.	PSI, PI
3	Hired or acquired patents of trademarks, products or processes.	PSI, PI, EI
4	Made collaboration agreements with research centers, universities and consulting firms.	EI
5	Made research for innovation.	PSI
6	Hired companies to do engineering research.	EI
7	Developed patents of trademarks, products or processes.	PSI, PI
8	Due to lack of resources stopped planning innovative projects or ceased to find substitutes that failed.	PSI, PI
9	Qualified full time staff dedicated to find solutions or improvements in quality control.	PSI, PI, OI
10	Qualified full time staff dedicated to find solutions or improvements in production processes efficiency.	PSI, PI, OI
11	Qualified full time staff dedicated to find solutions or improvements in innovation of products, services or processes.	PSI, PI, OI
12	With regular use of computer equipment.	PI
13	With regular use of the internet.	PI, EI
14	Used communication networks: broadband internet.	PI, EI
15	Used communication networks: intranet.	PI
16	Used communication networks: extranet.	PI, EI
17	Made by internet: banking and financial operations.	EI
18	Made by internet: procedures with government.	EI
19	Made by internet: purchase or sale of products or services.	EI
20	Made by internet: information search.	EI
21	Made by internet: management activities for the firm (planning, organization, direction and control).	PI

Source: based on economic census of Mexico, 2009.

Notes: Each question is classified by the type of innovation: PSI (product and service innovations), PI (process innovations), OI (organizational innovation), EI (external relationship innovations). "Core Innovation" index includes questions 1 and 5.

Lastly, we analyse the responses for Mexican firms' innovation activities at the sector and branch levels, using Soete and Miozzo's taxonomy (see classification codes in Table 3). For the final part of the study, we use only the aggregate indices ("Aggregate Innovation" and "Core Innovation"). First, for each census, we obtain the average percentage of those indices at sector and branch levels. Second, we use Soete and Miozzo's categories to classify sectors and branches. Third, for each category we choose the sectors and branches having value greater than or equal to the average aggregate indices. Finally, we calculate the category's percentage of innovation (in all cases higher percentages correspond to higher degrees of innovation).

It is important to point out that in the case of "Network firms", we find it difficult to distinguish physical networks from informational networks. This sector and these branches have therefore been catalogued as "Network firms"[7].

TAB. 3 – Classification codes based on Soete and Miozzo's taxonomy.

Code	Type
DS	Dominated by suppliers
PER	Personal services
PUB	Public and Social services
N	Network firms
PN	Physical networks
IN	Informational networks
SC	Specialized suppliers and science-based services

Source: based on Soete and Miozzo (1990) taxonomy.

---

7 The sector is Administrative and Support and Waste Management and Remediation Services for both censuses. The branches are: Retail trade in supermarkets; Retail trade in department stores; Parks with recreational facilities and electronic gaming also for both censuses. "Ambulances, organ banks and other ancillary services to medical treatment" for the 2004 Census and "Foreign package delivery services" for the 2009 census.

3. RESULTS

The results for the sector level analysis (2004 Census), show that Sector 51 (Information) has the greatest number of innovation activities, with an "Aggregate Innovation" index of 5.78 while Sector 72 (Accommodation and food services) has the lowest, at 1.37. The "Core Innovation" index (representing the use of "core" innovation activities) shows that Sector 52 (Finance and insurance) is the highest performer with an index of 1.81. The lowest innovator is again Sector 72, at 0.65. Meanwhile, the activities performed most across all sectors fall under "Adapted their goods or services to changes in the preferences of their customers" (PSI innovation type) and "Trained staff in the use of new technologies and work processes" (PI and OI types). The least performed activity is "Registered products or other works of intellectual creation to intellectual property institutes" (PSI and PI types). This tells us that different forms of innovation are present in services, though some service characteristics render a contrast with manufacturing difficult.

For the sector level analysis (2009 Census), Sector 52 (Finance and insurance) is most innovative, with an "Aggregate Innovation" index of 11.68, while the least innovative sector (as in the previous census) is Sector 72, at 3.83. Sector 52 (Finance and insurance) again has the highest "Core Innovation" index, and the lowest is once again Sector 72. In this census, the most common activity performed is "Made by Internet: information search" (EI type). The least performed are "Hired or acquired patents of trademarks, products or processes" (PSI, PI and EI types), "Hired firms to do engineering research" (EI type) and "Developed patents of trademarks, products or processes" (PSI and PI types).

Branch level analysis (2004 Census), shows that Branch 5151 (Transmission of radio and television programmes, except via the internet) has the highest "Aggregate Innovation" index, with Branch 5172 (Cellular and other wireless telecommunications, except satellite services) coming in second place. Branch 7213 (Pensions and guest houses, apartments and houses furnished with hotel services) has the lowest "Aggregate Innovation" index. Branch 5172 (Cellular and other wireless telecommunications, except satellite services) has the highest

"Core Innovation" index, with Branch 5151 (Transmission of radio and television programmes, except via the internet) in second place. These two branches switch places on the "Aggregate Innovation" index, and this result is consistent with the sector analysis, with Sector 51 (Information) rated the most innovative.

It is interesting to note that Branch 7222 (Self-service restaurants and with food to take-out) came in fourth place, with Branch 5415 (Computer consultancy services) coming in fifth. Once more, Branch 7213 has the lowest index. Interestingly, Branch 6219 (Ambulances, organ banks and other ancillary services to medical treatment) ranks very low. The analyses from the 2004 Census for branches thus show behaviour quite similar to that revealed in the innovation activity analysis at the sector level, in the 2004 and 2009 censuses.

Lastly, branch level analysis (2009 Census) shows that Branch 5221 (Multiple banking) scored the highest "Aggregate Innovation" index, Branch 5241 (Institutions of insurance and bonding) in second place. And Branch 4872 (Tourist transport by water) scored lowest. Branch 5221 again scored highest on the "Core Innovation" index and Branch 5241 came in second place on the "Aggregate Innovation" index. Branch 4852 (Non-urban collective fixed route passenger transportation) had the lowest index. The activity most performed for almost all branches is question number 20 ("Made by internet: information search", EI type).

For the second part of the study, we drew up Table 4 (2004 Census) and Table 5 (2009 Census) to analyse the degree of innovation at both sector and branch levels, using Soete and Miozzo's taxonomy.

Table 4 (2004 Census) shows the degree of innovativeness using Soete and Miozzo's taxonomy, subdivided into sector level and branch level. In our analysis of the "Aggregate Innovation" index at sector level, we found (as do most innovation studies) that the most innovative firms belong to the "Specialised suppliers and science-based services" trajectory, with 100% of these sectors having a value that is greater or equal to the average. The second most innovative sector is "Network firms" with 66.7%. The least innovative sector is "Supplier-Dominated" firms with 16.7%. The "Personal services" category innovates more in core activities than "Public and Social services" does (25% vs. 0%, respectively).

At branch level, the various categories innovate as they do at sector level, although the percentages show less dispersion, no branch has scores at 100% or 0%. Furthermore, we can see that all "Network firms" and "Specialised suppliers and science-based services" groups have more types of innovation (in both "Aggregate Innovation" and "Core Innovation" indices) than "Dominated by suppliers" firms.

TAB. 4 – Innovation in Mexican services sectors and branches
(Soete and Miozzo's taxonomy), 2004 Census.

Sector level (13 sectors)	Sectors with more or equal value than aggregate average	"% of Aggregate Innovation"	Sectors with more or equal value than core average	"% Core Innovation"
	Average index = 3.3		Average index = 1.10	
Dominated by suppliers	1	16,7	1	16,7
Personal services	0	0,0	1	25,0
Public and Social services	1	50,0	0	0,0
Network firms	1	66,7	4	66,7
Physical networks	0	0,0	0	0,0
Informational networks	3	100,0	3	100,0
Specialized suppliers and science-based services	1	100,0	1	100,0

Branch level (96 branches)	Branches with more or equal value than aggregate average	"% of Aggregate Innovation"	Branches with more or equal value than core average	"% Core Innovation"
	Average index = 3.49		Average index = 1.10	
Dominated by suppliers	7	17,9	13	33,3
Personal services	2	6,7	7	23,3
Public and Social services	5	55,6	6	66,7
Network firms	26	60,5	21	48,8
Physical networks	15	57,7	12	46,2
Informational networks	9	69,2	7	53,8
Specialized suppliers and science-based services	11	78,6	10	71,4

Source: based on economic census for Mexico (2004) and Soete and Miozzo taxonomy (1990).
Notes: The figures correspond to the obtained category percentage for sectors or branches with major or equal value against "Aggregate Innovation" or "Core Innovation" sector and branch averages respectively. Higher percentages are consistent to higher degrees of innovation.

Table 5 (2009 Census) also uses Soete and Miozzo's taxonomy to show the degree of innovativeness. In the "Aggregate Innovation" index at sector level, the ranking among categories is the same as it was in 2004: "Specialised suppliers and science-based services" are the most innovative (100%), followed by "Network firms" (66.7%) and "Supplier Dominated" firms (20%). In addition, "Personal services" still scores 0%, as it did in 2004, whereas "Physical networks" go from 0% to 33.3%. "Public and Social services" increase from 50% to 100%. With the exception of "Personal services", all categories increased their aggregate score. In terms of the "Core Innovation" index, "Network firms" seem less innovative than they were in 2004 (50% vs. 66.7%).

At branch level, ranking in terms of innovativeness is maintained. As with 2004 Census, there is less dispersion at the branch level.

TAB. 5 – Innovation in Mexican services sectors and branches
(Soete and Miozzo's taxonomy), 2009 census.

Sector level (12 sectors)	Sectors with more or equal value than aggregate average Average index = 7.26	"% of Aggregate Innovation"	Sectors with more or equal value than core average Average index = 0.30	"% Core Innovation"
Dominated by suppliers	1	20	1	20
Personal services	0	0	0	0
Public and Social services	1	100	1	100
Network firms	4	66,7	3	50
Physical networks	1	33,3	1	0
Informational networks	1	100	0	100
Specialized suppliers and science-based services	2	100	2	100

Branch level (64 branches)	Branches with more or equal value than aggregate average Average index = 7.34	"% of Aggregate Innovation"	Branches with more or equal value than core average Average index = 0.30	"% Core Innovation"
Dominated by suppliers	5	31,3	4	25
Personal services	3	21,4	2	14,3
Public and Social services	2	100	2	100
Network firms	26	66,7	13	33,3
Physical networks	14	56	5	20
Informational networks	10	100	7	70
Specialized suppliers and science-based services	8	88,9	8	88,9

Source: based on economic census for Mexico (2009) and Soete and Miozzo taxonomy (1990).
Notes: The figures correspond to the obtained category percentage for sectors or branches with major or equal value against "Aggregate Innovation" or "Core Innovation" sector and branch averages respectively. Higher percentages are consistent to higher degrees of innovation.

CONCLUSION

In this paper, we have extended innovation studies to the service sector in developing countries. As the share of services in these countries' GDP approaches that of developed countries, the service innovation topic is gaining in prominence. We used data from the 2004 and 2009 Economic Censuses of Mexico to identify which sectors and branches are most innovative in this country. We compared innovation in Mexican firms using both the North American Industry Classification System (NAICS) and Soete and Miozzo's technological trajectories mapping.

The results of the first part of the study (using NAICS) indicate that all service sectors innovate. Service sectors traditionally seen as "the most innovative" (Information, Finance and Insurance, Professional, Scientific and Technical Services) are still ahead, undertaking the bulk of innovation-related activities, according to the two surveyed censuses. Breaking down sectors into branches allows a closer view of how innovation activities are distributed, with some branches appearing more innovative than the sectors they belong to. Branch level analysis is thus more accurate than sector level analysis.

By analysing how Mexican firms innovate, we found that firms tend to underexploit certain actions, such as "Registered products or other works of intellectual creation to intellectual property institutes". This finding is in agreement with the conventional innovation surveys conducted to capture technological innovations, rather than the intrinsic characteristics of services. For the 2009 census, another underused category is "Activities with the involvement of other external agents or external relationship innovations". This can be attributed to firms' lack of confidence to explore the potential of the Open Innovation approach.

It should be observed that in developing countries like Mexico, "service firms collaborate with customers and suppliers more than through in-house R&D" according to Tether's (2005) study on European countries.

Moreover, Mexican firms in all sectors and branches state that they include an innovation department. However, due to the specificities of services, we infer that many of these departments are in fact flexible project groups or "innovation structures" – as Djellal and Gallouj (1999) called them – rather than permanent physical areas.

Though the use of computer equipment and the internet is considered essential to services innovation specifically, the responses to questions 7 to 10 (2004 Census) and 12 to 21 (2009 Census) show that this kind of equipment is not broadly used in all sectors and branches. Nevertheless, in the 2009 Census, we can see extensive use of ICTs by most firms, although different firms may use them differently.

Lastly, using Soete and Miozzo's mapping, we were able to confirm that the most innovative sectors and branches are "Specialised suppliers and science-based services" followed by "Network firms", while the least innovative are those labelled as "Supplier Dominated". In any case, contrary to the assertions of the technologist/assimilation approach, we found the service sector to be heterogeneous in terms of its innovative activities (Gallouj, 2002). We therefore advocate for analyses that are both finer, and more disaggregated, to portray service firms' innovations more accurately.

REFERENCES

AGHION P. and DURLAUF S. (2005), *Handbook of Economic Growth*, Amsterdam, North Holland Elsevier Publishers.

AYYAGARI M., DEMIRGÜÇ-KUNT A., and MAKSIMOVIC V. (2011), "Firm Innovation in Emerging Markets: the Role of Finance, Governance, and Competition", *Journal of Financial and Quantitative Analysis*, vol. 46, n° 6, p. 1545-1580.

BAUMOL W. (2002), *The Free-market Innovation Machine: Analysing the Growth Miracle of Capitalism*, Princeton, NJ, Princeton University Press.

CAINELLI G., EVANGELISTA R. and SAVONA M. (2006), "Innovation and Economic Performance in Services: A Firm Level Analysis", *Cambridge Journal of Economics*, vol. 30, n° 3, p. 435-458.

CASTELLACCI F. (2008), "Technological Paradigms, Regimes and Trajectories: Manufacturing and Service Industries in a New Taxonomy of Sectoral Patterns of Innovation", *Research Policy*, vol. 37, n° 6, p. 978-994.

CHESBROUGH H. (2006), *Open Innovation: A New Paradigm for Understanding Industrial Innovation*, Oxford, Chesbrough.

DJELLAL F. and GALLOUJ F. (1998), *Innovation in service industries in France: results of a postal survey*. SI4S project, European Commission, DG XII, TSER program, July.

DJELLAL F. and GALLOUJ F. (1999), "Services and the Search for Relevant Innovation Indicators: A Review of National and International Surveys", *Science and Public Policy*, vol. 26, n° 4, p. 218-232.

DJELLAL F. and GALLOUJ F. (2001), "Patterns of innovation organisation in service firms: postal survey results and theoretical models", *Science and Public Policy*, vol. 28, n° 1, p. 57-67.

FAGEBERG J. (1988), "Why growth rates differ?", in DOSI G., FREEMAN C., NELSON R., SILVERBERG G and SOETE L (eds.). *Technological Change and Economic Theory*, London, UK, Pinter, p. 432-457.

FREEMAN C. (1982), *The Economics of Industrial Innovation*, London, UK, Pinter.

FREEMAN C. (1994), "Critical Survey: The Economics of Technical Change", *Cambridge Journal of Economics*, vol. 18, n° 5, p. 463-512.

FREEMAN C. and SOETE L. (eds.) (1987), *Technical Change and Full Employment*, Oxford, Basil Blackwell.

FREEMAN C. and SOETE L. (1997), *The Economics of Industrial Innovation*, London, UK, Pinter.

FUGLSANG L. (ed.) (2008), *Innovation and the Creative Process: Towards Innovation with Care*, Cheltenham, UK and Northampton, MA, USA, Edward Elgar.

GALLOUJ F. (1999), "Les trajectoires de l'innovation dans les services : vers un enrichissement des taxonomies évolutionnistes", *Economies et Sociétés, Série EGS*, n °1, 5, p. 143-169.

GALLOUJ F. (2002), *Innovation in the Service Economy*, Cheltenham, UK and Northampton, MA, USA, Edward Elgar.

GALLOUJ F. and DJELLAL F. (2010), *The handbook of innovation and services: a multidisciplinary perspective*, in GALLOUJ F. and DJELLAL F. (eds.), Cheltenham, UK and Northampton, MA, USA, Edward Elgar.

GALLOUJ F., WEINSTEIN O. (1997), "Innovation in Services", *Research Policy*, vol. 26, n °4-5, p. 537-556.

GRILICHES Z. (1986), "Productivity, R&D and Basic Research at the Firm Level in the 1970s", *American Economic Review*, vol. 76, n° 19, p. 141-154.

GRILICHES Z. (1998), *R&D and Productivity: The Econometric Evidence*, Chicago, University of Chicago Press.

HERZOG P. (2008), *Open and Closed Innovation: Different Cultures for Different Strategies*, Germany, Gabler Verlag.

LAKSHMANAN T. (1987), "Technological and institutional innovation in the service sector", conference "Research and Development, Industrial Change and Economic Policy", Karlstad, Sweden, June.

MILES I., KASTRINOS N., FLANAGAN K., BILDERBEK P., DEN HERTOG P., HUNTINK W. and BOUMAN M. (1994), *Knowledge-intensive business services: their role as users, carriers and sources of innovation*. Manchester, PREST.

MILES I. (1995), *Services innovation: Statistical and conceptual issues*, report to OECD NESTY Working Group on innovation surveys. Manchester, PREST.

MILES I. (2005), "Innovation in services", in *The Oxford Handbook of Innovation*, Oxford, Oxford University Press.

MILLS P. (1986), *Managing Service Industries: Organizational Practices in a Postindustrial Economy*, Cambridge, MA, Ballinger Publishing Company.

MIOZZO M. AND SOETE L. (2001), "Internationalisation of Services: A Technological Perspective". *Technological Forecasting and Social Change*, vol. 67, n° 2-3, p. 159-185.

NATIONAL INSTITUTE OF STATISTICS AND GEOGRAPHY (INEGI) (2004), *2004 Economic Censuses methodology*, México, INEGI.

NATIONAL INSTITUTE OF STATISTICS AND GEOGRAPHY (INEGI) (2009), *2009 Economic Censuses methodology*, México, INEGI.

NATIONAL INSTITUTE OF STATISTICS AND GEOGRAPHY (INEGI) (2002), *North American Industry Classification System* (NAICS), México, INEGI.

NATIONAL INSTITUTE OF STATISTICS AND GEOGRAPHY (INEGI) (2007), *North American Industry Classification System* (NAICS), México, INEGI.

OECD (2000), *Innovation and Economic Performance. Science, Technology and Industry Outlook 2000*, Paris, OECD.

OECD (2011), "Science, Technology and Industry Scoreboard 2011", available at: http://dx.doi.org/10.1787/sti_scoreboard-2011-en (retrieved on June 20, 2019).

PAVITT K. (1984), "Sectoral Patterns of Technical Change: Towards a Taxonomy and a Theory", *Research Policy*, vol. 13, n° 6, p. 343-373.

PAVITT K., ROBSON M. and TOWNSEND J. (1989), "Technological Accumulation, Diversification and Organisation in UK Companies", *Management Science*, vol. 35, n° 1, p. 81-99.

SCHUMPETER J. (1942), *Capitalism, Socialism, and Democracy*, New York, Harper and Brothers.

SILVERBERG G. and SOETE L. (eds.) (1994), *The Economics of Growth and Technical Change*, Aldershot, Edward Elgar.

SOETE L. and MIOZZO M. (1990), *Trade and development in services: a technological perspective*, Maastricht, Netherlands, MERIT.

SOLOW R. (1957), "Technical Change and the Aggregate Production Function", *Review of Economics and Statistics*, vol. 39, n° 3, p. 312-320.

SUNDBO J. (1998), *The Organization of Innovation in Services*, Roskilde, Denmark, Roskilde University Press.

TETHER B. (2005), "Do Services Innovate Differently? Insights from the European Innobarometer Survey", *Industry and Innovation*, vol. 12, n° 2, p. 153-184.

TETHER B. and HOWELLS J. (2007), "Changing Understanding of Innovation in Services. From Technological Adoption to Complex Complementary Changes to Technologies, Skills and Organization", in DTI 2007. "Innovation in Services", DTI Occasional Paper n° 9, p. 21-62.

THE WORLD BANK (2018), "World Bank national accounts data". Available at: http://databank.worldbank.org/data/reports.aspx?source=2&country (retrieved on July 8, 2019).

ZAGACETA-GARCÍA J.C. (2016), *Service firm innovation: Disaggregated classification analysis for México*. 26th Annual RESER (European Association for Research on Services) Conference, September.

APPENDIX

1A. Sector level innovation indices (NAICS), 2004 census

Soete and Miozzo's code	Sector	Description	"Core Innovation" (max value= 3)	"Aggregate Innovation" (max value= 10)
PN	43	Wholesale trade	0,92	3,09
PER	46	Retail trade	0,99	2,37
IN	51	Information	1,74	5,78
IN	52	Finance and Insurance	1,81	5,11
PN	53	Real Estate and Rental and Leasing	0,68	2,06
SC	54	Professional, Scientific and Technical Services	1,26	4,11
IN	55	Management of Companies and Enterprises	1,20	4,83
N	56	Administrative and Support and Waste Management and Remediation Services	1,14	3,90
PUB	61	Educational Services	1,08	3,65
PUB	62	Health Care and Social Assistance	1,04	2,76
PER	71	Arts, Entertainment, and Recreation	1,13	2,49
PER	72	Accommodation and Food Services	0,65	1,37
PER	81	Other Services (except Public Administration)	0,71	1,74

Source: based on economic census for México (2004) and Soete and Miozzo's taxonomy (1990).

Notes: Sector 48-49 (Transportation and Warehousing) is not included in the 2004 census. "Administrative and Support and Waste Management and Remediation Services" sector has been catalogued like "Network firms" instead of separate it into the two groups from Soete and Miozzo's taxonomy: "Physical networks" or "Informational networks". "Core Innovation" index includes questions 1, 2 and 6. The averages for the "Core Innovation" and "Aggregate Innovation" indices are 1,10 and 3,33, respectively.

2A. Branch level innovation indices (NAICS), 2004 census (continued)

Soete and Miozzo's code	Branch	Description	"Core Innovation" (max value= 3)	"Aggregate Innovation" (max value= 10)
PN	4311	Wholesale trade of grocery and food	0,85	2,99
PN	4312	Wholesale trade of beverages and tobacco	0,96	3,72
PN	4321	Wholesale trade of textile products and footwear	0,99	3,00
PN	4331	Wholesale trade of pharmaceutical products	1,11	4,22
PN	4332	Wholesale trade of perfumery and jewelry items and other clothing accessories	1,10	3,25
PN	4333	Wholesale trade of discs, toys and sporting goods	1,44	3,90
PN	4334	Wholesale trade of stationery, books, magazines and newspapers	1,02	3,92
PN	4335	Wholesale trade of minor household appliances and white goods	1,10	3,80
PN	4341	Wholesale trade of agricultural raw materials	0,89	2,48
PN	4342	Wholesale trade of raw materials for industry	0,91	2,96
PN	4343	Wholesale trade of waste materials	0,63	1,67
PN	4351	Wholesale of machinery and agricultural, forestry and fishing equipment	0,85	3,50
PN	4352	Wholesale of machinery and equipment for the industry	0,90	3,98
PN	4353	Wholesale of machinery and equipment for services and commercial activities	1,09	4,24
PN	4354	Wholesale trade of machinery, furniture and general-use equipment	1,11	4,53
PN	4361	Wholesale trade for trucks	1,28	5,07
PN	4371	Intermediation to the wholesale trade	1,13	4,70
PER	4611	Retail trade for food	0,79	1,63
PER	4612	Retail trade of beverages and tobacco	0,73	1,52
N	4621	Retail trade in supermarkets	1,20	3,94
N	4622	Retail trade in department stores	1,45	5,26
PER	4631	Retail trade of textile products, except clothing	0,67	1,82
PER	4632	Retail trade of clothing and clothing accessories	1,18	2,47
PER	4633	Retail trade of footwear	0,90	2,23
PER	4641	Retail trade of health care articles	1,05	2,83
PER	4651	Retail trade of perfumery and jewelry	0,86	2,51
PER	4652	Retail trade for recreation articles	1,33	3,01
PER	4653	Retail trade of stationery, books and newspapers	1,09	2,48
PER	4659	Retail trade of pets, gifts, religious items, crafts, articles in importing stores and other personal items	0,85	1,87
PER	4661	Retail trade of home furniture and other household appliances	0,97	2,80
IN	4662	Retail trade of computers, phones and other communication devices	1,02	3,58
PER	4663	Retail trade of interior decoration items	0,92	2,14
PER	4671	Retail trade for hardware stores and glass	0,92	2,42
PN	4681	Retail trade for cars and light trucks	1,18	3,84
PER	4682	Retail trade of spare parts for cars, light trucks and trucks	0,87	2,51
PER	4684	Retail trade of fuels and lubricating oils	0,80	2,90
IN	5111	Edition of newspapers, magazines, books and the like, except via the Internet	1,81	5,88
SC	5121	Film and video industry	0,94	4,46
SC	5122	Sound industry	1,13	4,28
SC	5151	Transmission of radio and television programmes, except via the Internet	2,14	6,99
SC	5172	Cellular and other wireless telecommunications, except satellite services	2,19	6,92
SC	5175	Cable television programmes, except via the Internet	1,41	4,85
SC	5181	Internet access and search online services	1,81	5,85
SC	5182	Electronic processing of information, hosting of web pages and other related services	1,51	5,94
IN	5224	Brokerage credit and financial services not stock exchange	0,79	2,10
IN	5239	Other investment and brokerage services	1,94	6,68
IN	5241	Institutions of insurance and bonding	1,41	6,15
PN	5311	Rent without intermediation of dwellings and other real state	0,57	1,39
PN	5312	Real estate and real estate brokers	0,65	3,03
PN	5324	Rental of industrial, commercial and services machinery and equipment	1,07	3,37
IN	5411	Legal services	0,90	3,12

Source: based on economic census for Mexico (2004) and Soete and Miozzo taxonomy (1990).   (Continued)

Notes: Sector 48-49 (Transportation and Warehousing) is not included in the 2004 census. "Retail trade in supermarkets"; "Retail trade in department stores"; "Ambulances, organ banks and other ancillary services to medical treatment"; "Parks with recreational facilities and electronic gaming" branches have been catalogued like "Network firms" instead of separate them into the two groups from Soete and Miozzo's taxonomy: "Physical networks" or "Informational networks". "Core Innovation" index includes questions 1, 2 and 6. The averages for "Core Innovation" and "Aggregate Innovation" indices are 1.10 and 3.49, respectively.

2A. Branch level innovation indices (NAICS), 2004 census

Soete and Miozzo code	Branch	Description	"Core Innovation" (max value= 3)	"Aggregate Innovation" (max value= 10)
IN	5412	Accounting, audit and related services	1,11	4,49
IN	5413	Services in architecture, engineering and related activities	1,16	4,69
SC	5415	Computer consultancy services	1,83	6,64
SC	5416	Administrative, scientific and technical consulting services	1,06	4,84
SC	5417	Scientific research and development services	1,44	5,52
SC	5418	Advertising services and related activities	1,69	4,84
SC	5419	Other professional, scientific and technical services	1,25	3,11
PN	5511	Corporate management and business	1,20	4,83
IN	5611	Business management services	1,06	3,14
PN	5612	Facilities support services	0,89	2,63
IN	5613	Employment services	1,05	3,24
IN	5614	Support service of secretarial, photocopying, collection, credit research and similar activities	1,03	4,18
PER	5615	Travel agencies and reservation services	1,29	3,72
PER	5616	Research, protection and safety services	1,34	3,84
PER	5619	Other support business services	1,07	2,92
PER	5621	Wastes management and remediation services	0,95	3,18
PUB	6111	Schools of basic, secondary and special education	0,99	3,47
PUB	6112	Career and Technical Schools	1,80	5,13
PUB	6113	Professional degrees and graduated schools	1,63	6,02
IN	6114	Commercial schools, computer and training for executives	1,60	5,60
PUB	6116	Other educational services	1,23	3,38
PUB	6117	Education support services	1,43	4,11
PUB	6211	Medical consulting offices	0,62	2,01
IN	6215	Medical and diagnostic laboratories	1,29	3,70
N	6219	Ambulances, organ banks and other ancillary services to medical treatment	0,33	2,14
PUB	6221	General hospitals	1,10	3,57
PUB	6223	Hospitals in other medical specialties	1,19	3,73
PER	6232	Homes for the care of people with mental retardation, mental health and substance abuse problems	1,00	2,91
PUB	6241	Guidance and social work services	0,94	1,71
PER	7113	Sponsors of artistic shows, sports and the like	0,81	2,53
PN	7121	Museums, historical sites, botanical gardens and the like	1,52	3,99
N	7131	Parks with recreational facilities and electronic gaming	0,94	1,80
PN	7139	Other recreational services	1,19	2,79
PER	7211	Hotels, motels and the like	0,42	1,67
PER	7213	Pensions and guest houses, apartments and houses furnished with hotel services	0,12	0,34
PER	7221	Restaurants with waiter service	1,28	2,60
PN	7222	Self-service restaurants and with food to take-out	1,85	3,53
PER	7223	Custom-made food preparation services	1,12	3,10
PER	8111	Repair and maintenance of automobiles and trucks	0,91	2,10
SC	8112	Repair and maintenance of electronic equipment and precision equipment	0,95	2,71
SC	8113	Repair and maintenance of agricultural, industrial, commercial and services machinery and equipment	0,98	2,67
PER	8122	Laundries and dry cleaners	1,12	2,57
PER	8124	Parking lots for cars	0,22	0,60
PER	8131	Commercial, industrial, recreational and professional organizations and associations	0,64	2,26
PER	8132	Religious, political and civil organizations and associations	0,44	1,68

Source: based on economic census for Mexico (2004) and Soete and Miozzo taxonomy (1990).
Notes: Sector 48-49 (Transportation and Warehousing) is not included in the 2004 census. "Retail trade in supermarkets"; "Retail trade in department stores"; "Ambulances, organ banks and other ancillary services to medical treatment"; "Parks with recreational facilities and electronic gaming" branches have been catalogued like "Network firms" instead of separate them into the two groups from Soete and Miozzo's taxonomy: "Physical networks" or "Informational networks". "Core Innovation" index includes questions 1, 2 and 6. The averages for "Core Innovation" and "Aggregate Innovation" indices are 1.10 and 3.49, respectively.

3A. Sector level innovation indices (NAICS), 2009 census

Soete and Miozzo's code	Sector	Description	"Core Innovation" (max value= 2)	"Aggregate Innovation" (max value= 21)
PN	43	Wholesale trade	0,23	7,64
PER	46	Retail trade	0,14	6,76
PN	48-49	Transportation and Warehousing	0,10	4,16
IN	51	Information	0,43	8,86
IN	52	Finance and Insurance	0,88	11,68
PN	53	Real Estate and Rental and Leasing	0,17	6,83
SC	54	Professional, Scientific and Technical Services	0,42	8,02
N	56	Administrative and Support and Waste Management and Remediation Services	0,30	7,93
PUB	61	Educational Services	0,41	8,21
PER	71	Arts, Entertainment, and Recreation	0,22	6,51
PER	72	Accommodation and Food Services	0,10	3,83
PER	81	Other Services (except Public Administration)	0,20	6,68

Source: based on economic census for Mexico (2009) and Soete and Miozzo taxonomy (1990).

Notes: Sectors 55 Y 62 (Management of Companies and Enterprises and Health Care and Social Assistance, respectively) are not included in the 2009 census. "Administrative and Support" and "Waste Management and Remediation Services" sectors have been catalogued like "Network firms" instead of separate it into the two groups from Soete and Miozzo's taxonomy: "Physical networks" or "Informational networks". "Core Innovation" index includes questions 1 and 5. The averages for the "Core Innovation" and "Aggregate Innovation" indices are 0.30 and 7.26, respectively.

4A. Branch level innovation indices (NAICS), 2009 census (continued)

Soete and Miozzo's code	Branch	Description	"Core Innovation" (max value= 2)	"Aggregate Innovation" (max value= 21)
PN	4311	Wholesale trade of grocery and food	0,21	6,98
PN	4312	Wholesale trade of beverages and tobacco	0,30	7,91
PN	4321	Wholesale trade of textile products and footwear	0,29	7,57
PN	4331	Wholesale trade of pharmaceutical products	0,29	8,26
PN	4333	Wholesale trade of discs, toys and sporting goods	0,31	8,29
PN	4334	Wholesale trade of stationery, books, magazines and newspapers	0,32	8,03
PN	4341	Wholesale trade of agricultural raw materials	0,27	7,52
PN	4342	Wholesale trade of raw materials for industry	0,20	7,49
PN	4352	Wholesale trade of machinery and equipment for the industry	0,11	8,02
PN	4353	Wholesale trade of machinery and equipment for services and commercial activities	0,31	8,96
PN	4354	Wholesale trade of machinery, furniture and general-use equipment	0,26	8,75
PER	4611	Retail trade for food	0,11	4,99
N	4621	Retail trade in supermarkets	0,17	5,53
N	4622	Retail trade in department stores	0,40	7,91
PER	4632	Retail trade of clothing and clothing accessories	0,21	5,67
PER	4641	Retail trade of health care articles	0,15	5,27
PER	4652	Retail trade for recreation articles	0,17	6,34
PER	4661	Retail trade of home furniture and other household appliances	0,14	6,32
IN	4662	Retail trade of computers, phones and other communication devices	0,28	8,28
PER	4671	Retail trade for hardware stores and glass	0,15	6,61
PN	4681	Retail trade for cars and light trucks	0,17	8,96
PER	4682	Retail trade of spare parts for cars, light trucks and trucks	0,13	6,72
PER	4684	Retail trade of fuels and lubricating oils	0,09	6,60
PN	4841	General freight trucking	0,10	5,24
PN	4842	Specialized freight trucking	0,07	4,17
PN	4851	Urban and suburban collective transport of passengers from fixed-route	0,09	2,84
PN	4852	Non-urban collective fixed route passenger transportation	0,07	2,85
PN	4871	Tourist transport by land	0,16	4,45
PN	4872	Tourist transport by water	0,15	2,02
PN	4885	Intermediation services for freight transport	0,26	8,98
N	4921	Foreign package delivery services	0,23	6,65
IN	5111	Edition of newspapers, magazines, books and the like, except via the Internet	0,41	8,91
SC	5151	Transmission of radio and television programmes, except via the Internet	0,43	8,35
SC	5171	Wireline telecommunications operators	0,48	9,12
SC	5172	Cellular and other wireless telecommunications, except satellite services	0,46	9,39
IN	5221	Multiple banking	1,30	13,51

Source: based on economic census for Mexico (2009) and Soete and Miozzo taxonomy (1990).   (Continued)

Notes: Sectors 55 Y 62 (Management of Companies and Enterprises and Health Care and Social Assistance, respectively) are not included in the 2009 census.

"Retail trade in supermarkets"; "Retail trade in department stores"; "Foreign package delivery services"; "Parks with recreational facilities and electronic gaming" branches have been catalogued like "Network firms" instead of separate them into the two groups from Soete and Miozzo's taxonomy: "Physical networks" or "Informational networks".

"Core Innovation" index includes questions 1 and 5. The averages for the "Core Innovation" and "Aggregate Innovation" indices are 0.30 and 7.34, respectively.

4A. Branch level innovation indices (NAICS), 2009 census

Soete and Miozzo code	Branch	Description	"Core Innovation" (max value= 2)	"Aggregate Innovation" (max value= 21)
IN	5224	Brokerage credit and financial services not stock exchange	0,62	10,35
IN	5241	Institutions of insurance and bonding	1,00	12,43
PN	5311	Rent without intermediation of dwellings and other real state	0,13	5,52
PN	5312	Real estate and real estate brokers	0,21	7,29
PN	5324	Rental of industrial, commercial and services machinery and equipment	0,17	7,39
IN	5411	Legal services	0,25	7,91
IN	5413	Services in architecture, engineering and related activities	0,40	8,96
SC	5414	Specialized design	0,43	7,79
SC	5415	Computer consultancy services	0,84	10,84
SC	5416	Administrative, scientific and technical consulting services	0,40	8,96
SC	5418	Advertising services and related activities	0,55	8,79
SC	5419	Other professional, scientific and technical services	0,24	5,74
IN	5611	Business management services	0,32	8,46
PN	5612	Facilities support services	0,34	8,34
IN	5613	Employment services	0,28	7,58
PER	5615	Travel agencies and reservation services	0,29	7,64
PER	5616	Research, protection and safety services	0,34	8,47
PER	5619	Other support business services	0,38	8,76
PUB	6111	Schools of basic, secondary and special education	0,35	7,99
PUB	6113	Professional degrees and graduated schools	0,60	9,47
IN	6114	Commercial schools, computer and training for executives	0,40	7,67
N	7131	Parks with recreational facilities and electronic gaming	0,26	5,93
PN	7139	Other recreational services	0,20	7,00
PER	7211	Hotels, motels and the like	0,10	3,81
PER	7221	Restaurants with waiter service	0,23	6,34
PN	7222	Self-service restaurants and with food to take-out	0,08	2,46
SC	8113	Repair and maintenance of agricultural, industrial, commercial and services machinery and equipment	0,33	8,42
PER	8131	Commercial, industrial, recreational and professional organizations and associations	0,16	6,11

Source: based on economic census for Mexico (2009) and Soete and Miozzo taxonomy (1990).

Notes: Sectors 55 Y 62 (Management of Companies and Enterprises and Health Care and Social Assistance, respectively) are not included in the 2009 census.

"Retail trade in supermarkets"; "Retail trade in department stores"; "Foreign package delivery services"; "Parks with recreational facilities and electronic gaming" branches
have been catalogued like "Network firms" instead of separate them into the two groups from Soete and Miozzo's taxonomy: "Physical networks" or "Informational networks".

"Core Innovation" index includes questions 1 and 5. The averages for the "Core Innovation" and "Aggregate Innovation" indices are 0.30 and 7.34, respectively.

CHALLENGES FOR SERVICE INNOVATION IN DEVELOPING COUNTRIES

The cases of Mexico and Latin America

Leonel CORONA-TREVIÑO
CEPCyT, Faculty of Economics,
UNAM

INTRODUCTION

The primary objective of this article is to focus on innovation and service innovation across Latin America as a whole and in Mexico, in particular. While studies on innovation do exist, there is not enough awareness in either Latin America or Mexico of innovation's present-day importance as it relates to the growth of the service society. In 2018, Mexico's service economy generated 63% of gross domestic product (GDP), employing 61% of the economically active population (56 million people). Similarly, in 2017, the service economy across Latin America accounted for 62% of GDP (CEPAL, 2017c) and 65% of the active population (CEPAL, 2018a). A further objective of this article is to examine, in a prospective way, those trends that are particularly important for innovation and service innovation[1].

---

1   Prospective studies find a propitious moment when they are related to a commemorative event. As a matter of fact, Martin's 20 challenges (Martin, 2016) arrived after the 50th anniversary of the Science Policy Research Unit (SPRU) of the University of Sussex. Later, the publication of Djellal and Gallouj's paper on 15 service innovation challenges was presented at the 27th Annual RESER Conference in 2016 (Djellal and Gallouj, 2016). The present paper, proposing 22 challenges in innovation and service innovation for Mexico and Latin America, also came out in 2016, based on the studies conducted

To that end, we draw inspiration from two publications: Martin (2010) and Djellal and Gallouj (2016). Martin's work entailed 1) accounting for the evolution of innovation studies, highlighting the main advances and authors (Martin, 2010) and 2), using this information to draw up a list of 20 future challenges for innovation studies (Martin, 2016). Next, Faridah Djellal and Faïz Gallouj (2016), using the same methodology, described the evolution of service innovation as being based on the shift from "assimilation" to "demarcation" and "integration" perspectives, identifying 15 advances in service innovation studies; they then suggested 15 challenges for these studies[2].

Emulating the steps taken by Martin, and Djellal and Gallouj, the first task was to select certain leading economic and social problems that could be related to innovation and service innovation in Mexico and Latin America, using the latest available statistic (around the year 2018):

1. In Mexico, *urbanization* (cities with 10,000 or more inhabitants) stands at 80.15%, while across Latin America, 80.6% of the population lives in urban areas (World Bank, 2018b). Urbanization is increasing demand for services, and thus creates opportunities for service innovation.

2. Many people work in *informal* activities: 44% in cities (of more than 10,000 inhabitants) and 70% in rural areas and smaller cities. 27% of informal workers are part of the total employed population (INEGI, 2018a). Across Latin America, 48.4% of urban dwellers work in informal activities (CEPAL, 2017a). These are largely concentrated in commerce and services, so both could require service innovations.

3. *Violence* is widespread in Mexico. In 2018, there were 28,269 victims of crime[3] per 100,000 people, 97% of which never

---

during the 40th anniversary of Seacyt (Spanish acronym of the Seminar on Economics in Science and Technology), which was founded in 1976 at UNAM in Mexico, by Theotonio dos Santos (†) and Leonel Corona.

2   These results were later published in two separate publications, one devoted to advances in Services Innovation Studies (Djellal and Gallouj, 2018a), the other to challenges in this field (Djellal and Gallouj, 2018b).

3   This number of victims is measured by the perception of crimes having directly affected people or their homes in 2018. These crimes could be one or more per victim from a wide spectrum, such as total or partial theft of a vehicle, home burglaries, robbery or

came to trial (INEGI, 2018b). Across Latin America, the victimization rate is 36% (CEPAL, 2016b). There is therefore a significant increase in security services, which can be improved by technology and service innovations.

4. In 2018, *poverty* affected 42% of Mexico's total population of 125 million inhabitants (CONEVAL, 2018). Across Latin America, 30.2% of the population lives in poverty (CEPAL, 2019). In 2017, of Mexico's 11 million indigenous people[4], 72% were living in poverty (CONEVAL, 2018) – a much higher proportion than the 38% indigenous population in poverty found in some Latin American countries[5] (CEPAL, 2014). One solution could be to support collaborative economic activities based on techniques, technologies, and services suited to the different regional and indigenous contexts. These involve organisational innovations in services.

5. Income is *polarized*: higher-income households (30%) account for 63% of total income. Just 9% of total income finds its way to lower-income households (also 30%); this results in a Gini Index of 0.5 (INEGI, 2019). Across Latin America, higher-income households (30%) earn 56% of total income, with just 12% going to lower-income households (also 30%). This results in a Gini Index of 0.46 (CEPAL, 2018b). Another indicator of well-being polarization is expressed in access to information and communication technologies (ICT), as measured by the percentage of households having internet access at home: 52.2% across Latin America, and 50.9% in Mexico (CEPAL, 2017b). Frugal service and technology innovations could help provide access to communication and other resources in lower-income households (Koerich *et al.*, 2019).

---

assault on the street or on public transport, etc. ENVIPE (acronym in Spanish for the National Survey of Victimization and Perception on Public Safety (INEGI, 2018b).

4 2018 data about people that speak an indigenous language.

5 In Latin America, 38% of poverty in the indigenous population is the double of the poverty of the rest of population, 19% (Calvo-Gonzalez, 2016). Indigenous people as a percentage of the population: Bolivia (62%), Guatemala (41%) and Mexico (15%), which has the largest indigenous population with 17 million, followed by Peru (24%) with 7.5 million and Bolivia with 6.2 million. Data circa 2015 about people self-declared as indigenous (Cruz-Saco, 2018).

6. In Mexico, Central America and the Caribbean there is substantial dependence on foreign material imports for the *"maquila duty-free industry"*. In Mexico there are 2.7 million maquiladora workers, *i.e.* 5% of the total active population (INEGI, 2018a). Consequently, there are opportunities to both upgrade the internal position within those global production chains and offer incentives for local production by seeking innovations and service innovations.

7. Regarding *rule of law* and *public policy*, public spending amounts to 28.1% of GDP across Latin America, while it is 20.4% of GDP in Mexico (World Bank, 2017). Moreover, 70% of people aged 18 or over across Latin America, and 63% in Mexico are distrustful of political and state institutions (CEPAL, 2016a). In addition, on the list of countries categorised from lowest to highest levels of corruption, Mexico, with an index of 29, ranks 130th - the worst performance in the OECD. Some Latin American countries have better indexes, for example: Uruguay (71), Chile (67) and Costa Rica (56). The average corruption index for Latin America is 43 (Transparency International, 2019). The fight against corruption requires further effort; to a certain extent opportunities to innovate and apply service innovation in the distribution of public services and money do exist.

This article addresses both the need to highlight challenges requiring the attention of innovation (mainly service innovation) studies, and the need to consider some of Mexico's and Latin America's crucial political, economic and social problems – such as those mentioned above. Therefore, following the methodology of two prospective studies by Martin (2016) and Djellal and Gallouj (2018a; 2018b), we propose an agenda of 22 challenges that are faced by studies of innovation and service innovation, in the context of Mexico and Latin America.

This outline is organised into 4 parts: Part 1 is given over to a short literature review, largely based on the reviews by Martin (2016) and Djellal and Gallouj (2016, 2018a, 2018b). Part 2 is devoted to a discussion of the evolution of science, technology and innovation thinking across Latin America and in Mexico. In Part 3 we present and discuss the 22 challenges for service innovation studies identified for Mexico and Latin America. And in Part 4, we design four scenarios towards which economies can evolve, depending on how the challenges posed are taken up.

1. LITERATURE REVIEW: A COMPARISON OF METHODOLOGY

The literature[6] has suggested 20 innovation and 15 service innovation challenges for the future (Table 1). As already stated, these have been developed based on the steps initially taken by Martin (2010) which consist of: 1) surveying the evolution of thinking on innovation to highlight the main advances and authors and in light of these findings, draw up 2) a list of 20 future challenges for innovation studies (Martin, 2016). Furthermore, Djellal and Gallouj (2016, 2018a and 2018b) first characterized the main advances in service innovation studies, using the "assimilation, demarcation, inversion and integration" framework (Gallouj, 2010). They went on to identify 15 challenges for service innovation studies in the future.

In order to draw a comparison of the two lists of challenges, they are classified into seven domains in this paper, namely: Innovation, Environment, Social, Economy, State, Institutional, and Academia – while maintaining the original challenge numbers assigned by each list. It should also be noted that there is no direct relationship between the classified challenges. For some challenges proposed by one author, there is no counterpart on the other list. For example, Djellal and Gallouj postulate a challenge concerning the environment, while Martin does not explicitly take this into account, and conversely, neither Martin nor Djellal and Gallouj suggest any public service challenges (Table 1).

For the purpose of comparison, the 20 challenges for innovation studies classified by Domain are also found in certain Fields – beginning, appropriately, with Innovation in a general sense[7]. In the first

---

6   This section concentrates on the methodology used by Martin (2016) and taken up by Djellal and Gallouj (2016, 2018 a and b). Other aspects are found in specific sections of the present paper.

7   Notwithstanding the fact that the other domains also relate to innovation.

challenge "Dark" innovation is noted (to indicate that it is not easily detected). Innovation challenges relate to different contexts: Sectoral, Regional and Global. There are also focal points and interests in which certain innovations could be introduced. These domains could be related to Djellal and Gallouj's "Forgotten sectors"[8] and the problems of Developing/Emerging countries. In the case of Developing/Emerging countries, other sectors (in addition to Djellal and Gallouj's forgotten sectors) must also be included in such a category. Agriculture-related services, informal activities and housework, all of which are common in both Latin American and Mexican contexts, should be investigated via empirical research. In these countries, the assimilation of innovation capabilities (concentrated in sectors such as manufacturing and whose focus is cutting-edge technology) underscores the challenge of moving towards more domestic (or local) innovations in the services sector. From this perspective, the ability to boost these "Forgotten sectors", mainly through organisation and social innovations, could improve the situation in developing countries (Table 1).

The Environment domain faces challenges – such as global warming and climate change – that "have been recognized as a real threat to the viability and sustainability of the planet" (Lundvall *et al.*, 2018, p. 144). However, only Djellal and Gallouj list this as a challenge to service innovation studies. Martin does not directly mention this topic, although he does, within "Disciplinary sclerosis", advocate for the economy to be more attentive to other sciences, which could include ecology.

After the Environment, the Social Area carries significant weight for both authors. Martin's innovation targets social well-being rather than wealth per se, ensuring fair distribution in place of the "winner takes all" approach. However, he also recognizes that certain risks inherent to the innovation process do make it necessary to move towards socially responsible innovations. As might be expected, one third of the challenges suggested by Djellal and Gallouj concern Innovation in the Social domain – yet their proposal also includes new issues not commonly

---

8   Djellal and Gallouj (2016, p. 414) mention examples of this kind of sector, such as "religious organizations, prisons, driving schools, hairstyling services or beauty treatments, body care services, laundry services, funeral services, police, fire services, social housing services, non-profit organizations…"

addressed in economic thinking, such as Ageing population, Religion, Gender perspective and Ethical concerns. These social aspects are not explicitly considered in Martin's challenges, which explains why some boxes in Table 1 remain blank.

In Martin's column, the Economy domain relates to theory – or, more accurately, to a "paradigm". After the last major crisis in 2008, it became clear that conventional economic theory lacked the tools necessary to dealing with such a problem. In response, we must identify the causes, but we should leave aside "Ptolemaic economics" and rely more on an open-minded economy. Economic growth, while a necessary condition, should not be the sole focal point. The challenge is to reach "Sustainable development". For Djellal and Gallouj, in Domain 4 (Economy), the emphasis is on individuals and their interrelationships. They point out that employment (and the skills it generates) both highlight the role of entrepreneurship and present an important challenge for innovation studies. All these considerations are examined through the challenge of systemic evaluation, i.e. moving together towards a smart service ecosystem.

The other half of the fields are mainly institutional challenges. The first of these are those concerned with the state, policy, intellectual property and the openness of innovation. Those following concern the exploitation and cooperation purposes of innovation and, lastly, the academic sphere where the topics are elitism, disciplinary sclerosis and ethical research concerns.

In Table 1, Djellal and Gallouj's 15 challenges are also included in the above-mentioned fields: 1) Innovation includes the "forgotten sectors" (similar to Martin's "dark innovation") and the challenges faced by developing countries. 2) Half of the challenges are connected to the social field: social innovation, religion, population ageing, gender, ethical issues and evaluation challenges. 3) Topics such as employment, entrepreneurship, smart service ecosystem, and innovation networks are located within the economic challenges. 4) In academia, we find multidisciplinary challenges. Although the environmental challenge is added for service innovation, it clearly must also be related with innovation in general. Service innovation must also consider public services.

TAB. 1 – 20 challenges for innovation, and 15 for service innovation studies.

Domain	Martin's 20 Challenges for innovation studies*					Djellal and Gallouj's 15 Challenges for Service Innovation **	
	Martin's number	Field	Shift		Forces/ actions (1)	Djellal and Gallouj's number	Challenge
			From (Current)	To (Challenge)			
1. Innovation	1	Innovation in general	Visible	"Dark"	Revelation		
	2	Sectoral innovation	Manufacturing	Services	Integration approach (2)	12	Forgotten Sectors
	3	Focuses	High-tech innovations	High impact of mundane innovations	Interests, traditions (gender)		
	4	Regional	National and Regional	Global	Multi-scope analysis	3	Developing/ Emerging countries
2. Environment (3)	5	Ecology (4)	Innovation productivity	Green innovation	Ecological crisis	1	Two empty Rows in Blank

Notes: (1) Forces/actions are the author's interpretation. (2) "The integrative or synthetic perspective provides more a balanced view of innovation in services. It seeks to provide the same analytical frameworks for both goods and services, and for both technological and non-technological forms of innovation (3) "Environmental science focuses on the interactions between the physical, chemical, and biological components of the environment, including their effects on all types of organisms". (4) "Ecology is the scientific analysis and study of interactions among organisms and their environment". https://scienceprize.scilifelab.se/prize-categories-ecology-environment

Domain	Martin's number	Field	Shift		Forces/actions (I)	Djellal and Gallouj's number	Challenge
			From (Current)	To (Challenge)			
	8	Social (in general)	Wealth	Well-being	Democracy	2	Social innovation: skills and competences, entrepreneurship.
3. Social	9	Distribution	Winner takes all	Fairness for all	Looking for equality	4	Religious Trajectory
	7	Risk	Risk	Social responsibility	Government intervention	5	Population ageing
					Policy/ Education	6	Gender agenda
					Social awareness	7	Ethical and societal issues
4. Economy		Labour				9	Employment and skills
	17	Crisis	Causes of the current crisis		Identification	10	Smart service ecosystems
5. State	10	State	Fixer of failures	Entrepreneurial	Active Role	*This box is empty as there is no explicit content on the relation of Public service innovations (Djellal and Gallouj, 2018b). (5)*	
	11	Policy	Faith-based policy	Evidence based policy	Reality		

Notes: (5) Gallouj did not include public innovation in the challenges; there is however a current EU research project, 2020 CoVAL, that aims to find new ways of examining the co-creation of value and its integration in order to transform public administration services and processes (http:// www.co-val.eu/).

Domain	Martin's number	Field	Shift		Forces/ actions (1)	Djellal and Gallouj's number	Challenge
			From (Current)	To (Challenge)			
6. Institutional Rules	12	Appropriation of knowledge	Intellectual property	Open Source	Tensions Balancing**	11	Innovation networks and innovation systems
	14	Innovation purpose	Closed	Open innovation			
	13		Exploration	Exploitation			
	15		Competition	Cooperation			
7. Academia	16	Academic	Case study (policy)	Innovation theory (explanation)	Pricking academic bubbles	13	Multi-disciplinarity: towards a service science?
	18		Disciplinary sclerosis		Avoiding		
	20	Research	Integrity, sense of morality and collegiality		Maintaining	15	Service innovation degrees

Source: Table based on *Table 6 (Martin, 2016, p. 443) and **Box 1.3 (Djellal and Gallouj, 2018b, p. 5).

2. THE EVOLUTION OF SCIENCE, TECHNOLOGY AND INNOVATION THINKING IN LATIN AMERICA AND MEXICO

In terms of Mexico and Latin America, the seven Domains of Table 1 bring the 20 "Innovation Challenges" for the future (Martin, 2016) together with the 15 "Service Innovation Challenges" (Djellal and Gallouj, 2018b). Table 1 also suggests concepts specifically developed for service innovation, such as "assimilation/demarcation" and "inversion/integration" perspectives[9], which were adapted and supplemented in order to build Mexican and Latin American challenges for innovation and service innovation. This was achieved by reordering around the eight domains and consideration of the following two lines of analysis.

The first line of analysis is the evolution of economic thinking in Mexico and across Latin America, which has also generally followed a different emphasis, beginning in science and technology, which has both resulted in innovation and led to the National Innovation System (NIS).

The second line of analysis is a list of challenges drawn up and grouped both within each domain and within a specific field therein, on the basis of the social and economic problems of Mexico and Latin America. In drawing this up, we have taken into consideration both strengths and weaknesses, as well as the levers needed to improve each country's performance (Table 2).

A prospective analysis of the forces of change framing the challenges of innovation and service innovation was then applied. Four scenarios were designed, based on two axes: one axis of income concentration-distribution and one axis of regional divergence-convergence development. Consequently, there is A) a desirable scenario relating to the forces of change for the proposed challenges and standing in contrast to B) a starting scenario covering the main Mexican and Latin American economic and social problems (Figure 1).

---

9   These lines of analysis are based on the different analytical focus of service innovation: the technologist approach (assimilation), the service-oriented approach (demarcation/differentiation), the integrative approach (synthesis) and a fourth perspective, inversion, in light of the active role played by KIBS (Djellal and Gallouj, 2018a, 2018b).

Because the other two scenarios are a blend of C) a desirable and a contrasting current problematic situation and D) regional development with income inequality (Figure 1), they have been used implicitly.

2.1 THE EVOLUTION OF SCIENCE, TECHNOLOGY
AND INNOVATION THINKING ACROSS LATIN AMERICA

First, we present an evolution of economic innovation thinking that is based mainly on ECLAC[10] publications. Second, we have identified eight periods for Mexico; these include certain milestones in economic innovation thinking in the Seacyt-UNAM.

2.1.1. Latin America: science policy analysis of technology (1950-1979)

A science policy analysis of technology was conducted within a Latin American network. Its central objective was to compare the causes of backwardness in the region that could be attributed (according to this vision) to the lack of any industrial development up to the task of tackling the centre-periphery relationship (in which negative terms of trade for the periphery tend to decrease, and transfer more value to, the centre). On that basis, industrialization had been built around an "imports substitution policy", meaning that protective commercial import barriers had been imposed, to make room for an internal industrial sector.

"Dependency theory" focuses on external relations that limit development; external technology is one of its main mechanisms. This trend was oriented towards the interpretation of underdevelopment, and the need to change social relations. Although three forms featuring dependence are highlighted, only two are relevant to this analysis. The first of these is financial-industrial dependence, which is characterized by the dominance of large capital in hegemonic centres, and its expansion abroad to invest in raw materials and agricultural products that are consumed in hegemonic centres. This is known as "development out" (Novelo, 2014, p. 7). The second is technological-industrial dependence, which emerged in the post-war period and is characterized by the technological-industrial field of transnational companies that invest in

---

10   ECLAC, The Economic Commission for Latin America and the Caribbean (ECLAC) –
     the Spanish acronym is CEPAL.

industries for the internal market of periphery countries. The theory did not however work as described.

2.1.2. Debt crisis and the protection of scientific and technological capabilities (1980-1989).

With the debt crisis, most Latin American countries adopted neoliberal policies advocating that the state should reduce its participation in the economy and let the market operate on its own. These policies, supported by the International Monetary Fund (IMF), led to the privatization of public enterprises and the opening of economies to international markets, culminating in the abandonment of the "import substitution industrialization model". Nevertheless, some public resources were assigned to the protection of specific scientific and technological capabilities.

The main objective had been to achieve economic growth – but an increment in income concentration ensued. In other words, the opening the *black box* of economic development in terms of reaching growth goals was not accompanied by improved equality (Faynzylber, 1990).

To counter the growing neoliberal trend, Latin America was therefore obliged to adjust its policy recommendations. The recessive adjustment of the balance of payments would be replaced by an expansive adjustment, driving exports via the dynamization of investments in the tradeable goods sectors. One feasible solution was a debt renegotiation agreement between debtors and bankers, with less protectionism on the part of the central countries and a more flexible and pragmatic use of economic policy instruments.

2.1.3. Productive transformation with equity: neo-structuralism and openness to foreign technology (1990-2007)

During this period, human resources training and an active technology policy for long-term productive transformation were highlighted. Though industry remained the axis of productive transformation, its articulations with the primary sector and services stood out, through an integral productive reconfiguration around those branches that would allow technical progress to spread to all sectors of the economy. The provision of a balanced macroeconomic environment was also considered important. In addition, greater (though gradual and selective) economic openness was achieved as a way of introducing technical progress and increasing productivity.

In that context, the "great priority challenge" was "the recovery of politics as an innovative public action to establish a new balance that complements both state and market", rejecting "the univocal vision of globalization and neoliberalism" (Sunkel, 2006, p. 24). It was not a matter of returning to the period of state-centred structuralist thinking, because the international environment had completely changed (history is not reversible). In fact, public action by the state was needed because significant corrections to the market model were needed. In a globalized world, the state's forms of action had to be renewed. In short, the top priority challenge was to reinstate policy as an innovative public action, in order to establish a "new balance" that would "complement the state and the market in the context of globalization" (Sunkel, 2006, p. 24).

2.1.4. Returning to structuralism: public policy's attempt at boosting innovation (2008-today)

Having realised that Latin American countries needed to seek the growth that would allow them to achieve social, external and environmental balance (Bárcena, 2019), ECLAC initiated a transition from neo-structuralism to structuralism. However, ECLAC also stated the need for international governance to modify international power relations between the Centre and the Periphery. This is where innovation takes on an important role – as a mechanism that allows others to adopt the "core technologies" that will enable them to boost innovation and generate internal productive capacity.

Here again, the state is advised to play a more active role in both the economy and public investment. But not all Latin American countries are ready for this new way of thinking. So far, most – with the notable exceptions of Venezuela, Uruguay, Costa Rica, Cuba, and (since 2019) Mexico – have maintained their neoliberal economic policies, in which the role of the state is restricted to that of a mere corrector of market failures, and its entrepreneurial role is minimized. Public spending has been reduced accordingly, first and foremost impacting public investment – which has always been an important support to the development of new technologies and innovations. However, from the point of view of social goals, the quality of the technology has caused income inequality to rise. ECLAC also expressed the need for international governance. Sustained, balanced growth has been preserved at the cost of deterioration to the quality of life of most people. Various alternatives have been postulated in response to this, such as the idea of the state playing an active role in the economy, to boost innovation. This would be a move away from the orthodox thinking that is tied to the idea of a market failure corrector state.

2.2. THE EVOLUTION OF SCIENCE, TECHNOLOGY AND INNOVATION THINKING IN MEXICO

In light of the aforementioned four phases of Latin American thinking about innovation and economic evolution, this paper will describe below the eight stages in Mexico's use of Seacyt-UNAM for the pursuit of Science, Technology and Innovation research.

2.2.1. Science policy analysis of technology (1959-1979)

1. Gestation (1977-1979): Analysis of the basic economic and social problems of contemporary capitalism. Multinational corporations were considered cells of the system. A new social force of production was based on the scientific and technological revolution (Richta, 1969).

2.2.2. Debt crisis (1980-1989), though some scientific and technological capabilities were preserved

2. Take-off (1980-1983): Following the gestation phase of the political economy, the main subjects were the internationalization of capital, the crisis of capitalism and long waves. These topics were also being researched by SPRU (Freeman, 1984).

3. Internationalization (1984-1989): a Latin American research project on technological prospective was carried out by six groups. One of these focused on the political economy of technology, and was based at UNAM Mexico[11]. The Bariloche group worked on an alternative to

---

11 The other groups were CENDES in Venezuela, the Campinas University in Brazil, and the Bariloche Foundation in Argentina. The main results of this project are available in Herrera *et al.* (1994)..

the limits to growth (Meadows *et al.*, 1972), signposting a new society (Herrera, 1977).

2.2.3. Neo-structuralist openness to foreign technology (1990-2007)

4. Transition (1990-1995): Starting from the perspective that a crisis of economic theories had been caused by increasing the diversity and complexity of contemporary economic problems, a review of the concepts and economic problems relating to technology was conducted, from the standpoint of the main economic theories and approaches (Corona and Paunero, 2013).

5. Business Innovation (1996-2006): The ability to grasp and analyse real economic problems is essential to the development of new approaches; INDICO (Innovation – Diffusion and Competitiveness) – a business-centred index – was thus designed to measure a company's ability to innovate. (Corona-Treviño, 1997). It has also been applied internationally to compare innovation in the triple helix relationship of the new regulated market of NAFTA's three countries (Corona *et al.*, 2006).

2.2.4. A return to structuralism and a public policy attempt at boosting innovation (2008-present)

6. The 2008 economic crisis (2007-2013): three developments occurred in this period. The first was the collaboration that began in 2003 with a group of Management School professors examining approaches to innovation management. The second was a move towards prospective studies methodologies, and its implications as a tool to understand the 2008 world crisis, which began in the United States. One line of reasoning was the interdisciplinary approach to a broader outlook on innovation, centred on its role in the knowledge society. The third development was a deep dive into the agglomeration of regional companies, in a bid to look global but act locally, as well as generate solutions in the face of the economic crisis (Corona and Paunero, 2013).

7. Prospective studies and service innovation (2014-2018): some research has tackled the short- and long-term economic impacts of a prolonged economic crisis in Mexico as illustrated by the 36-year average of low (0.7%) annual per capita growth (World Bank, 2020). This

demonstrates the importance and necessity of: change to the production model; a profound examination of selected sectoral cases and dealing with growing insecurity and violence in Mexico (Kato Vidal, 2015). Such solutions require service organisation and innovation supported by information and communication technologies in Latin America (Cardoso, 2017).

8. Public services innovation in Mexico (2019-2020): Mexico's public sector is changing in line with the so-called 4th Transformation (4T)[12] by improving its ability to deal with certain historic societal demands such as well-being (education and healthcare), fairer distribution, justice, democracy, and combatting corruption (DOF, 2019).

3. 22 CHALLENGES FOR SERVICE INNOVATION STUDIES: MEXICO AND LATIN AMERICA

This paper's focus is on innovation and service innovation in Mexico and across Latin America. We should therefore consider Djellal and Gallouj's Challenge No. 3 (Table 1), which states that there is a service innovation gap in developing and emerging countries. Based on the economic line of innovation-related reasoning in this region, we propose a list of challenges designed to overcome the current situation through studies that help solve socioeconomic problems. In keeping with the Domains listed in Table 1, the challenges aimed at resolving the current situation in Mexico and across Latin America are described in Table 2. They seek to do so by either leveraging the forces of change or overcoming the obstacles[13].

---

12 The current Mexican government (2019-2025) has styled itself the "Fourth Transformation", following three major historical events: 1) Mexican Independence (1810-1821) after 300 years of Spanish colonization; 2) The Reformation (1858-1861) that followed the war between liberals and conservatives and ushered in the "Reform Laws" and established separation between church and state, and 3) The Mexican Revolution (1910-1917), in which armed conflict against the dictatorship of Porfirio Díaz led to Mexico's current constitution and the beginning of agricultural land distribution.

13 The Domains of Table 2 have been rearranged to better align them with Latin American and Mexican priorities. See the correspondence with Table 1 in each Domain.

3.1. INNOVATION

Any import of foreign technologies must be designed to lead to internal development capable of assimilating such technologies (C1). However, technology capacity development of this type can only have a broad impact where institutional channels capable of disseminating innovations both exist (via either private firms or public incentives), and result in a wider benefit (C3). The challenges, then, involve both technology and non-technology development, as well as its transfer – including from science. (C1) However, the diffusion of frugal innovations is mainly found locally, predominantly within a single country, and only in rare cases globally (Hossain *et al.*, 2016). Mechanisms therefore need to be created for both the diffusion of "frugal innovations" and for imitation capabilities – those that offer the highest benefits with the lowest use of resources (C2). However, absorption capacities are also required (C4). In addition, because there are clearly inherent risks in the innovative process, risk management capabilities can render innovation more feasible.

3.2. SOCIAL INNOVATION[14]

This specific domain is associated with multicultural Mexican characteristics. The local context must be approached in two ways. On the one hand, the preservation and protection of traditions require the active participation of clients, users and providers, so that as they engage in social innovation, their contributions allow for cultural expression (C6). In other words, innovation should permeate the country's cultures. On the other hand, the actors' participation should be flexible enough to open up the local context through dissemination mechanisms (C5). Indigenous peoples are an asset that preserves Mexican cultures in a purer way, but because they have also been marginalized, their cultures tend to disappear. Ideally a relationship can be forged between the innovation process and the cultures embodied by indigenous people.

Next, social innovation allows production to change in a way that recognizes the multicultural features of Mexican society, adapts to it and is capable of coming up with solutions that reduce poverty – indigenous poverty in particular.

---

14   For a comprehensive view of social innovation see Mulgan (2019). This corresponds to Domain 3 in Table 1.

Violence is a strong inherent cultural trait that must be taken into consideration in order to recognize it as a multidimensional problem. In this sense, suggesting social participatory options that include the specific cultural characteristics of Mexican and Latin American society ultimately represents a social innovation challenge. The mechanisms necessary to reducing rates of violence and poverty, especially among indigenous people, can be generated by community-based projects that are developed comprehensively and cover all sectors of society[15].

3.3. INNOVATION SYSTEMS[16]

Innovation systems can be analysed at three levels: national, regional and local. Correspondingly, outward extensions could exist, an important one being the Mexican diaspora (C8). Since there is abundant knowledge of the Mexican population in the United States, there is also the potential of increasing knowledge via connection services with in-country technology and scientific peers. As mentioned in the social innovation section above, the generation of effective channels of relations (C7) can both preserve a culture and use it as a springboard with which to empower the National Innovation System (NIS). The same thing happens with Latin American diaspora, in the sense that the population living abroad can be regarded as an opportunity to improve local, regional, national and Latin American innovation systems through the multidimensional exchanges that this population can provide.

The interrelations generated by innovation systems (both between and within countries) can help build their economic development through the diffusion of technology. In this way, solutions that reduce poverty could be found if an institutional environment were to exist allowing the results of innovation to be adapted to the sectors in which they are applied. Otherwise, income polarization could worsen, in the event that the highest-income segments of society were to monopolize the benefits of innovation systems.

---

15 An example is found in Cuetzalan, Puebla, Mexico, where different communities have organized to defend their lands and traditional culture, creating cooperatives around coffee production and commercialization (Cobo *et al.*, 2018).

16 Innovation systems correspond to 1.4 Regional and 7. Academia, in Table 1.

3.4. SECTORS: SERVICES[17]

Focusing on formal services, the servitization of manufacturing is an important process of the Division of Labour (C9). Mexico and Latin America, whose service sectors account for the largest share of the economy (62% of GDP in Mexico and 63% of GDP in Latin America), both participate in the New International Division of Labour through manufacturing. In other words, the region (mainly Mexico, Central America and some Caribbean countries) is presented as the factory of the world, especially in terms of the "maquiladora industry" (C10). In certain regions, tourism services are dominant as a result of their natural beauty and anthropological attractions (C11). Likewise, internationalization is flourishing, with offices, call centres, and research centres for multinational firms being set up in Mexico and across Latin America (C11). A further aspect is the internal division of services, in specific niches. All of these form an important focus for service innovation research (C11).

Urbanization is another source of services. Wherever the population is concentrated in specific locations, generating growing demand for services, this leads to the provision of those services, resulting in a growing circle of people migrating to urban areas, further increasing the degree of urbanization – and with it, the demand for services and all that this entails. Consequently, while both Mexico and Latin America as a whole have urbanization rates of close to 80% (World Bank, 2018b), this has not been used as leverage for improving services. The fact that urban concentrations are numerous, and that services are located in very specific big cities (Mexico City, as well as other Latin American cities and capitals), reveals a problem in terms of the redistribution and deconcentration of services. Although demand for services is located in urban areas, their supply needs to be expanded – which provides an opportunity for improvements through service innovations.

3.5. SERVICE INNOVATION[18]

From the assimilation/demarcation perspective (Gallouj, 2002, 2010), service innovation offers better opportunities for the product service system

---

17   Services are included in Field (1.2 Sector) of Table 1. It is separate because of its importance to service innovation.
18   Service innovation is also part of Field (1.2) of Table 1.

in terms of the internal domain of key technologies. The fields of e-banking, e-government, and e-city have different kinds of service innovations using ICT technologies (C12). These innovations could include market warnings and product maintenance, and even extend the life of goods. Although these and other Knowledge Intensive Business Services (KIBS) play a particularly important role in the knowledge society (C14), they currently represent an invisible service innovation opportunity (C15). Because it is difficult to include the use of more advanced services and technologies, informal activities (most of which have low productivity) are regarded as presenting a challenge to innovation in services. Only 50% of households in Mexico and across Latin America have ICT access[19]. There is a broad area in which innovation in services could be developed to improve access to existing ICT as well as to innovate in its use and development.

3.6. ECONOMY[20]

As a basic input to the productive system, energy is one of the most important sectors. However, it is not always produced internally. Latin America as a whole is a net importer (6.6% of energy is imported), while Mexico is a net energy exporter (-4.6%) (World Bank, 2018a). In 2015, just 9% of the energy consumed in Mexico came from renewable sources, whereas across Latin America, this indicator stood at 27.6% (World Bank, 2015). The challenge, then, is to render innovation (in both technologies and services) capable of providing solutions or alternatives to current electricity generation, so as to move towards natural resource sovereignty (C16). In other words, the aim is to reduce the heavy reliance on foreign energy services – a sector in which both Mexico and the region as a whole could be self-sufficient.

Mexico, like Central American and Caribbean countries, has a significant "maquiladora" industry that produces goods and services. This industry struggles to attract local suppliers, and its development of internal capabilities and spillover innovations is sparse (C17). It is also a strongly reliant on imports of products and services to the Mexican economy in general, which reduces the possibility of generating internal capabilities. However, the "maquiladoras" could be used as leverage for the achievement of internal capabilities, perhaps helping it switch from

---

19   Measured as a percentage of households with Internet access.
20   Economic and industrial sectors are included in Domain 4 of Table 1.

being a high-import industry to one with internal network providers. To that end, the Mexican economy faces the challenge of creating large, planned strategic investment projects to build domestic capability (C18).

In this case, low-productivity informal activities are seen as a challenge to innovation in services in the sense that it is difficult to introduce use of the most advanced technologies in this sector. In fact, high-tech exports as a percentage of manufactured products amounts to 21% in Mexico and 14.3% across Latin America (World Bank, 2018a). Therefore, were the informal sector to be absorbed by the formal economy, there could be improvement to endogenous capacities. Since nearly half of urban workers and 70% of rural workers are employed informally, one major challenge is to provide training in service and technology innovation (C19). The same goes for the "maquiladoras", whose production dynamics generate little or no innovation. There is also an opportunity here to both absorb this portion of the population and increase productivity.

3.7. INSTITUTIONS[21]

The economic and social rules for both Mexico and Latin America as a whole reveal a low Rule of Law Index[22]; Mexico stands at 44 and Latin America at 53 (World Justice Project, 2020). An institutional change would thus require, firstly, efficient organisation of those institutional rules and secondly – in order to apply the rules based on internal capacity – the generation of organisational innovation, either socially or privately. For this reason, top-down policies must be complemented by bottom-up communication channels. In addition, competition requires good-faith cooperation. To that end, the rules governing Public-Private-Partnerships (PPP) are in need of improvement (C20).

The same type of policies need to be applied in other areas (such as security, violence and poverty) in order to improve living standards and establish a solid institutional structure.

As a result, alongside a reduction in the state's role in the region, there has been a rise in mistrust of public institutions. This is due to problems such as corruption and unlawful relations between public and private agents. A focus on social equity and regional development

---

21   It groups Table 1's Domains: 5. State; and 6. Institutional rules.
22   The index goes from 0 to 100, where 100 is complete rule of law and 1 is total absence of rule of law.

is needed. Once economic progress has been achieved and the rule of law has been strengthened, income polarization could be reduced (C21). There are of course fields in which private initiatives will be essential to boosting studies of innovation in services (for example, the use of ICT or extending the life of goods), but the main issues are the institutionalization of innovation channels and taking into account the particular characteristics of Latin America as a whole and Mexico in particular – such as indigenous communities and their culture.

To sum up, an interrelationship between the private and public sectors, based on rule of law, represents a major challenge for service innovation in Mexico and across Latin America.

3.8. ENVIRONMENT[23]

Similarly, the quest for sustainable development demands specific pro-environment policies. According to the circles of sustainability method (James, 2015), the institutional settings of both Latin America and Mexico must include such aspects as culture (identity and engagement, creativity and recreation, and enquiry and learning) and ecology (built form and transport, embodiment and sustenance and emissions and waste) (C22). The forces of change are local awareness, coupled with the participation of local people who have been affected by different kinds of pollution, and international cooperation, which at times involves international environmental agencies.

The increasing environmental damage generated by human activities has led to imbalances in wildlife ecosystems. Greater contact with wild animals puts both fauna and humans at risk. One example of this is the recent COVID-19 pandemic, caused by the mutation of a virus originally hosted by bats. It is not the only such disease: 8 out of 10 emerging diseases occur due to invasive wildlife (López-Gatell, 2020). Indeed, other conditions related to wild animals such as rabies (bats), hantaviruses (rodents) and Lyme disease (ticks) are more commonly found in regions having high deforestation rates (Suzán, 2020).

In addition to the direct effects of the COVID-19 lockdown measures on economic activity and social welfare (Deloitte, 2020), it has also opened opportunistic windows for organized crime, which has been able

---

23   In table 1 it is Domain 2.

to adapt to the new circumstances by diversifying activities to cyber-crime, clandestine trafficking in drugs, medical supplies, etc. It has also taken advantage of the gap left by governments focused on the health and economic crisis, by attempting to become a "legitimate actor" in, for example, the provision of food and medicine (Mexico) or disinfection campaigns to protect controlled territories (Honduras) (AFP, 2020).

Innovation and service innovation studies thus face the challenge of taking the environment into account within the prevailing economic dynamics while minimizing the risks inherent in the exploitation of natural resources. In other words, of promoting sustainable development in harmony with nature while preventing the appearance of new diseases such as the COVID-19 virus.

TAB. 2 – 22 Challenges for Service Innovation Studies: Mexico and Latin America.

	C	Domain*	From... (current)...	... To... (challenge)	Through the Forces of/ Capabilities/Actors
1	1	Innovation	Import of technology and knowledge services	Development and management of technology and knowledge services	Risk Management
	2		Science	Diffusion of frugal innovations Internal capabilities	
	3		Frugal	Incentives to local innovation	
	4		Imitation	Absorption capacities	
2	5	Social innovation	local context	Channels to spread it	Culture Indigenous People
	6		Eventual participation of clients, users, providers	Institutionalize participation of clients, users, providers	
3	7	Innovation systems	National, NIS regional, local system,	Effective channels of relations	Research Centres Entrepreneurships Public policies
	8		ONIS, Open National Innovation System.	Open to Mexico's diaspora	
4	9	Sectors: Services	Manufacturing	Servitization	Urbanization: Big cities Urban Culture
	10		Factories worldwide	International offices, Call centres	
	11		Tourism	Niches: medical, cultural, sport, ecology, research	

C		Domain*	From... (current)...	... To... (challenge)	Through the Forces of/ Capabilities/Actors
5	12	Service innovation	ICT	Service innovation applied to: e-banking, e-government, e-city	Diffusion of ICT's applications: Robotization
	13		Maintenance	Extend the life of goods	
	14		KIBS	Knowledge Society	
	15		"Dark"	Visible service innovation	
6	16	Economy	Energy generation and services	Internal energy production and services	Natural resource sovereignty and control, use and conservation
	17		Strong dependence of maquiladoras industry on foreign product and service inputs	Maquiladoras as a leverage for the development of internal capabilities	Maquiladoras
	18		Large project investment	Strategic project based on internal capabilities	State Participation
	19		Informal economy	Improved informal with new partnerships	Popular economy Skills and competences, Entrepreneurship
7	20	Institutions	Top-down policies	participation: bottom- up	Rule of Law
	21		Competition	cooperation: PPP public–private partnership.	
			Polarization of income and regional disparities	Social equity and regional development	
8	22	Environment	Over-exploitation of natural resources	Sustainable Development	Local awareness and participation International cooperation

*The Domains of Table 2 relate to Table 1 as follows: 1. Innovation (1); 2. Social innovation (3); 3. Innovation systems (1.4 regional; 7. Academia); 4. Sectors: Services (1.2 Sector); 5. Service innovation (as part of 1.2); 6. Economy (4); 7. Institutions (5. State; 6. Institutional rules); 8. Environment (2. Environment).

Source: the author, based on science, technology and innovation thinking and Challenge 3 "Service innovation and developing/emerging countries" (Djellal and Gallouj, 2016).

4. SCENARIOS FOR SERVICE INNOVATION CHALLENGES

The impact of the 22 challenges in innovation studies will depend both on the extent to which they are applied by decision-makers and on how the milieu evolves. If a desirable scenario for Mexico emerges, followed by "Regional development and inclusive growth" that is focused on a sustainable development model, then the challenges of innovation and service innovation studies will produce better results (Scenario A in Figure 1). This requires transparency in the use of public funds and mechanisms for evaluating social and public policies during the implementation process of the sustainable model[24].

The opposite scenario is "Social and Economic Polarization", which prolongs the problems relating to income and regional concentration. Reflecting Mexico's current reality, this situation is correlated with non-implementation of the anticorruption policies designed to avoid this undesirable situation (Scenario B). The COVID-19 crisis has accentuated existing structural problems in economies worldwide, including in Latin America. There is a need to link the short- to medium- and long-term measures designed to guarantee rights by strengthening the welfare state and providing universal social protections in such a way that it "counteracts the loss of sources of labour income and supports demand by safeguarding household income and consumption, while at the same time facilitating access to health" (ECLAC, 2020).

Inequality puts the poorest sectors of the population at a disadvantage when dealing with the health crisis, with the risk that their already precarious situation may worsen (García, 2020). To move from this Scenario to Scenario A, in the context of "The Great Lockdown"[25], the application of countercyclical policies aimed at abandoning the policy of fiscal discipline has been called for in order to allocate financial resources that promote economic growth (OXFAM, 2020).

---

24 Corruption in general is not good for society, yet rules have produced the opposite of their intended effects. One example of this is taxation that leads to ways of avoiding it; achieving zero tolerance then becomes very costly (North, 1990).
25 Name given to the COVID-19 crisis by the IMF.

The other two hybrid scenarios point to a positive objective, i.e. a mix of a desirable goal with an unattained axis, consisting of resolving regional disparities (scenario D) by building up communications, Internet infrastructure and widespread access to the Internet, without overcoming income concentration. Scenario C increases production policies and income distribution, without tackling regional disparities in Mexico and Latin America (Figure 1).

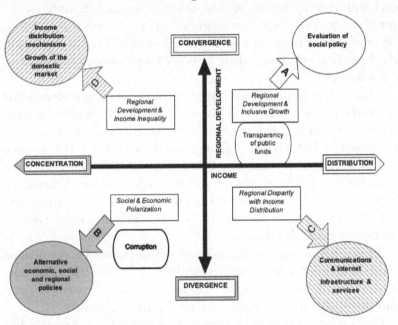

FIG. 1 – Mexico: Scenarios relating to income distribution and regional development (Source: the author).

CONCLUSION

The state of the art of innovation and service innovation can in part be explained by certain important commemorative events[26]. The intersection of innovation and service innovation occurs on an initial level with the application of innovation to service – mainly rooted in technology. Yet thanks to contributions from service innovation, the original concept of innovation now has an additional dimension which generates an "integrating" concept for technology and services, at another level.

This article has analysed advances in innovation concepts for Latin America as a whole and Mexico in particular, beginning with a description of the evolution of Latin American economic thinking, based on ECLAC, through four phases: A) 1959-1979: Science policy analysis of technology; B) 1980-1989: Debt crisis and the preservation of some scientific and technological capabilities; C) 1990-2007: Neo-structuralism and openness to foreign technology; and D) 2008-present: Returning to structuralism: public policy's attempt to boost innovation.

These phases were established in order to examine eight periods based on milestones in innovation thinking in Mexico. They also take into account the broad change in labelling, from "science policy research since the 1950s" to "innovation studies" in the 21st century.

One finding is that service innovation across Latin America and in Mexico is incipient, in comparison with Europe as well as – from a theoretical standpoint – even less tangible in respect of its economic and social awareness. This is despite the fact that both Latin American and Mexican economies are mostly service-oriented.

The 22 challenges for innovation and service innovation across Latin America and in Mexico could thus be compared with both Martin's 20 innovation challenges and Djellal and Gallouj's 15 service innovation challenges in similar domains and specific fields (Table 3). These were also drawn up with "the intention... not so much to come up with a

---

26   See note 1.

definitive list but rather to stimulate debate among innovation scholars about the future of our field" (Martin, 2016, p. 432).

In addition to applying what Martin and Djellal and Gallouj suggested were "key challenges for the field of IS (Innovation Studies) over the coming decades" (Martin, 2016, p. 433), the proposed challenges also include a framework of scenarios for the problems. This frames the challenges on the basis of one axis of income concentration-distribution and another relating to regional convergence-divergence. The desirable scenario is a sustainable development model featuring "regional development and inclusive growth" (to neutralize loss of labour while preserving income, consumption, and access to health during the COVID-19 crisis. The opposite scenario reflects the current situation of social and economic polarization caused by the concentration of both income and regions.

Results show that the main challenges listed by both Martin, and Djellal and Gallouj are generally valid for Latin America and Mexico. However, both the emphasis and the kind of social and economic angles vary, depending on the contextual scenarios of Mexico and Latin America. In such cases, domains and fields may or may not vary, whereas the challenges are, as a rule, different.

Consequently, given the structural economic and health crisis in Mexico and across Latin America, the forces of change must be reoriented towards the desirable scenario of institutions being able to improve the rule of law, increase participation for everyone (particularly indigenous people and their access to modern ICT services) and empower the local economy – in part by linking it to the dynamics of modernity, and using the "maquiladora" industry's leverage. Furthermore, a policy that could mark a turning point on environmental issues and urbanization is needed. This policy should be capable of tackling the chaotic concentration of large cities in Mexico and across Latin America by means of reinforcing the welfare state and supporting universal social protections.

I am grateful to anonymous referees of this paper for their stimulating and thought-provoking comments and criticisms who provided good ideas for improving this paper. Thanks to Alexis Camacho (Conacyt's scholarship holder) who helped me to analyse data and literature. Thanks also to Bruce McCann and Jane Roffe for their English editing of this article.

Tab. 3 – 22 Challenges for innovation and service innovation studies across Latin America and in Mexico.

Field	22 Challenges for Latin America and Mexico
1. Innovation	Develop risk management capabilities to suit different types of innovation and its diffusion, such as:
	1. Technology management and technology transfer 2. Frugal and local innovation 3. Absorption innovation capacities 4. Incentives to innovation development
2. Social Innovation	Take advantage of multicultural context in Latin America and Mexico
	5. To build channels to spread social innovation locally 6. Increased participation of indigenous people through flexible institutionalization
3. Innovation Systems	Foster networking in innovation systems
	7. Improve the linking mechanisms for regional, national and local innovation systems 8. Linking academic with the Mexican diaspora for research and production problems
4. Services	Develop innovation service; Latin America and Mexico are service economies and there is a growing urbanization in big cities.
	9. Inputs to manufacturing servitization 10. Facilitate the location of international research centres, and other service (call centres, etc.) 11. Enable the niche service sectors: medical, cultural, ecology, research
5. Innovation Systems	Foster the trend of specific and complex application of TICs
	12. Automation must be carefully assessed as a major impact on service employment and people's qualifications 13. Facilitate the creation and sustainability of KIBS (Knowledge Intensive Business Service) 14. To make visible different kinds of "dark innovations" services
6. Economy and Industrial Sectors	Raise awareness and participation among people at local and national levels, and take advantage of international cooperation agreements
	15. Service innovation related to energy generation 16. The maquiladora industry could be a leverage to increase internal production 17. Implement large investment projects to develop internal resources: qualifications of personnel and local firms 18. The informal economy is an important part of the economy which needs special legislation for productive development

Field	22 Challenges for Latin America and Mexico
7. Institutional: State	Institutionally apply the rule of law, leading to:
	19. Facilitation of (non-corrupted) PPP (Private-Public Partnerships) to set up efficient organisations. 20. Increased social participation in social and economic problems (bottom-up). 21. Regional, national and local policies to diminish income polarization and regional disparities.
8. Environment	Both local participation and international cooperation are needed.
	22. Sustainable development with social and regional equity

Source: based on Table 2.

REFERENCES

AFP (2020), "Pandemia de Covid-19 y América Latina, una ventana de oportunidad para el crimen organizado", *El Economista*, 16 May 2020: https://www.eleconomista.com.mx/internacionales/Pandemia-de-Covid-19-y-America-Latina-una-ventana-de-oportunidad-para-el-crimen-organizado-20200516-0011.html, Accessed June 10, 2020.

BÁRCENA A. (2019), *Cambio de época y nuevo modelo de desarrollo: la interpretación estructuralista*, Conferencia magistral en Facultad de Economía, UNAM, México, October 30.

CARDOSO F. H. (2017), "The Future of Latin America in the Global Economy. An Interview with Fernando Henrique Cardoso", in *Alternative pathways to sustainable development: lessons from Latin America*, International Development Policy series, n° 9, Geneva, Boston: Graduate Institute Publications, Brill-Nijhoff, p. 16-22.

CALVO O. (2016), "¿Por qué la población indígena tiene mayor probabilidad de ser pobre?", Banco Mundial Blogs, blogs.worldbank.org/es/opendata/por-qu-la-poblaci-n-ind-gena-tiene-mayor-probabilidad-de-ser-pobre, Accessed February 10, 2020.

CEPAL (2014), "Population living in extreme poverty and poverty by ethnicity, sex and geographical area", CEPALSTAT, https://cepalstat-prod.cepal.org/cepalstat/tabulador/ConsultaIntegrada.asp?idIndicador=3342&idioma=e, Accessed February 10, 2020.

CEPAL (2016a), "Distrust in the political and state institutions by sex", CEPALSTAT: https://cepalstat-prod.cepal.org/cepalstat/tabulador/ConsultaIntegrada. asp?idIndicador=995&idioma=i, Accessed February 10, 2020.

CEPAL (2016b), "Victimization rate by sex". CEPALSTAT: https:// cepalstat-prod.cepal.org/cepalstat/tabulador/ConsultaIntegrada. asp?idIndicador=1842&idioma=i, Accessed February 10, 2020.

CEPAL, (2017a), "Estadísticas e indicadores sociales". CEPALSTAT. https://cepalstat-prod.cepal.org/cepalstat/tabulador/ConsultaIntegrada. asp?idIndicador=252&idioma=e, Accessed February 10, 2020.

CEPAL (2017b), "Percentage of households with Internet access at home". https://cepalstat-prod.cepal.org/cepalstat/tabulador/ConsultaIntegrada. asp?idIndicador=1877&idioma=i, Accessed February 10, 2020.

CEPAL (2017c), "PIB anual por actividad económica a precios constantes en dólares. CEPALSTAT". https://cepalstat-prod.cepal.org/cepalstat/tabulador/ConsultaIntegrada.asp?idIndicador=2216&idioma=e, Accessed February 10, 2020.

CEPAL (2018a), "América Latina y El Caribe: Perfil regional económico". CEPALSTAT. https://estadisticas.cepal.org/cepalstat/Perfil_Regional_ Economico.html?idioma=spanish, Accessed February 10, 2020.

CEPAL (2018b), "Distribution of national income of the households by income deciles, by geographical areas". CEPALSTAT. https://cepalstat-prod.cepal. org/cepalstat/tabulador/ConsultaIntegrada.asp?idIndicador=3390&idioma=i, Accessed February 10, 2020.

CEPAL (2019), "Crece la pobreza extrema en América Latina". https://news. un.org/es/story/2019/01/1449412, Accessed February 10, 2020.

COBO R., PAZ L. & BARTRA A. (2018), ¡Somos Tosepan! 40 años haciendo camino, Mexico City: Union de cooperativas Tosepan, Circo Maya Fundación, Rosa Luxemburgo.

CONEVAL (2018), Social Development Policy Evaluation Report. Mexico City.

CORONA TREVIÑO, L. (1997), Cien empresas innovadoras en México, México: M.A. Porrúa, UNAM.

CORONA L. & PAUNERO X. (2013), Ante la crisis: estrategias empresariales de innovación en México y España, México: UNAM Siglo XXI.

CORONA L., DOUTRIAUX J., & MIAN S. (2006), Building knowledge regions in North America: Emerging technology innovation poles, Cheltenham, U.K, Northampton, MA, USA, Edward Elgar Publishers.

CRUZ-SACO M. A. (2018), Indigenous communities and social inclusion in Latin America, New York: United Nations Expert Group Meeting on Families and Inclusive Societies.

DELOITTE (2020), Barómetro de empresas. https://www2.deloitte.com/content/ dam/Deloitte/es/Documents/acerca-de-deloitte/Deloitte-ES-Barometro-de-empresas-COVID-19-20200329.pdf, Accessed March 29, 2020.

DJELLAL F. & GALLOUJ F. (2016), "Fifteen advances and fifteens challenges for service innovation studies", 26th RESER Conference, What's ahead in service research? New perspectives for business and society, 8-10 September, Naples, Italy.

DJELLAL F. & GALLOUJ F. (2018a), "Fifteen advances in service Innovation Studies", in SCUPOLA A., FUGLSANG L. (eds), Integrated Crossroads of Service, Innovation and Experience Research-Emerging and Established Trends, Cheltenham, UK, Northampton, MA, USA, p. 39-65.

DJELLAL F. & GALLOUJ F. (2018b), "Fifteen challenges for Service Innovation Studies", in GALLOUJ F., DJELLAL F. (eds), A Research Agenda for Service Innovation, Cheltenham, UK, Northampton, MA, USA, Edward Elgar Publishers, p. 1-26.

DOF (2019), Plan Nacional de Desarrollo 2019-2024. Diario Oficial de la Federación https://www.dof.gob.mx/nota_detalle.php?codigo=5565599& fecha=12/07/2019, Accessed May 11, 2020.

ECLAC (2020), "The Social challenge in times of COVID-19", *Special Report COVID19 No 3*, Economic Commission for Latin America and the Caribbean, Santiago, Chile, 12 May 2020.

FAYNZYLBER F. (1990), "Industrialización en América Latina: de la 'caja negra' al 'casillero vacío': comparación de patrones contemporáneos de industrialización", *Cuadernos de la CEPAL No.60* 176 p. Santiago de Chile: Naciones Unidas-CEPAL.

FREEMAN C. E. (1984), *Long Waves and the International Diffusion of the Automated Labour Design Innovation and Long Cycles in Economic Development*, London, Royal College of Arts.

GALLOUJ F. (2002), *Innovation in the Service Economy*, Cheltenham, UK and Northampton, MA, USA, Edward Elgar.

GALLOUJ F. (2010), "Services innovation: assimilation, differentiation, inversion and integration", in BIDGOLI H. (Ed), *The Handbook of Technology Management*, Hoboken, New Jersey John Wiley and sons, p. 989-1000.

GARCÍA A. (2020), "La crisis por Covid-19 profundizará la desigualdad y la pobreza en América Latina", *El Economista*, 21 April, 2020: https://www.eleconomista.com.mx/politica/La-crisis-por-Covid-19-profundizara-la-desigualdad-y-la-pobreza-en-America-Latina-Cepal-20200421-0076.html, Accessed May 11, 2020.

HERRERA A. (1977), *Catastrofe o nueva sociedad?: modelo mundial latinoamericano*, IDRC, International Development Research Center, Ottawa, Canada.

HERRERA A., CORONA L., DAGNINO R., GALLOPIN G., GUTMAN P. & VESSURI H. (1994), *Las nuevas tecnologías y el futuro de América Latina: riesgo y oportunidad*, Mexico: Universidad de las Naciones Unidas, Siglo XXI.

HOSSAIN M., SIMULA H. & HALME S. (2016), "Can frugal go global? Diffusion patterns of frugal innovations", *Technology in Society*, vol. 46, n° 1, p. 132-139.

INEGI (2018a), *National Occupation and Employment Survey.* https://www.inegi.org.mx/sistemas/Infoenoe/Default_15mas.aspx, Accessed May 11, 2020.

INEGI (2018b), *National Survey of Victimization and Perception on Public Security.* https://www.inegi.org.mx/temas/manufacturasexp/default.html#Tabulados, Accessed May 11, 2020.

INEGI (2019), Press release no. 384/19 (31 July 2019). https://www.inegi.org.mx/contenidos/saladeprensa/boletines/2019/EstSociodemo/enigh2019_07.pdf, Accessed May 11, 2020.

JAMES P. (2015), *Urban Sustainability in Theory and Practice: Circles of Sustainability* (First ed.), New York, Routledge.

KATO VIDAL E. L. (2015), "Violence in Mexico: An economic rationale of crime and its impacts", *EconoQuantum, Revista de Economia y Negocios*, vol. 12, n° 2, p. 93-108.

KOERICH G. & PELLIZAARO DE LORENZI É. C., "Frugal Innovation: origins, evolution and future perspectives", *Cuadernos EBAPE.BR*, nº 4, Rio de Janeiro, Oct./Dec. 2019.

LUNDVALL B.-Å., CHAMINADE C. & HANEEF S. (2018), *Advanced Introduction to National Innovation Systems*, Cheltenham-Northampton: Edward Elgar.

LÓPEZ-GATELL H. (2020), "Riesgo de que se presenten nuevas enfermedades como el virus SARS-CoV-2", in MIRANDA F. (Ed), Conferencia de prensa de la Secretaría de Salud de México. México. https://www.milenio.com/politica/lopez-gatell-enfermedades-emergentes-invasion-vida-silvestre, Accessed May 11, 2020.

MARTIN B. R. (2010), "Science policy research – having an impact on policy?" *OHE Seminar Briefing*, nº 7, Office of Health Economics, London.

MARTIN B. R. (2016), "Twenty challenges for innovation studies", *Science and Public Policy*, vol. 43, nº 3, p. 432-450.

MEADOWS D., MEADOWS D. L., RANDERS J. & BEHRENS W. (1972), *The Limits to Growth*, New York, Universe Books, A Potomac Association Book.

MULGAN G. (2019), *Social Innovation: How Societies Find the Power to Change*, London, UK, Policy Press.

NORTH D. (1990), *Institutions, institutional change and economic performance*, Cambridge, Cambridge University Press.

NOVELO F. (2014), *El desarrollo económico y social en América Latina: El doble atraso* (p. 21), Serie Estudios y perspectivas, México: ONU-CEPAL.

OXFAM (2020), "Crisis de desigualdad en tiempos de Coronavirus". OXFAM: https://www.oxfammexico.org/sites/default/files/Posicionamiento%20OMX%20ante%20emergencia%20COVID19.pdf, Accessed May 11, 2020.

RICHTA, R. (1969), *Civilization at the Crossroads: Social and Human Implications of the Scientific and Technological Revolution*, New York, Routledge International Arts and Sciences Press.

SUNKEL O. (2006), "En busca del desarrollo perdido", *Problemas del Desarrollo*, vol. 37, nº 147, 13-44.

SUZÁN, G. (2020), Necesario monitorear si humanos transmiten SARS-CoV-2 a animales. (DGCS, Entrevistador), *Gaceta UNAM*: https://www.gaceta.unam.mx/necesario-monitorear-si-humanos-transmiten-sars-cov-2-a-animales/, Accessed May 11, 2020.

TRANSPARENCY INTERNATIONAL (2019), "Corruption Perceptions Index", Transparency International: https://www.transparency.org/cpi2019, Accessed February 19, 2020.

WORLD BANK (2015), *Indicators*. https://datos.bancomundial.org/indicador/, Accessed February 19, 2020.

WORLD BANK (2017), *Indicators.* https://datos.bancomundial.org/indicador/, Accessed February 19, 2020.

WORLD BANK (2018a), *Exports of high-tech products (% of exports of manufactured goods).* https://datos.bancomundial.org/indicador/TX.VAL.TECH. MF.ZS?locations=MX-ZJ&view=chart, Accessed February 19, 2020.

WORLD BANK (2018b), *Indicators.* https://datos.bancomundial.org/indicador/, Accessed February 19, 2020.

WORLD BANK (2020), *World Development Indicators (WDI).* https://databank. worldbank.org/source/world-development-indicators, Accessed February 19, 2020.

WORLD JUSTICE PROJECT (2020), *Rule of Law Index.* Washington: WJP.

FOSTERING "CO-SOCIALIZATION" BETWEEN PATIENT AND NURSE TO MITIGATE THE RISKS OF DIGITALIZING HEALTH CARE SERVICES

Magali Dubosson[a],
Emmanuel Fragnière[a&b],
Anne-Sylvaine Héritier[a],
Samuele Meier[a],
Charles Wainwright[c]
[a]University of Applied Sciences and Arts Western Switzerland (HES-SO),
[b]University of Bath, School of Management,
[c]Oxial

INTRODUCTION

Psychosocial risks are defined as risks to mental, physical and social health arising from employment conditions and from organizational and relational factors that may interact with mental functioning (Gollac and Bodier, 2011). In other words, working in a stressful environment increases the risk of suffering from physical illness or psychological distress (Clarke and Cooper, 2004). In practice, psychosocial risks are described by terms such as burnout, poor performance, deteriorated work environment, negative stress, illness, and turnover (INRS, 2006). In the service sector, frontline employees, that is, those who deal directly with customers, may be suffering from intense stress pressures (Miller *et al.*, 1988). Yet these frontline workers are expected to perform tasks and roles that a robot cannot perform, such as expressing empathy or solving complex new situations requiring creativity. Solving client problems can provide a sense of competence, accomplishment, and growth (Dormann and Zapf, 2004). Instead of focusing on these rewarding and positive aspects, frontliners may still be forced to cope with stressful situations due to overdemanding customers (Kim and Stoner, 2008) or misunderstandings about role perception (i.e. role conflict or role ambiguity) that could lead to a decrease in performance, job satisfaction, and organizational commitment (Brown and Peterson, 1993).

When employees feel that they are unable to close a gap between their abilities and the requirements or expectations of their organization, it may lower their efficiency at work and cause health problems (Toderi *et al.*, 2015). Moreover, burnout often affects the best staff, namely those who are unusually skilled and who take the initiative (improvise) in the case of service failures (Malakh-Pines *et al.*, 1981). In the era of the fourth industrial revolution, with massive amounts of digital technology being integrated into each and every aspect of daily life that can be digitalized by converting analog information into digital form (Gray and Rumpe, 2015), these frontline jobs are placing employees under even more intense stress (Ahlers, 2016). Human resources have to be seen as strategic and, in this context (Noe, 2017), it is imperative to effectively prevent and mitigate psychosocial risks.

In a Swiss research project involving more than 5,000 employees, a process of human risk management was used to enhance performance, to maintain or improve health, to reduce absenteeism, and to boost business profits[1]. In Switzerland, the majority of the workforce is employed in the service sector. In this research, we chose to focus on the population of nurses. The objective of this exploratory study is twofold: on the one hand, we aim to explore and better understand the professional context of nurses who are on the front line in the increasingly technological and digitalized environment of health care, and, on the other hand, we want to assess the propensity of nurses to regularly reveal information about their feelings and attitudes regarding their professional life in order to estimate the level of psychosocial risk and thus better embrace the digitalization of these professional services.

---

1   Promotion santé suisse & Association d'assurances (2011).

The paper is organized as follows. In Section 2, we present a literature review that explains the specific challenges encountered by nurses in an increasingly digitalized working environment. In Section 3, we explain the methodology that has been employed to collect data among nurses, which is based on a focus group approach. In Section 4, we describe the main results based on the transcripts of the focus group. In Section 5, a discussion develops several research ideas and finally a model derived from the SECI model (Socialization, Externalization, Combination, Internalization), in order to better take into account the practitioner dimension (*i.e.*, tacit knowledge) of the nursing profession in the digitalization of the health sector. In Section 6, we conclude and provide suggestions for further research.

1. LITERATURE REVIEW

The world of labor has undergone many changes in recent years, leading to new health risks (EUOSHA, 2007). Technology and social development have influenced the relationship between people and their work, so that managing psychosocial risks in the workplace has become an increasing challenge (Jain *et al.*, 2011). Research in the psychosomatic field (Honkonen *et al.*, 2006; Kendal-Tackett, 2009) has highlighted an association between psychological health and physical body response. Clarke and Cooper (2004) have shown that working in a stressful environment increases the risk of suffering from physical illness and/or from psychological distress. According to Chiarini (2012), disorders like anxiety, depression, sleep disorders, and burnout are among the most common work-related pathologies. Subsequently, stress and psychosocial risks are linked to lower productivity, high absenteeism, and high staff turnover (Hassard *et al.*, 2014).

Moreover, consistency between the actual job and employee's perceived work experience of the employee could act as a catalyst of strain because stress occurs when a gap is observed between role expectations and actual role performance (Lambert and Lambert, 2001). Thus, when employees feel that they are unable to make up the difference between the requirements or expectations placed on them, it may reduce their work efficiency and cause health problems (Toderi *et al.*, 2015). The introduction of new technologies is often seen as a positive element that supports employees' work. However, it appears that in some circumstances the introduction of new technologies may lead to increased stress (Tovey and Adams, 1999; Jennings, 2008), lower job satisfaction, and increased psychosomatic complaints (Korunka *et al.*, 1995).

Jobs in the service sector have become the main source of employment in Western countries (Zeithaml and Bitner, 2006), and in Switzerland approximately 75% of the working force is employed in this area (Office fédéral de la statistique, 2017). In this sector, frontline employees suffer from intense stress pressures (Miller *et al.*, 1988). Indeed, although customer relationships can be a source of satisfaction, it has been observed that this same relationship can also be a significant source of stress (Tolich, 1993), dissatisfaction and pain (Korczynski and Bishop, 2008), or burnout (Dormann and Zapf, 2004). Furthermore, if the job leaves an employee stuck between customer and management pressures, the work can be experienced as a conflict between quality and quantity objectives (Korczynski, 2008). Frontline workers must provide high-quality services to customers, but at the same time they have to meet the quantitative targets imposed by management. The way of dealing with the discrepancy between the reality of work as experienced by the employee and the constraints imposed by management is crucial. Thus, another element that has been highlighted as influencing employee stress is the management style that could mitigate or exacerbate such constraints (Leveck and Jones, 1996; Weinberg and Creed, 2000; Laschinger *et al.*, 2001; Hall, 2007).

Nursing is typically a service sector profession where frontliners perform tasks, such as communicating with empathy or understanding a patient's needs, that a robot cannot do. At the same time, nurses deal with industry-specific stressors such as patients' physical and mental pain, coping with death, extended working hours, work-life conflict, insufficient staff, inappropriate management style, physical labor, multidirectional interpersonal relationships (patient, relatives, co-workers, superiors), rising health care costs, inability to provide high-quality service, increased paper burdens, increased reliance on technology (Heim, 1991; Lambert and Lambert, 2001; Jennings, 2008; McVicar, 2016) and the overall digital transformation of the health sector (Agarwal *et al.*, 2010).

A major concern is the observable effects of these stressors on staff in terms of employee dissatisfaction (Zangaro and Soeken, 2007), burnout (Bakker *et al.*, 2005), intentions to quit their job (Jennings, 1994), and on patient outcomes as they are compromising the quality of services provided to patients (Leiter *et al.*, 1998; Vahey *et al.*, 2004). Coping with stressors is a major concern in the health care sector that must be dealt with to prevent employee health problems and staff turnover, as well as to reinitiate a cycle of positive interactions (*i.e.*, co-creation) between nurses and patients. When patients receive better service, they will express fewer complaints, and the staff will respond more positively, leading in turn to better service (Rust *et al.*, 1996).

For employers, the costs arising from the damaging impact of stress are very high. Often burnout affects the best personnel, those who are typically the most skilled and who take the initiative (*i.e.*, improvise) when there are service-related problems (Malakh-Pines *et al.*, 1981).

2. METHODOLOGY

In this exploratory study, we wanted to analyze nurses' perception of their work and their representation of the psychosocial risks they faced. We chose to conduct a focus group since it is an effective qualitative method for assessing social representations among the health sector (Flynn *et al.*, 2018). Focus groups allow researchers to gather the expression of ideas presented in a social context (for instance, in a conversation between colleagues) and thus to study conversational practices that are used to discuss a particular topic. Focus groups make it possible to analyze how these representations are built, transmitted and transformed (Linell, 2001). Moreover, it is a simple and practical way to gather information from several people at once, with each person responding individually one at a time (Kitzinger *et al.*, 2004).

A focus group normally involves between 4 and 12 participants (Krueger, 2014) and a moderator. The role of the moderator is to ask questions, listen, keep the conversation going. and ensure that everyone has a chance to participate. The moderator has to explain the objectives and the conditions of the study because, as Krueger (2014, p. 34) states, "those who participate in the study must be informed of the study's rewards and risks, told the study is voluntary and confidential, and told they can quit participating at any time. In addition, the participants sign a statement that they are aware of these features."

To engage participants who are more reflexive, Krueger (1998) suggests introducing activities such as listing, sorting, and ranking. These kinds of activities can take various forms by adapting them to the recruited sample and to the specific field of investigation. These activities can also be used at various stages of the focus group session, for example, as a warm-up, as a transition to another topic, or to summarize what has been discussed during the session (Colucci, 2007). We decided to use a card-ranking exercise to summarize the discussion. For this task, participants were provided with a list of terms, written on cards to be ranked according to a given dimension.

Our focus group brought together 10 young nurses—9 women and 1 man—working in western Switzerland and was hosted at the Haute Ecole de Santé in the small city of Sion. In one of the classrooms, we arranged the chairs in a circle (as suggested by Krueger [2014]), so that everyone could see each other. The moderator was seated among the participants. A recorder was placed in the middle of the interaction area, and a camera recorded the discussions to provide a second source of high-quality transcripts. Once the participants were seated, the conditions for participation and the sequence of the proceedings were explained to them. All participants agreed and signed a document summarizing the conditions of participation. Then the camera and the audio recorder were switched on. The focus group was conducted over a one-hour period.

Prior to this event, six researchers had built up a discussion guide with a series of questions designed to elicit participants' feelings and insights about the human risks incurred in a hospital environment where information technology is becoming increasingly prevalent. This issue was addressed through the following main questions:

1. In the context of your job, did you observe any human-related risk?
2. How would you feel if your hospital started collecting information about employees and teams in order to prevent psychosocial risks?

3. What information about yourself and your work environment would you be willing to share?
4. Which incentives would make you feel motivated to provide that information?

When all the topics of the guide had been addressed, we introduced the card ranking activity. Each participant received 40 cards with a brief description of hypothetical work situations that could be an indication of a positive or negative attitude or behavior: for example, "unable to cope with the demands of patients," "having poor relationships with colleagues," "lack of time to do the job." These work situations were identified through a review of the literature on stress and well-being at work. Participants were asked to divide the cards into three categories: "not important," "neutral," and "important." To help them in their reflection and to contextualize their thinking, we proposed the following scenario: "You work in a team at the hospital in close collaboration with a colleague who has a work-related problem. You have plenty of opportunities to carefully observe this person's behavior. She or he trusts you and talks to you. What are the most important indicators that may explain this situation? Or what could be a good indicator of the situation?" The answers were collected and the participants discussed them so as to come to a consensus on what should be considered the most important and least important elements. Participants were also asked to explain the reasons underlying their assessment. The content of the discussion was fully transcribed and analyzed through the framework-analysis method.

3. RESULTS

Our results are presented hereafter, categorized according to the frameworks found through the analysis of the participants' discussions. Each dimension is interpreted and supported by concrete examples from the participants' verbatim. Each quotation is preceded by a letter (A, B, C, etc.), which stands for the name of the otherwise anonymous participant.

3.1. MOTIVATIONS FOR WORKING AS A NURSE

Most participants expressed a desire to be in direct contact with people, to be helpful by spending time dealing directly with the patients.

> B: *"I like everything about medicine, care and especially contact with patients."*

They see this job as a vocation, where it is crucial to help another person get better.

> E: *"It's a bit like a [nursing] vocation. But there's also human contact, everything medical and technical."*

Knowledge directly related to the medical profession also seems to be a very important motivation.

> L: *"I'm interested in everything related to anatomy and physiology."*

One person also mentioned the possibility of having a full and broad career based solely on a bachelor's degree. In summary, the motivations for performing these tasks are a combination of emotional, rational, and technical elements.

> F: *"The human contact, the fact that you can also be a senior. There are many areas in which you can evolve. It's interesting."*

3.2. THE MOST IMPORTANT HUMAN-RISK FACTORS

Work overload leads to conflicts with colleagues, decreased motivation, poor performance, and prevents nurses from being more in touch with patients.

> G: *"In everyday life, all these factors such as understaffing and the overload of work in some sectors; it's also difficult... It is now ... and here."*
> B: *"Just the overload, it causes conflicts between colleagues and then we don't want to go to work. There are tensions, in fact."*

With the integration of more technologies, the profession is also changing as many other professional activities are evolving. Nurses have to perform more and more paperwork (for which they can blame the "bureaucracy"). One reason for this is the digitalization of processes in hospitals, which calls for more information on what is being done and who is responsible for what.

> F: *"Maybe it's because we don't have much time. We don't have time to spend with patients, and maybe that's what the patients want. Actually, we're not very useful because the nurse is not in contact with the patient; she's busy doing paperwork."*

Distancing from the patients is often a source of frustration for our participants because they can't assume the role they had in mind when they started this job (see dimension above). Furthermore, a deteriorated work quality elicits ongoing negative comments from patients, their relatives, and stakeholders involved. This lack of recognition for the work of staff and the negative comments from patients, family, doctors, and superiors is a major source of negative attitudes and behaviors, such as demotivation and conflicts.

Most of the time, nurses suffer from a lack of autonomy combined with a high level of responsibility. The status of their profession does not reflect the added value they bring. As a result, they suffer from a lack of recognition since they are relegated to a role with very little latitude for action, a strong allegiance expected from doctors, confined in a posture that could be labeled as a "medical delegation role."

> C: *"There is also the lack of recognition for the work of the staff because we see that some nurses or health care workers do a great deal of work but are neither valued nor rewarded by anyone... neither by the patients, nor the family, nor the doctor."*
> G: *"Patients being treated or their families... I think they don't really realize the workload we have. They are people that we just see for a short period of time and they don't know that this might be our seventh workday in a row, that we've had to work harder each day to take care of them. Then, on top of that, they ask us to make a little extra effort or provide one more care when we can't stand it anymore."*
> E: *"There is also the lack of recognition in comparison to all other health care professions. For example, the physiotherapist, the occupational therapist, the dietician, they have all been recognized as proper disciplines. Nurses are still somewhat dependent on the doctor. They [doctors] never share information with nurses. We always have the same role, a kind of medical delegate who has to smile. We can't change the way we are perceived by patients, relatives, or other health care colleagues."*

Depending on the care unit in which they work, nurses experience different levels of stress. For example, working in a rehabilitation sector is less stressful than working in a sector where the nurse has to deal with the death of patients.

G: *"In some sectors I know that there are nurses who are severely affected by death. Our job is very difficult with all these deaths, all the stress involved..., if on top of that you're tired and you have a stressful workplace, it's even more difficult."*

Working hours are an important factor exerting work pressure in the workplace. Shift work schedules are often irregular and involve alternating day and night shifts, which leads to significant fatigue.

E: *"There are also working hours. There are units where you work eight hours a day, sometimes ten hours, sometimes twelve hours. You have day shifts, night shifts..."*

Our participants believe that teamwork plays a protective role. However, for this to happen, the team must get along well and be able to work together. Otherwise, it is not possible to support and help each other. If the team does not play its role, there is a risk that patients will not receive adequate service. In fact, nursing teams play a central role. Teams that do not function well, where the atmosphere is not good, quickly become dysfunctional and inefficient. As soon as team spirit is no longer present, the team's ability to carry out its mission decreases extremely rapidly.

C: *"I find that it depends a lot on the team we are part of, because the team is meant to be around to help, to support each other. If doesn't work, if there are tensions, clans and divisions in the team, if you feel bad, you don't feel safe. If there is no one to rely on or tell things to... I would say that that's also the role of the superior. They [the superiors] are in a higher position, to value us, or to tell us if it's going well or not. But not to constantly blame us because that puts an additional strain on the team."*

G: *"I think it's certainly important for the patients, particularly since we have to take care of a lot of patients..., when we get along well and there's a good atmosphere at work, among colleagues. When they [the patients] arrive in a care unit where there's a good team rather than if it's already tense... it also affects the patients."*

Burnout and depression are the most visible symptoms of these problems. But it is often too late to act. Our participants think that it is ironic that in the health sector, those who take care of other people' health are not able to promote and set up the conditions necessary to ensure their own health.

C: *"I was in a team that didn't work well in the end; nobody got along with anybody. I was trying to do things right, and so were the others. Some of them were exhausted.*

I left the team, and sometime later I heard that the whole team had been replaced. There were a lot of depressed people and burnouts."
G: *"In addition, as professionals, we are supposed to have high medical standards. Whereas precisely when there are people who are exhausted or people who are not well in the unit… It is even more negative in the field of health… That's a pity."*

To sum up, psychosocial risks are generally generated by working conditions, the organization of the hospital, the hierarchical relationships, and the nature of the work itself. The consequences of psychosocial risks are described in terms such as burnout, poor performance, poor work quality, negative stress, illness, and turnover. Good relationships with colleagues could help to better support and protect themselves in a dysfunctional environment and provide a better level of patient care.

3.3. COLLECTING PERSONAL INFORMATION

One of the main inhibitors to sharing reliable information is the fear of being judged and punished on the basis of the answers provided. There is therefore a risk of not answering questions truthfully.

F: *"It depends on people's personalities… some people may be more assertive and others a little more shy. And they won't have the courage because they're afraid…"*
L: *"Actually, it's better if it [a survey] is anonymous. When it's anonymous, we can say what we like because we know anyway, if there's retaliation afterwards, it can't fall on us because nobody knows who said what. So the fact that it's anonymous could lead me to get something off my chest …"*

An important factor for improving the quality of the information provided is the organization in charge of the survey. Even if there is a statement of confidentiality of respondents and responses, participants are suspicious if their employer is involved in the process. They prefer an outsourced administration of the questionnaire that would handle the entire process, from collection, through analysis, up to reporting the results.

Nurses would be willing to get involved in such feedback on a long-term basis provided that the information is actually used by management to improve the administration of the organization. If managers do not strictly adhere to this commitment, there is a risk that the participation rate will drop to a very low level, or a risk that "employees do not play by the rules." It is therefore essential to provide clear evidence that the information collected is not only used for statistical purposes, but is actually used to support relevant actions.

Participants also suggested that someone should come and explain the information collection process. This would be an essential factor in ensuring the success of the operation. This should avoid the trap of an impersonal and cold memo.

> H: *"What could also be motivating for me is the follow-up. If we know that something will be implemented, that everything we say will be taken into account, it would motivate me to say what I feel and what is going on. More than if it's just to gather information for statistics. We will act according to the rules if we know what's really being taken into account and if afterwards there are things that will be implemented."*
> E: *"I think we've all completed questionnaires at the hospital or elsewhere. In fact, they just send us the questionnaire without telling us what it is for... We have questionnaires filled out... but at least give some feedback... it's for statistics, yeah, statistics, what's the point?"*
> I: *"I think the questionnaire is quite impersonal. I would really like to have someone like you in front of me and then discuss, and then I could really say what I think. A questionnaire, you fill it out in two seconds. It's not precise enough."*

The questionnaire might initially be administered in a structured form with closed-ended questions either remotely via the internet or by mail (traditional or electronic), but it is also important to establish individual human contact between the person collecting the information and the respondent. Direct personal contact humanizes the relationship and also encourages the deepening of responses through a qualitative approach.

> H: *"I think it's better on paper because it's something we could do at home, for example, but otherwise, I don't think we should take our problems back home. When I fill it in, I start thinking about these problems even more than I do at the office... I think that's a real shame."*

The time required for data collection is crucial. Indeed, depending on the collection method, it can take more or less time. If the data collection system takes too long, there is a risk of additional workload. If at the same time, there is no rush. Taking the time to "ritualize" the process can then be an advantage in making the data collection system more acceptable and convincing.

> G: *"I think it will be complicated for this profession. Our tasks are already taking up a lot of time, and all the nurses I know have already a huge overload of work. If*

we tell them that they have to take time away from their work, if we don't give them time to do it... they won't find the time."

The time needed to complete the questionnaire must be integrated into the normal course of a work day. It should be considered as a legitimate work activity, just as important as any other task mentioned in the job description. For example, employees could schedule to spend three minutes filling in the questionnaire each week at the end of the week before leaving work.

H: *"I think we always have five minutes to fill out a questionnaire. It's quick to answer. If we want things to change, we have to participate. At the end of our day, take three minutes before leaving to read a questionnaire and complete it... anyway, we often finish late, so three minutes more or three minutes less..."*

During the focus group discussion, participants reacted positively to the idea of implementing a process for regularly collecting personal information. In particular, they felt that if information was collected about their stress and fatigue levels, it would be positive because they would feel listened to, recognized, and valued. They highlighted the importance of ensuring that these data collections are anonymous and that they reflect the specificities of the different sectors in which nurses are working. It is important to gather everyone's point of view and not to hide it in a global perspective. The individual case must be treated in all its uniqueness and complexity. This would also allow the point of view of minorities to be respected and valued.

3.4. RANKING OF PSYCHOSOCIAL RISK FACTORS

This section summarizes the results of the ranking activity conducted by the focus group. Table 1 presents a synthesis of the results of the participants' rank order of factors and of the discussion to reach consensus. The results are clear and consensual. Indeed, all of them chose "no longer have the patience to handle patients' requests" and then "no longer see any sense in my work" as psychosocial risk factors. This shows that nurses attach great importance to their mission and that their priority goes first and foremost to the patients, well before the institution. The profession is chosen and practiced as a true vocation.

Among the factors that play a minor role, the "fear of losing my job at any time" is completely ignored. This fact was at first surprising when compared with other studies conducted in other contexts and considering the relatively low remuneration of the nursing profession. Upon further consideration, we think that this can be attributed to the special situation of the Swiss labor market for nurses. Participants explained that if they lose their job or decide to resign, they will soon find a new job, as nurses' qualifications are highly sought after nowadays.

These attitudes are quite consistent. Nursing is a difficult job, but it can be highly rewarding. To enjoy it, nurses choose to stay or resign based on their perception of their ability to properly fulfill their role as caregivers for their patients.

TAB. 1 – Most and least important factors leading to psychosocial risk.

Importance	Factors	Votes
+	No longer have the patience to handle patients' requests	4
	No longer see any sense in my work	2
	Don't like my job	1
	Lack of time to do my work	1
	No boundaries between private life and work	1
	Feeling exploited	1
−	Fear of losing my job at any time	5
	Feeling ignored by superiors	1
	No fair reward	1
	Lack of control over work	1
	Unpleasant or unnecessary comments from the superior	1
	Take no pride in my job	1

4. DISCUSSION

The results from our focus group confirm the main stressors observed in the literature (Heim, 1991; Lambert and Lambert, 2001; Jennings, 2008; McVicar, 2016). Among the most important stressors, participants mentioned working hours; night shifts; lack of recognition from physicians, patients, and their relatives; emotional strain related to death; lack of autonomy; and overload of paperwork. In this stressful environment, the ultimate line of defense seems to be your team, as long as the work atmosphere is good. If it is not, co-worker problems are the element most often associated with burnout and job dissatisfaction (Khamisa *et al.*, 2015). Other research studies highlight the importance of social support in mitigating unhealthy work conditions (Constable and Russel, 1986; Lambert and Lambert, 2001; Jennings, 2008; Johansen and Cadmus, 2016). The main risk of unhealthy workplaces is the inability to provide adequate patient care.

Psychosocial risks must therefore be managed by collecting information about individuals and teams. Focus group participants endorsed a process for sharing information about their workplace situations. This would make them feel more listened to, considered, and valued. But this process has to meet certain conditions. The procedure must guarantee anonymity and, to that end, it would be preferable that it be conducted by an organization independent from the institution. The information transmitted must be used fairly quickly and effectively for communication and action. It is necessary to give a real sense of purpose to the process. However, this approach must under no circumstances lead to an added burden in an already overloaded work environment.

In this context, we want to apply the paradigm proposed by Rust *et al.* (1996) where the notion of "employee as servant" becomes "employee as customer" of the employer. From this perspective, a frontline employee has to be considered not only as a person who must listen to managers, but above all as a person to whom managers must listen, since she or he is often in the best possible position to assess the organization's needs for improvement and the methods implemented to meet client needs and expectations (Manz and Sims, 1993). Very often, the employee has implicitly found means and solutions to meet the day-to-day needs of customers.

The consequences of psychosocial risks are often manifested as mental and physical problems for employees, resulting in a loss of human capital for the company. This is a business problem since turnover can threaten the "stability and development of enterprises" (Wang *et al.*, 2011).

Employee turnover erodes the knowledge base and the knowledge creation process (SECI) as theorized by Nonaka *et al.* (2000). In fact, the know-how acquired and accumulated by individuals through their work experience and the organizational routines that are implemented to carry out the daily activities of the company are compromised by the loss of human capital. The production of new knowledge is also at risk.

The SECI model is based on four processes (see Figure 1), namely socialization, externalization, combination and internalization. Socialization is the process of converting new tacit knowledge through the sharing of experiences. Externalization is the process of articulating tacit knowledge into explicit knowledge. This step helps to crystallize knowledge. Combination is the process of converting explicit knowledge into more complex and structured sets of explicit knowledge. Through internalization, the explicit knowledge created is shared within an organization and converted into tacit knowledge by individuals. According to the SECI model, newly created knowledge, in order to be relevant, must go through these steps of "knowledge transformation."

FIG. 1 – The SECI model (Nonaka *et al.*, 2000).

Our interviews highlighted two important factors contributing to the mitigation of human risks in the hospital environment, which are the work team, which plays a role as a buffer in the event of a problem, and working in direct contact with patients, which gives real sense to his or her work. Our participants talked about feeling a strong sense of mission to do this work. Organizing teamwork enables the sharing of knowledge and practices, and if it works well with a positive atmosphere, it will play its role of protection against the pressures of an unhealthy work environment. There is also another level of socialization that occurs in the nurse–patient relationship. This level of socialization is the one that will truly convey a sense of meaning to the work provided that nurses feel that they are able to carry out their mission.

However, this dual level of socialization is increasingly undermined by the introduction of technology and especially by the paperwork it paradoxically requires (see Figure 2). At the stages of internalization and externalization, information technology is strongly leveraged to collect, process, structure, and store explicit knowledge. Participants in our study complained about increasing demands for getting involved in these information management processes. According to them, getting entangled in paperwork implies a significant risk of degradation of socialization processes. Indeed, there is a risk of pulling the nurse team away from the patients to feed the paper-intensive system. Having to deliver downgraded work will lead to frustration that will grow even more as a result of negative comments from the patient, the patient's relatives, colleagues, and superiors. If patients perceive a poor quality of care, there is also a risk of compromising the recovery process by preventing a beneficial co-production process. Risks affecting the socialization loop around patient care may, in turn, lead to conflict within the work team, which will affect the team's production capacity and patient care as well.

At the level of socialization, technology is rather used as an increasingly essential tool for care. Socialization in itself is based on the sharing of implicit practices and knowledge that will be taken up and used implicitly. There is therefore no exploitation of information technology in this sharing. Rather, IT is seen as a necessary evil, imposed for purely organizational reasons external to the employees' genuine vocation as nurses, at the upstream and downstream stages of internalization and externalization.

FIG. 2 – Risk of undermining the dual process of socialization (source: authors).

It is therefore essential to manage human risks that could prevent these two socialization processes from taking place. For this reason, it is important to be able to collect information to detect problems experienced by nurses in relation to the sense of meaning found in the work and the working atmosphere. The participants in our study warmly endorsed an approach to collecting data (internalization according to the SECI model) that could measure the factors that foster this dual socialization process and prevent factors that could damage it. Managing these aspects more effectively might also lead to higher recognition of the work done and of the people who give so much. For the hospital, it would make it possible to respond to recurring problems of turnover, burnout, negative stress, and absenteeism among other losses.

CONCLUSION

As the literature shows and our results confirm, a crucial point for the nurse is to consistently meet the patient's requests effectively and with empathy. The nurses want to fulfill their role as caregivers even if it is difficult. All the stressful dimensions that have been identified in this research prevent the nurse from being closer to and connecting with patients. Technology that is gradually pervading the entire workspace further disrupts and obstructs the nurse–patient relationship. ICTs are currently experienced as an additional stress factor that increasingly dehumanizes the relationship with the patient as it results in even more paperwork and bureaucracy instead of real interaction. The main consequence of the identified human risks is that the service provided is insufficient for all parties, leading to a risk of dissatisfaction for all.

Employees are eager to be involved, under certain conditions, in the collection and transmission of data that could be useful to improve the quality of service. This is in line with our assumption that a digitalized service can be successfully implemented when it is used to support the core mission of a particular job. By this logic, a device (tool and process) to manage human risks so as to detect them early would be an essential mechanism to improve the efficiency of the hospital through a preventive rather than reactive system.

It is for this reason that our theoretical development has been based on the SECI model (socialization, externalization, combination, internalization) of knowledge creation developed by Nonaka et al. (2000). Indeed, the profession of nurse is a professional service, where the nurse physically interacts with the patient to provide care. The digitalization of hospital processes and particularly of the management and planning of nursing teams means that the nurse is involved less and less in the phases of socialization in terms of knowledge creation and more and more involved in phases of externalization and internalization. As a result, the nurse loses the strong attention she or he used to have with patients. By coupling the nurse's SECI loop with the patient's SECI loop in the socialization phase, we believe we can better mitigate the risks of a drop in the quality of care that might be caused by the strong digitalization of the health care sector.

This research is part of a larger project whose objective is to develop a tool and processes to prevent human risks in the workplace. These exploratory results must be compared with the results of complementary work carried out in different fields. They will also have to be verified and confirmed by quantitative surveys in order to be generalized. Further research in this area will verify whether they contribute to reducing turnover and maintaining a useful knowledge base in companies.

REFERENCES

AGARWAL R., GAO G., DESROCHES C. & JHA A. K. (2010), "Research commentary – The digital transformation of healthcare: Current status and the road ahead", *Information Systems Research*, vol. 21, n° 4, p. 796-809.

AHLERS E. (2016), "Flexible and remote work in the context of digitization and occupational health", *International Journal of Labour Research*, vol. 8, n° 1-2, p. 85-101.

BAKKER A. B., LE BLANC P. M. & SCHAUFELI W. B. (2005), "Burnout contagion among intensive care nurses", *Journal of advanced nursing*, vol. 51, n° 3, p. 276-287.

BROWN S. P. & PETERSON R. A. (1993), "Antecedents and consequences of salesperson job satisfaction: Meta-analysis and assessment of causal effects", *Journal of Marketing Research*, vol. 30, n° 1, p. 63-77.

CHIARINI B. (2012), *Projet de sensibilisation des médecins* à la santé au travail, *Thèse de Doctorat*, Université de Lausanne. https://serval.unil.ch. (retrieved on January 15, 2020).

CLARKE S., COOPER C. L. (2004), *Managing the Risk of Workplace Stress: Health and Safety Hazards*, London, Routledge.

COLUCCI E. (2007), "'Focus groups can be fun': The use of activity-oriented questions in focus group discussions", *Qualitative Health Research*, vol. 17, n° 10, p. 1422-1433.

CONSTABLE J. F. & RUSSELL D. W. (1986), "The effect of social support and the work environment upon burnout among nurses", *Journal of Human Stress*, vol. 12, n° 1, p. 20-26.

DORMANN C. & ZAPF D. (2004), "Customer-related social stressors and burnout", *Journal of Occupational Health Psychology*, vol. 9, n° 1, p. 61-82.

EUOSHA - European Agency for Safety and Health at Work (2007), *Expert Forecast on Emerging Psychosocial Risks Related to Occupational Safety and Health*, European Risk Observatory Report, Office for Official Publications of the European Communities, Luxembourg.

FLYNN R., ALBRECHT L. & SCOTT S. D. (2018), "Two approaches to focus group data collection for qualitative health research: Maximizing resources and data quality", *International Journal of Qualitative Methods*, vol. 17, n° 1, p. 1-15.

GOLLAC M. & BODIER M. (2011), *Mesurer les facteurs psychosociaux de risque au travail pour les maîtriser*, Rapport du Collège d'expertise sur le suivi des risques psychosociaux au travail, faisant suite à la demande du Ministre du travail, de l'emploi et de la santé, Paris, France.

GRAY J., RUMPE B. (2015), "Models for digitalization", *Software & Systems Modeling*, vol. 14, n° 4, p. 1319-1320.

HALL D. (2007), "The relationship between supervisor support and registered nurse outcomes in nursing care units", *Nursing Administration Quarterly*, vol. 31, n° 1, p. 68-80.

HASSARD J., TEOH K., COX T., COSMAR, M., GRÜNDLER R., FLEMMING, D., COSEMANS B. & VAN DEN BROEK K. (2014), *Calculating the cost of work-related stress and psychosocial risks*, Technical Report, Publications Office of the European Union, Luxembourg.

HEIM E. (1991), "Job stressors and coping in health professions", *Psychotherapy and psychosomatics*, vol. 55, n° 2-4, p. 90-99.

HONKONEN T., AHOLA K., PERTOVAARA M., ISOMETSÄ E., KALIMO R., NYKYRI E., AROMAA A. & LÖNNQVIST J. (2006), "The association between burnout and physical illness in the general population – results from the Finnish Health 2000 Study", *Journal of Psychosomatic Research*, vol. 61, n° 1, p. 59-66.

INRS (2006), « Stress et risques psychosociaux : concepts et prévention », Documents pour le médecin du travail, n° 1 06, 2ᵉ trimestre, http://www.inrs.fr/htm/stress_risques_psychosociaux_concepts_prevention.html (retrieved on January 15, 2020).

JAIN A., LEKA S. & ZWETSLOOT G. (2011), "Corporate social responsibility and psychosocial risk management in Europe", *Journal of Business Ethics*, vol. 101, n° 4, p. 619-633.

JENNINGS B. (1994), "Stressors of critical care nursing", in THELAN L., DAVIE J., URDEN L., LOUGH M. (eds), *Critical care nursing. Diagnosis and management*, St Louis, MO, Mosby, p. 75-84.

JENNINGS B. M. (2008), "Work stress and burnout among nurses: Role of the work environment and working conditions", in HUGHES R.G. (ed.), *Patient safety and quality: An evidence- based handbook for nurses*, Agency for Healthcare Research and Quality, Rockville (USA), p. 135-158.

JOHANSEN M. L. & CADMUS E. (2016), "Conflict management style, supportive work environments and the experience of work stress in emergency nurses", *Journal of Nursing Management*, vol. 24, n° 2, p. 211-218.

KENDALL-TACKETT K. (2009), "Psychological trauma and physical health: A psychoneuro-immunology approach to etiology of negative health effects and possible interventions", *Psychological Trauma: Theory, Research, Practice and Policy*, vol. 1, n° 1, p. 35-48.

KHAMISA N., OLDENBURG B., PELTZER K. & ILIC D. (2015), "Work related stress, burnout, job satisfaction and general health of nurses", *International Journal of Environmental Research and Public Health*, vol. 12, n° 1, p. 652-666.

KIM H. & STONER M. (2008), "Burnout and turnover intention among social workers: Effects of role stress, job autonomy and social support, *Administration in Social Work*, vol. 32, n° 3, p. 5-25.

KITZINGER J., MARKOVA I. & KALAMPALIKIS N. (2004), « Qu'est-ce que les focus groups ? », *Bulletin de Psychologie*, vol. 57, n° 3, p. 237-243.

KORCZYNSKI M. (2008), "Understanding the Contradictory Lived Experience of Service Work: The Customer-Oriented Bureaucracy", in MACDONALD C. & KORCZYNSKI M. (eds), *Service work: Critical perspectives*, New York, NY and London, Routledge, p. 73-90.

KORCZYNSKI M. & BISHOP V. (2008), "The job centre: abuse, violence and fear on the frontline", in FINEMAN S. (ed), *Emotions in Organizations: Critical Voices*, Oxford, Blackwell, p. 74-87.

KORUNKA C., WEISS A., HUEMER K. H. & KARETTA B. (1995), "The effect of new technologies on job satisfaction and psychosomatic complaints", *Applied Psychology*, vol. 44, n° 2, p. 123-142.

KRUEGER R. A. (1998), "Developing questions for focus groups", in MORGAN D. L., KRUEGER R. A. & KING J. A. (eds), *Focus group kit* (Vol. 3), Thousand Oaks, CA, Sage.

KRUEGER R. A. (2014), *Focus groups: A practical guide for applied research*, Thousand Oaks, CA, Sage publications.

LAMBERT V. A. & LAMBERT C. E. (2001), "Literature review of role stress/strain on nurses: an international perspective", *Nursing & Health Sciences*, vol. 3, n° 3, p. 161-172.

LASCHINGER H. K. S., FINEGAN J., SHAMIAN J. & WILK P. (2001), "Impact of structural and psychological empowerment on job strain in nursing work settings: expanding Kanter's model, *JONA: The Journal of Nursing Administration*, vol. 31, n° 5, p. 260-272.

LEITER M. P., HARVIE P. & FRIZZELL C. (1998), "The correspondence of patient satisfaction and nurse burnout", *Social Science & Medicine*, vol. 47, n° 10, p. 1611-1617.

LEVECK M. L. & JONES, C. B. (1996), "The nursing practice environment, staff retention, and quality of care", *Research in Nursing & Health*, vol. 19, n° 4, p. 331-343.

LINELL P. (2001), "A dialogical conception of focus groups and social representations", in LARSOON U.S. (ed.), *Socio-Cultural Theory and Methods: An Anthology*, University of Trollhättan/Uddevalla, Trollhättan, p. 163-206.

MALAKH-PINES A., ARONSON E. & KAFRY D. (1981), *Burnout: From tedium to personal growth*, New York, Free Press.

MANZ C.C. & SIMS H.P. JR (1993), "Business without Bosses: How Self-managing Teams Are Building High-performing Companies", New York, NY, John Wiley & Sons.

MC VICAR A. (2016), "Scoping the common antecedents of job stress and job satisfaction for nurses (2000–2013) using the job demands – resources model of stress", *Journal of nursing management*, vol. 24, n° 2, p. 112-136.

MILLER A., SPRINGEN K., GORDON J., MURR A., COHEN B., DREW L. (1988), "Stress on the Job", *Newsweek*, April 25, p. 40-45.

NOE R. A., HOLLENBECK J. R., GERHART B. & WRIGHT P. M. (2017), *Human resource management: Gaining a competitive advantage*, New York, NY, McGraw-Hill Education.

NONAKA I., TOYAMA R. & KONNO N. (2000), "SECI, Ba and leadership: a unified model of dynamic knowledge creation", *Long Range Planning*, vol. 33, n° 1, p. 5-34.

OFFICE FÉDÉRAL DE LA STATISTIQUE (2017), Mémento statistique de la Suisse 2017, Confédération suisse.

PROMOTION SANTÉ SUISSE & ASSOCIATION SUISSE D'ASSURANCES (2011), Projet SWiNG – Rapport final de l'évaluation, 2008-2011. https://promotionsante. ch/assets/public/documents/fr/6-ueber-uns/downloads/Alt_PSY_BGM/2011-07_Projet_SWiNG_rapport_final.pdf (retrieved on January 15, 2020).

RUST R. T., STEWART G. L., MILLER H. & PIELACK D. (1996), "The satisfaction and retention of frontline employees: A customer satisfaction measurement approach", *International Journal of Service Industry Management*, vol. 7, n° 5, p. 62-80.

TODERI S., GAGGIA A., BALDUCCI C., SARCHIELLI G. (2015), "Reducing psychosocial risks through supervisors' development: A contribution for a brief version of the Stress Management Competency Indicator Tool", *Science of the Total Environment*, 518-519, p. 345-351.

TOLICH M. (1993), "Alienating and liberating emotions at work", *Journal of Contemporary Ethnography*, vol. 22, n° 3, p. 361-381.

TOVEY E. J. & ADAMS A. E. (1999), "The changing nature of nurses' job satisfaction: an exploration of sources of satisfaction in the 1990s", *Journal of Advanced Nursing*, vol. 30, n° 1, p. 150-158.

VAHEY D. C., AIKEN L. H., SLOANE D. M., CLARKE S. P. & VARGAS D. (2004), "Nurse burnout and patient satisfaction", *Medical Care*, vol. 42, n° 2 (Suppl. 2), p. 1157-1166.

WANG X., WANG H., ZHANG L. & CAO X. (2011), "Constructing a decision support system for management of employee turnover risk", *Information Technology and Management*, vol. 12, n° 2, p. 187-196.

WEINBERG A. & CREED F. (2000), "Stress and psychiatric disorder in healthcare professionals and hospital staff", *The Lancet*, vol. 355, n° 9203, p. 533-537.

ZANGARO G.A. & SOEKEN K.L. (2007), "A meta-analysis of studies of nurses' job satisfaction", *Research in Nursing & Health*, vol. 30, n° 4, p. 445-458.

ZEITHAML V. A., BITNER M. J., GREMLER D. D. & PANDIT A. (2006), *Services marketing: Integrating customer focus across the firm*, Boston, MA McGraw-Hill/Irwin.

PUBLIC SERVICE INNOVATION NETWORKS (PSINs)

An instrument for collaborative innovation
and value co-creation in public service(s)

Benoît DESMARCHELIER,
Faridah DJELLAL,
Faïz GALLOUJ
Université de Lille, Clersé-CNRS

INTRODUCTION

Paradigm shifts in the field of public administration, over the past decades, have brought the issue of innovation to the forefront. Initially considered as incongruous in the field of public services, this issue has become central and has been the object of a growing number of studies, particularly at the instigation of the European Commission. As paradigms have shifted, innovation in public services has become a new focus of "Innovation Studies" and "Service Innovation Studies" (SIS), with particular attention paid to both the nature of the innovation and the modalities of its implementation (Desmarchelier *et al.*, 2019a). Thus, in the paradigm of *traditional public administration*, innovation is seen in terms of the industrial rationalization of production processes and the introduction of technical systems aimed at providing citizens with homogeneous quasi-products. This innovation activity is embedded in a top-down, linear organization of innovation, from which the user is, for the most part, excluded. In the *new public management paradigm*, innovation remains linear (non-interactive), and the logic at work is still that of the assimilation of services to goods (industrialization). New public management simply introduces market management techniques into public services. The paradigm of *new public governance* currently favoured in all developed economies fundamentally changes the perspective of innovation, in that it rejects the assimilation of public services to goods but instead considers them as services (demarcation perspective). Thus, by loosening the traditional industrialist, technologist and market biases (which characterize the two previous paradigms), this new paradigm transfers into public services management the advances achieved in service economics and management. From the point of view of innovation, the new public governance paradigm fundamentally changes the focus regarding the nature of innovation and its modes of organization. Indeed, in accordance with Service Innovation Studies (SIS), first of all, innovation in public services is defined in a broad and open way in order to encompass both technological and non-technological dimensions (new service, new process, new organization). Secondly, according to the logic of services, the production of public service like innovation in public services are envisaged above all as collaborative activities, which require interactions between multiple agents and first and foremost the citizen. Thus, innovation networks are core components of new public governance, to such an extent that this new paradigm is also sometimes referred to as "networked governance".

This article, which is based on a review of the literature and on empirical work carried out under two European funded projects (ServPPIN and COVAL[1]), is devoted to these new collaborative innovation activities, which we denote by the term "Public Service Innovation Networks" (PSINs). PSINs are multi-agent collaborative arrangements that develop within *public services* (sectoral perspective) or *public service* (functional perspective), spontaneously or at the instigation of (local, national or European) public policies. They bring into play a variable number of public and private agents, especially citizens, in order to co-produce innovations and ultimately contribute to the co-creation of value. Our goal in this article is to deepen the definition and description of PSINs,

---

1   ServPPIN: The Contribution of Public and Private Services to European Growth and Welfare, and the Role of Public-Private Innovation Networks, FP7-SSH project 2008-2011. – COVAL: Understanding value co-creation in public services for transforming European public administrations, H2020 project 2017-2020.

especially in comparison with other known network forms, including Traditional Innovation Networks (TINs) and Public Private Innovation Networks in Services (PPINSs) (see Gallouj *et al.*, 2013; Desmarchelier *et al.*, 2019b). Our goal is also to examine in particular how PSINs are formed and function in order to co-create, more or less effectively, value in public service(s) through innovation. The article is organized into two sections. Section 1 examines the concept of PSINs from a morphological or structural point of view, and Section 2 from a dynamic point of view (formation and functioning, evolution in space and time, assessment).

1. PSINs THROUGH MORPHOLOGICAL/ STRUCTURAL VARIABLES

A PSIN can be described using the following three variables: 1) the actors involved; 2) the interactions between these actors; 3) (the characteristics of) the innovation carried out by the network. The first two variables are topographical, while the third is functional. On the basis of a review of the theoretical and empirical literature, we discuss each of these variables, striving to identify what can distinguish PSINs from other types of networks.

1.1 THE ACTORS INVOLVED

Not all multi-stakeholder collaborations for innovation are innovation networks, but all innovation networks are made up of a number of actors. These actors, in varying numbers, are different in nature (belong to different categories) and occupy different places in the network.

1.1.1 The nature of the actors

In traditional innovation networks (TINs), the main actors belong to the triad manufacturing firms, public administrations and research organizations, with manufacturing firms being or likely to be the main nodes of the network. In so-called Public Private Innovation Networks in Services or PPINSs (Gallouj *et al.*, 2013), market service firms, public administrations and third sector organizations occupy a prominent place. PSINs for their part involve *public actors* (public administrations at the national, regional or local level) and *private actors* (including business actors *i.e.* private firms, NGOs, associations, foundations, social enterprises, individual service consumers/users and individual citizens). The nature of the actors involved in innovation networks and PSINs can be distinguished according to several levels of analysis: the *sector* of activity of the organization (public/private, market/non-market, manufacturing/service), the type of *organization* (a firm, an association, a mutual insurance company, a foundation), the status of the *individual* (a basic employee, a public manager, a citizen, a user, an elected politician). The nodes of PSINs and among them PSINSIs (that is, PSINs dedicated to social innovation) can be organizations or individuals. Thus, unlike TINs, PSINs and PSINSIs are sometimes multi-agent/individual rather than multi-organizational collaborations.

Because they are different in nature, the actors of the network can obey different "institutional logics": public, private/market, private/non-profit (Friedland and Alford, 1991; Thornton *et al.*, 2013; Vickers *et al.*, 2017). The network is thus a "hybrid organization" (Vickers *et al.*, 2017; Battilana and Lee, 2014; Billis, 2010) where different complementary or competing institutional logics interact. However, the organizations that constitute the network are also hybrid organizations, just like the individual himself/herself, who is at the same time citizen, consumer and producer. This plurality of institutional logics, expressed at different levels, is both a positive and negative factor for collaboration. We will come back to this in section 2.2.

1.1.2 The role of citizens

The role of citizens as important actors in value co-creation and collaborative innovation in public services, that is, in PSINs (and even more in PSINSIs) is often emphasized for most PSINs identified in the literature (Agger and Hedensted Lund, 2017). When analysing PSINs, especially in terms of social innovation, it is useful to distinguish three types of citizens, depending on how they are affected by the problem that gives rise to the innovation implemented by the network:

– Type 1: the citizen is directly affected by the problem. Examples include dependent elderly people, drug addicts, early school leavers, refugees, homeless people, and so on.
– Type 2: the citizen is indirectly affected by the problem. This type mainly includes relatives and family of type 1 citizens.
– Type 3: the citizen is neither directly nor indirectly affected by the problem, but he/she is sensitive to it by empathy and solidarity or for ideological, philosophical or political reasons.

These three types of citizens can take part in the innovation process in different ways. Given their vulnerability and lack of resources, type 1 citizens, rarely (or passively) take part in the collaborative innovation process in the network. However, type 2 and 3 citizens can take part in all stages of the innovation process, individually or collectively (as part of third sector organizations).

The literature considers that the participation of citizens in public innovation networks may lead to a selection bias, thought to be potentially prejudicial to innovation (Fung, 2003; Carpini et al., 2013; Agger and Hedensted Lund, 2017). The concern is that it is always the same (or the same types of) citizens (those that Fung (2003) calls the "usual suspects") who take part in the innovation processes, namely the most resourceful citizens. The knowledge and preferences of other citizens (the least resourceful) are likely to be excluded, which is detrimental to innovation. Although the "usual suspects" can be sources of innovation, they can also be relatively conservative and contribute to locked-in innovation trajectories and competency traps.

1.1.3 The number of actors

The number of actors involved in the network can of course vary greatly. It might nevertheless be assumed that TINs are generally used as a meso-economic level concept that fit into (local, regional, national, global) innovation systems, which can bring together a large number of actors. PPINSs mobilize relatively fewer actors and PSINs for their part are a microeconomic level unit, which can be limited to a small number of actors. A general idea that comes up frequently in the literature is that the capacity for innovation increases with the number and diversity of actors involved in a network (Franke and Shah, 2003; Ansell and Torfing, 2014; Bland *et al.*, 2010; Agger and Hedensted Lund, 2017). While this hypothesis may be well-founded for TINs oriented towards complex, highly R&D-intensive technological innovations, it is not clear that the same is true for PSINs.

1.1.4 The importance, influence and power of the actors

It is obvious that all actors do not play the same role, or occupy the same place, or have the same influence and power in a network. There are some actors who play the role of mediators, linchpins between different actors, facilitate mediation and "translation" (Callon, 1986), exert leadership, and so on. Social Network Analysis (SNA) provides useful and well known tools to measure the level of influence, importance and power of a given actor. The most important of these tools is the measurement of the centrality of the actor. SNA distinguishes several different types of centrality indicators, in particular:

– Degree centrality, which measures the number of direct links connecting a node/actor to neighbouring nodes/actors. In the field of innovation networks, it reflects the ability of a given actor to gain access to external knowledge (Schön and Pyka, 2012).

– Closeness centrality, which accounts for the geodesic distance (shortest path) to reach an actor/node. The importance of the actor is therefore expressed by its proximity to all other actors, reflecting its higher capacity to receive or distribute information.

– Betweenness centrality, which measures the importance of an actor through the number of times it acts as an intermediary in the relationship between other actors.

In a discussion of network topology/morphology, it is the distribution of these indicators among agents that is important. This distribution provides information on the growth patterns of the network and its solidity/vulnerability, and therefore its ability to last over time (Barabasi and Albert, 1999).

As we have just seen, the importance of an actor is closely linked to the quantity and quality of its interactions with other actors. We discuss this question of interactions between actors in more detail below.

1.2 INTERACTIONS BETWEEN ACTORS

In an innovation network, the function of the economic agents involved is to interact with others, within the innovation process. Interaction can be defined, generally speaking, as a process of exchange of information, knowledge, civility and task achievement (Gallouj and Weinstein, 1997). But this interaction can take different forms, vary in intensity and involve a variable number of actors, be enshrined in a particular temporality, introduce a hierarchy between agents and rely on special tools. Social network analysis provides valuable tools for describing, mapping and measuring these interactions (see also previous point). It is important to note that, in the case of social innovation, interaction (especially with the citizen) is consubstantial with innovation. It is not just a form of innovation production, but an important result of innovation.

1.2.1 The nature of the interaction

The literature uses many different terms or concepts to define this interaction between agents within a network: cooperation, coordination, collaboration, partnership, and so on. These different terminologies are often used as synonyms. But in some cases, efforts are made to differentiate them and designate different modes of interaction.

Keast *et al.* (2007) consider that the first three terms (the "3Cs") are not interchangeable, but have different content and objectives, and increasing levels of connection, which reflect a connectivity (or integration) continuum (cooperation --> coordination --> collaboration). *Cooperation* is a simple mechanism for the exchange of information and knowledge. *Coordination* is an (intermediary) mechanism for linking actions, and achieving coherence, which makes it possible to create synergies and to avoid repetitions/redundancies in a process. *Collaboration* is a higher level of interaction that goes beyond simply exchanging information/knowledge, pooling resources and avoiding redundancies. It is a strong and enduring commitment to jointly develop solutions to shared problems. In other words, cooperation is a communication mechanism, coordination a regulatory mechanism and collaboration an operational mechanism.

If it is accepted, this distinction, calls for a number of comments. These three modes of interaction are, of course, at work in all networks, especially PSINs. They are not independent of each other. Cooperation and coordination, as defined, are necessary but not sufficient, conditions for the establishment and proper functioning of an innovation network and in particular a PSIN. The collaboration mechanism for its part incorporates the other two mechanisms, *i.e.* cooperation and coordination. After all, by getting involved in the concrete achievement of innovation tasks (collaboration), the agents necessarily exchange information and knowledge (cooperation) and establish a division of tasks (coordination). Collaboration is the central element of PSINs. It is therefore collaboration that makes the network.

Collaboration often has the connotation of a consensual and peaceable relationship, undoubtedly because it is implicitly viewed in opposition to another form of interaction: competition. If this were the case, it would be detrimental to innovation. After all, conflict/opposition are drivers of innovation, while reaching a consensus consumes resources and most often results in incremental innovations, after getting everyone to agree on the lowest common denominator (Sørensen and Torfing, 2013). Collaboration thus benefits from being considered, not as a consensual relationship, but as a process organizing and managing conflicts, oppositions and differences, in order to catalyse creativity and generate innovative solutions.

When it comes to collaborating in the field of innovation, other terms (from different research traditions: service economics and management, innovation economics and management, design thinking and participatory design) are also frequently used. These include co-production (of innovation), co-creation and co-innovation to express the idea of collaboration to innovate, and co-initiation, co-design and co-implementation to describe collaboration at a particular stage of the innovation process (Agger and Hedensted Lund, 2017).

The literature provides a discussion of the distinction between co-production and co-creation in services in general and public services in particular. Thus, in their systematic review of the literature on co-production and co-creation with citizens in public innovation, Voorberg *et al.* (2015) point out that, in most cases, co-production and co-creation are used as interchangeable concepts. Both encompass the different activities of the citizen: the citizen as co-implementer (he/she carries out certain public service implementation tasks in place of the provider); co-designer (the citizen participates in the design of the content and delivery process of the service, but public administration is the leader); initiator (it is the citizen who initiates the new public service and defines its characteristics, and the public administration is the follower). On the basis of this observation, for the sake of clarification, Voorberg et al. (2015) use the term co-production for the (co-) implementation activity of the citizen and the term co-creation for his/her involvement in co-design and (co-)initiation activities.

Some authors use the concept of co-production only to describe the participation of the direct user/consumer/customer/client in the production/delivery of the service (Pestoff et al., 2006), while others give it a broader meaning, integrating the indirect participation of other individual or collective actors, for example the family or an association (Alford, 2014; Bovaird, 2007; Sicilia et al., 2016).

In a report entitled "Together to improve public services: partnership with citizens and civil society", OECD (2014, p. 17) defines co-production as "the direct involvement of individual users and groups of citizens in the planning and delivery of public services". According to OECD (2014, p. 17, Politt et al., 2006), this is a generic term that encompasses various other activities/concepts that "reflect the different stages and types of citizen involvement and input": co-design, co-creation, co-delivery, co-management, co-decision, co-evaluation and co-review. Thus, in this definition, co-creation is a component of co-production, while in others, co-creation is the higher level concept encompassing co-production.

The literature also proposes typologies of co-production. For example, Loeffler (2009) distinguishes between substitutive co-production and complementary co-production. In the former case, an agent (for example, a citizen or user) performs a task that was previously performed by someone else (for example, a public official). In the latter case, an agent (the citizen) performs a new activity, complementary to that of the other agent (the public official).

Beyond the difficulty in accurately defining co-production and co-creation, another difficulty is added when considering the target of these two activities.

When the term co-production is used alone, as is often the case in service economics, it refers to the operational process of production of the service, in which the customer is often involved in a natural or compulsory way. For example, a student co-produces the education service by attending classes and learning lessons. The citizen co-produces the "crime prevention" service by being vigilant and reporting any suspicious event to the police. Although the idea of co-production aims to differentiate services from goods, the industrial connotation of this concept (if only semantically) is obvious. This has led some service marketing scholars to replace the term production by *servuction* (Eiglier and Langeard, 1987). Similarly, when the term co-creation is used alone, it often refers to the idea of contributing to the innovation activity (creation referring to creativity).

However, the terms co-production and co-creation are often used in conjunction with the target of the activity, for example, innovation or value (co-production/co-creation of value or innovation). Reference is thus often made to *value co-production* and *value co-creation* (without actually defining what value means[2]). Some authors use these two terms as synonyms (Gebauer *et al.*, 2010). Others (Lusch and Vargo, 2006) substitute value co-creation for value co-production, rejecting the latter term to the extent that it reflects a Goods-Dominant Logic (GDL) conception of value generation. Yet others see co-production as a dimension/channel of value co-creation (Hardyman *et al.*, 2015), just like co-innovation.

1.2.2 The intensity of the interaction

The question of the intensity of the interaction between two agents is difficult to approach and measure because it can be addressed according to at least three perspectives.

First of all, it can be addressed *through the nature of the activities carried out* in the interaction. We have already implicitly addressed this issue in the previous discussion of the nature of the interaction. After all, some forms of interaction are, by nature, more intense than others. Thus, in the distinction established by Keast *et al.* (2007), cooperation is the least intense mode of interaction, since it is limited to a simple exchange of information, whereas collaboration is the most intense, since it implements richer activities and supposes a greater and more lasting commitment of the stakeholders.

---

2   We will return to this question in section 2.5.

Secondly, it can be addressed *through a temporal dimension*. The interactions within the network are, after all, embedded in different temporal patterns. PSINs may be interaction/collaboration systems that are temporary/short-term or permanent/long-term (such as R&D departments). Whether the networks are temporary or permanent, the interactions can be either continuous (full-time work of actors) or sporadic (part-time work). Thus, Pestoff and Brandsen (2008, see also Pestoff, 2009) distinguish three types of interactions between public authorities and citizens, according to a growing time scale: i) sporadic and distant, ii) intermittent and/or short-term, iii) intensive and/or enduring.

Finally, it can be addressed *by the formal or informal nature of the relationship*. Mention can be made here of the distinction between weak and strong ties made by Granovetter (1973). According to Granovetter, the strength of ties in a network is not synonymous with performance. On the contrary, weak ties are likely to be more efficient because they make it possible to connect a given agent embedded in a given network to other agents involved in other networks.

1.2.3 The number of interactions and network density

PSINs are generally characterized by a relatively small number of interactions (number of total links), at least in comparison with traditional innovation networks, which are part of innovation systems at different geographical levels. This is of course linked to the relatively small number of agents involved (see previous point). But, beyond this general observation, there is a great variability in the number of interactions, depending on the PSINs considered.

The density of the interactions or of the network[3] reflects the number of links between the different nodes of the network. In SNA, it is measured by the ratio of the number of links established to the number of possible links in a network. The density of the network provides elements of interpretation on the speed of circulation of information and knowledge flows in the network, a speed which is also measured by the average shortest path length (Newman, 2003).

---

3   The characteristics of the actors (individual perspective) and the characteristics of the network as a whole (network perspective) should not be confused here and elsewhere.

The literature on TINs argues that interactions are more frequent when knowledge is poorly codified or tacit. This is the case, for example, in the field of biotechnology. Extrapolating this argument to PSINs, which are established in knowledge and innovation fields that are hardly visible and poorly codified in their form and content, one can assume that they are characterized by a higher relative density of links (a high ratio of the number of links to the number of actors), even though, in view of lesser availability of financial resources, there are likely to be fewer actors in PSINs.

1.2.4 The instruments of interaction

ICTs, online public services and social media are increasingly common instruments of interaction. The major public changes that are illustrated by revolutions (see the experience of the Arab Spring) are nowadays increasingly based on social media. The possibility of connecting has significantly increased the ability of citizens to get involved, give their opinions and express their "voice" in Hirschman's sense (Hirschman, 1970).

1.3 INNOVATION IN THE NETWORK

The innovation that is the purpose of the network can be considered from the angle of its nature, its process and its mode of organization and its appropriation regime.

1.3.1 The nature (type) of innovation

Traditional innovation networks (TINs) are characterized by a technological bias. After all, their main purpose is the production of technological innovation. PPINSs break away from this bias, insofar as, without neglecting technological innovations, they also take seriously the production of non-technological innovation in the networks (Gallouj et al., 2013; Desmarchelier et al., 2019b). PSINs, for their part, while they fall within the scope of the same open perspective (in theory encompassing technological innovation and non-technological innovation), are actually putting more emphasis on non-technological innovation in all its forms: a new service, a new process, a new delivery mode, a new organization, a new public reform, a new public policy and so on. Whatever their type, these different innovations can be classified according to their degree of novelty. Thus, the traditional distinctions between incremental innovation and radical innovation or between innovation adopted (by PSINs) and innovation designed/produced (by them) apply to public service innovations.

Generic and longstanding examples of innovation in public services illustrating the diversity of forms include the following (Sørensen and Torfing, 2013):

- new policy areas (preventive care, active employment policy and climate change mitigation);
- new services (online education, digital services, neighbourhood renewal programs, new elder care services);
- new managerial systems (elaborate systems of performance management, performance-related wage-systems and quasi-markets);
- new organizational modes (one-stop service agencies, public-private partnerships).

The network itself, it should be noted, can be considered not only as a mode of innovation, but as a form of innovation strictly speaking. This is what Gallouj *et al.* (2013) call *network innovation*. Network innovation is thus a particular case of organizational innovation, in which the development of the network is itself the innovative object (the goal of the innovation process). An example is the case of an innovative care network initiated by a third-sector organization for the care of the elderly.

1.3.2 The innovation process: a non-linear or open innovation model

The NPG paradigm, in which networks occupy a central place in the production of public value and public innovation, falls within the scope of an evolutionary and neo-Schumpeterian perspective of innovation, but also within the broader perspective of complex adaptive systems (Holland and Miller, 1991). Thus, innovation is not only considered as a definitively constituted result, but as a non-linear, interactive or open and path-dependent process. This innovation carried out by the network is embedded in a set of interrelated activities, a more or less explicit process that is traditionally described by the following steps/activities that may overlap, be performed in parallel, allow feedback, etc.:

- Identification/initiation: this activity consists of becoming aware of a problem to be solved, a need to be satisfied or a challenge to be met and deciding to initiate an innovation process to cope with it.
- Development/design: this is a creative activity that consists in generating new ideas to solve the problem in question.
- Experimentation: the selection and testing of a solution.
- Implementation: the execution of the solution within the organization.
- Dissemination: this activity aims to scale up the chosen solution, within the organization itself or beyond it.

The innovation model at work in PSINs (and PSINSIs) is a highly non-linear or open model. It is opposed to the traditional linear model which assumes a sequential (and specialized) organization of the innovation process, greatly limiting the interactions and feedback between the R&D, production and marketing phases. In management sciences, this linear model is illustrated by a well-established theoretical tradition that considers the production of new goods or services according to the New Product (or New Service) Development methodology, which implements planned and systematic processes. The open innovation perspective includes a number of unplanned or emerging models, which have been observed in market services, but which apply to public services, for example, the rapid application model, bricolage innovation and *ad hoc* innovation. In the rapid application model, planning does not precede production, as in the traditional linear model (Toivonen, 2010). Once the idea has appeared, it is immediately developed as part of the service delivery. Thus, the service delivery process and the innovation process are mingled (Toivonen et al., 2007). The bricolage innovation model describes change and innovation as the consequence of unplanned on-the-job activities involving trial-and-error and adjustment to random events (Sanger and Levin, 1992; Fuglsang, 2010; Styhre, 2009). Fuglsang and Sorensen (2011) point to the importance of "capability of bricolage" in the activity of in-home caregivers for the elderly, who have to "solve unexpected problems with available resources". "*Ad hoc* innovation" (Gallouj and Weinstein, 1997) can be defined as the interactive process of constructing a (novel) solution to a given problem. This process, which requires the participation of the customer/user/citizen himself/herself, is described as *ad hoc* because it is "unprogrammed" or "emerging", which means that it merges with the service provision process from which it can be dissociated only a posteriori. *Ad hoc* innovation is recognized as such only after the fact.

Finally, non-linearity is a shared characteristic of highly complex and dynamic innovative processes related to the most advanced fields of Science and Technology (and implemented in traditional innovation networks – TINs) and less dramatic social processes falling within the scope of Human and Social Sciences (and implemented in PSINs and PSINSIs).

The literature is unanimous in concluding that the collaboration/ interaction between agents is able to reinforce each of the activities/stages of the innovation process (Roberts and Bradley, 1991; Roberts and King, 1996; Hartley, 2005; Nambisan, 2008; Eggers and Singh, 2009; Bommert, 2010; Sørensen and Torfing, 2013). Thus, the *identification of the problem* is facilitated by pooling the experiences and skills of multiple public and private agents. The *development of new ideas* is fertilized/catalysed by the confrontation of opinions and perspectives of different actors. *Experimentation* of innovation is facilitated when the partners are interested stakeholders in a jointly developed solution. Such partners are undoubtedly reliable ambassadors for this innovation and promoters of its *diffusion*.

Another interesting point is the extent to which different categories of actors in the network are involved at different stages of the innovation process. Empirical investigations identify different levels of involvement of different actors in each activity, according to their public or private status (Sørensen and Torfing, 2010). By focusing on innovation in public services related to crime prevention in a local context, the Danish CLIPS project (Sørensen and Torfing, 2013) emphasizes that private stakeholders are more involved in collaboration at the implementation stage of the solution than at the initiation and design stages. It also points out that the end user (here "at risk youth") rarely comes into play in the project because the associations are the key nodes of the network.

1.3.3 *Appropriation of the results of an innovation resulting from a collaborative process*

In innovation networks, the difficult question of the appropriation regimes for co-produced innovation no longer arises at a bilateral level, but at a multilateral level, which of course increases the problems of leakage and coordination.

However, in PSINs, given the nature of the innovation in question (namely a public service innovation (PSI), whether it is a social innovation or not), traditional appropriation does not apply. After all, unlike economic innovation, which the innovators strive to personally appropriate and protect against imitation by competitors, public service innovators and social innovators are eager to see their innovation imitated. An indicator of the success of such innovations is even their ability to be scaled up and adopted by other organizations.

2. PSINs THROUGH DYNAMIC VARIABLES

The dynamic variables describe the network in action (in space and time) and its results. The following variables are considered: 1) the mode of formation of the network, 2) its mode of functioning, 3) its integration in time (its life cycle), 4) its integration in space (the geography of PSINs), 5) the assessment of its performance.

2.1 THE MODE OF FORMATION OF THE NETWORK

Regarding network formation, the literature generally distinguishes *planned* or *engineered* networks from *spontaneous* or *emergent* networks (Doz et al., 2000; Schön and Pyka, 2012; Green et al., 2013).

Planned networks are formed under the impetus of an initiating or enabling agent (in theory, any type of agent: individual, public organization, private firm, NGOs, etc.) who will invite other potential stakeholders to join the network. In this kind of network formation, the initiating actor invites actors he himself knows and whom he expects to bring useful skills for carrying out the innovation project. However, the invited actors do not necessarily know each other.

Spontaneous networks emerge in a self-organized way from the convergence of the initially non-coordinated activities of different agents facing a given problem, on a given territory (a district, a city, a region, etc.). The initiation of the network probably takes place between agents who already know each other, in one way or another (see Figure 1). *Self-organization* is a principle inspired by the natural and physical sciences (Von Bertalanffy, 1968; Prigogine and Stengers, 1984), which describes the intrinsic capacity of the elements that make up a system to organize themselves, to create order and adjust, spontaneously. The principles that underlie self-organization are *local interaction* (that is to say between the basic elements making up the system), *non-linearity* (the existence of feedback loops in the exchanges), *thermodynamic openness* (the exchange with the environment) and *emergence*, *i.e.* the fact that a higher order level may spontaneously arise from interactions at lower levels (Forrest and Jones, 1994; Pyka and Windrum, 2000).

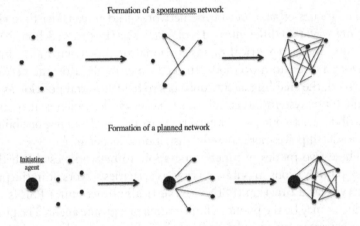

FIG. 1 – Formation of a spontaneous network and a planned network.

The works devoted to PSINs have a different vision of this distinction between planned networks and spontaneous networks, which reflects the concern to move beyond the simple definition of the universe of theoretical possibilities, to be in line with the empirical reality. After all, they generally consider that *spontaneous* (self-organized) networks are networks involving citizens (not government). In PSINs, "self-organization" or "self-governance" often denotes the emergence of a convergent collective action among private agents, without government participation (Bekkers *et al.*, 2014). Such networks emerge spontaneously in order to address given social problems for which public solutions are lacking or ineffective. *Planned* networks, on the other hand, are often initiated by the public administration itself. Although the prevalence of these configurations would probably be confirmed by statistical analyses, the fact remains that others are possible. Thus, the empirical literature also provides examples of PSINs planned by private actors.

2.2 THE FUNCTIONING MODE OF THE NETWORK

We focus here on the way, once formed, PSINs are managed and governed and on the factors that can hinder their proper functioning.

2.2.1 Management and governance of PSINs

The modes of *formation* of the networks lead to consider (in a simplifying way) two different modes of *functioning* (Pyka and Schön, 2009; Sundbo, 2009): a vertical or institutional or top-down mode and a horizontal or bottom-up mode. In the former mode, after the network is formed, the enabling agent continues to hold a central position as the conductor or system integrator. In the latter mode, which is also called "distributed network", local interactions are favoured and responsibilities and leadership are more shared ("distributed leadership").

These two modes of functioning apply to networks established to develop innovations in public services as activities/sectors or in the public service as a function (PSINs). In vertically functioning PSINs, the conductor may be the public administration or a private agent. The public administration may be absent from those functioning horizontally (in this case, the PSIN, very often, replaces a failing public administration).

A review of the case studies in the literature reveals a number of real (and no longer theoretical) configurations of PSINs, characterized by different modes of formation and functioning (see Figure 2).

– Thus, so-called planned networks can be planned by a public agent or a private agent (citizen, NGO, etc.). When the initiator is a public agent, two different configurations are identified, which refer to different modes of functioning.

In the first configuration, the initiating public agent encourages and promotes the emergence of the network, without becoming concretely involved himself. Without directly participating in the network, he ensures what is known as governance of governance or metagovernance (Bekkers *et al.*, 2014; Sørensen, 2006; Sørensen and Torfing, 2010), which strives to establish the favourable general conditions for the formation and functioning of the network. The public actor creates all the conditions conducive to the interaction between the different actors engaged in the network, by elaborating a "political, institutional and discursive framework for collaborative innovation" (Torfing, 2010, p. 12), in other words, a collaborative innovation-friendly ecosystem. He plays the role of "civic enabler" of the collaboration (Sirianni, 2009). This first configuration may encompass two different types of PSINs: distributed PSINs, which function according to a bottom-up, local logic, and verticalised PSINs in which a given private actor takes the lead over the others and plays the role of conductor.

In the second configuration, the initiating public agent surrounds himself with private actors and/or other public actors[4] and gets involved in the network himself. The network functions vertically, with the initiating public agent continuing to play the role of conductor in the functioning of the network (i.e. the development of innovation). It should be noted that public organizations can involve other stakeholders (especially citizens) at different moments in the innovation process and for different tasks (see § 1.3). They can, for example, involve them in the co-design of the innovation or handle the design themselves, and mobilize the other actors (the citizens) only during the implementation phase in order to test the new service and suggest improvements. A functioning mode, in which the initiating public agent, himself operationally involved in the network, would let it function horizontally straightaway is theoretically conceivable. We did not include this configuration in Figure 2 because we did not identify any empirical cases. The fact that the public agent is an operationally involved initiator ("hands-on initiator") tends to verticalise the network, at least at first[5].

In the same way, when the initiator is a private agent (mainly citizens or NGOs), two configurations are also identified. In the first configuration, the initiating private agent invites other agents including public agents to join him to form a network. But he remains leader in

---

4   The collaboration of exclusively public actors can be considered as a PSIN when the different public actors belong to different public organizations.
5   Of course this situation can change over time.

the functioning and governance of the network (vertical functioning and governance). In the second configuration, he also invites other agents (including public agents), but the interaction and functioning are from the outset carried out according to a democratic mode of distributed governance (horizontal functioning).

– Regarding **spontaneous networks,** agents spontaneously converge to build them without necessarily including public agents, and this is not necessarily the consequence of public metagovernance. PSINs, in this case, are distributed PSINs (horizontal functioning). Private actors, in particular citizens, who are the collective promoters of such networks, ensure their distributed governance. These situations arise when private agents replace the public service organizations that are unable to deal with a given problem, for various reasons (lack of resources, lack of skills, politically sensitive subject, etc.). Using the distinction previously established between complementary and substitutive co-production, (§ 1.3), it may be said that these networks are substitutive rather than complementary PSINs.

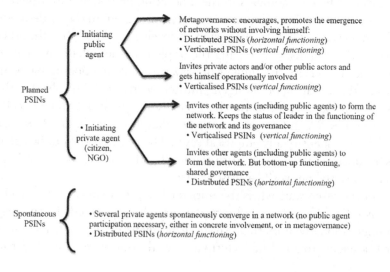

FIG. 2 – Modes of formation and modes of functioning of PSINs.

This mapping of PSINs gives rise to a number of remarks:

- Planned PSINs (whether initiated by a public or private agent) are not necessarily PSINs whose functioning is verticalised. They can function from the outset in a distributed way.
- It is necessary to distinguish *de facto* horizontality (the network is made up of entities or individuals, which claim from the outset their autonomy or which are from the outset autonomous) from *constructed* horizontality, when a dominant entity (often the public administration) strives to establish horizontal relationships through employee empowerment and collaborations with stakeholders (because it considers such a configuration more effective in terms of collaboration or mission achievement).
- In PSINs which concern social innovation (PSINSIs), the functioning and leadership seem to be mostly horizontal.
- The functioning modes are not fixed. They can evolve over time (see § 2.3 about the life cycle of PSINs). For example, planned networks, initiated and governed by public administration, can evolve into self-organized networks. Conversely, spontaneous networks, formed without public administration, can and often do include it, at a given moment, whether as a standard member or as a conductor.

2.2.2 Obstacles to the functioning of innovation networks and the linkage of institutional logics

The NPG paradigm and the literature on innovation networks in general highlight the benefits of networking for innovation. But there are fewer works that identify the problems posed by networks. Bland *et al.* (2010) identify three barriers to networked innovation: 1) the diversity of inputs (information, knowledge, expertise) of the various actors in the network, which can be the source of a communication breakdown; 2) conflicting goals resulting from the diverse interests of the actors, 3) coordination problems that can blur the division of responsibilities ("no one in charge").

Djellal and Gallouj (2013), in their paper on PPINSs, emphasize that the main challenge faced by this type of network is a meta-challenge, insofar as it encompasses most of the others. It is the opposition of so-called "cultures" which designate a complex set of institutional and organizational arrangements, contradictory conceptions of products, services, missions and performance (definition and assessment). Conflicting managerial and/or organizational "cultures" are a classic barrier to collaboration between public and private organizations.

In the same way, a PSIN links different "cultures" or "institutional logics" belonging to the public/State sector, private/market sector and non-profit/civil society (Vickers et al., 2017). Institutional logics can be defined as a set of beliefs, assumptions, values, norms, rules, goals and practices that structure the cognition and behaviour of individuals and organizations (Friedland and Alford, 1991; Thornton and Ocasio, 1999; Thornton et al., 2013; Besharov and Smith, 2014). Although the term "hybrid organization" is generally used to describe organizations (hierarchies) linking different types of institutional logics such as social enterprises, hospitals, universities, micro-finance companies, etc. (see Vickers et al., 2017; Battilana and Lee, 2014; Billis, 2010), it can be applied without difficulty to PSINs and PSINSIs. The networks are based on the assumption that the diversity of the institutional logics at work is a source of innovation through cross-fertilization of different knowledge and skills. But this diversity can also be a source of conflicts and barriers to innovation. The question is therefore how to link these different institutional logics (norms, objectives, preferences, practices) in order to make them favourable to public service innovation. In other words, the question is to understand how the tensions are solved and the compatibilities and compromises are built. This question of the interaction of institutional logics is related to the question of performance assessment, which we will discuss in section 2.5.

Besharov and Smith (2014) have put forward a matrix of institutional logics in organizations that applies without problem to cross-sector collaborative partnerships (Voltan and De Fuentes, 2017) and consequently to PSINs, which are our focus here. This matrix, which seeks to account for the heterogeneity of institutional logics within organizations and to identify the levels of conflict between institutional logics, combines two variables: the degree of logic compatibility and the degree of logic centrality. Compatibility reflects the coherence between institutional logics and the way in which they reinforce themselves within organizational actions. Centrality reflects the domination of one logic over others. It is defined as "the degree to which multiple logics are each treated as equally valid and relevant to organizational functioning" (Besharov and Smith, 2014, p. 367). Centrality is high when several institutional logics play an important role, and it is low when one logic dominates. The logic compatibility-centrality matrix makes it possible to highlight four ideal-types of organizations (for us, PSINs), namely "contested", "estranged", "aligned" and "dominant", reflecting different levels of conflict. The *contested* PSIN is characterized by a low degree of compatibility of institutional logics, a high degree of centrality and therefore a high level of conflict. The *estranged* PSIN, locus of a moderate conflict level, is characterized by a low degree of compatibility and a high degree of centrality. The *aligned* PSIN is characterized by a low level of conflict related to high levels of both compatibility and centrality. Finally, conflict is absent from the *dominant* PSIN, characterized by a high degree of compatibility and a low degree of centrality. This matrix should not give a fixed picture of the configurations and their level of conflict. Conflicting PSINs (contested and estranged PSINs) can be successful in terms of innovation, and non-conflicting PSINs (aligned or dominant PSINs) can be failures. It is therefore important to consider how these more or less conflicting interactions of institutional logics are managed.

2.3 THE INTEGRATION OF THE NETWORK
IN THE TIME FRAME (ITS LIFE CYCLE)

Innovation networks and in particular PSINs are not static. They evolve over time. They are born, reach maturity and can disappear. The number of actors, the nature of the interactions, the functioning, mode of management and governance, etc. change over time. Schön and Pyka (2012) (see also Green *et al.*, 2013) consider that the industry life cycle concept can be transposed to networks.

The *emergence stage* which corresponds to network formation can be achieved spontaneously by self-organization or be planned by a particular actor (initiator, enabler), as noted in section 2.1.

In the *growth stage*, the number and variety of actors involved in the network increases. This increase can be achieved by two different mechanisms (see Figure 3): i) in the planned network, it can be achieved by the invitation of new actors by the key actor, ii) in the spontaneous network, by a snowball mechanism in which the last entrant, himself invited by the previous entrant, invites new entrants, and so on. It is the first mechanism that seems the most likely in PSINs initiated by a public actor. But, of course, these two mechanisms are only ideal-types, which can mingle with one another (hybridize). For example, in the last case mentioned, there is no reason why other actors than the public actor could not invite other members. There is also no reason why an actor established for some time cannot invite someone else and no reason why new stakeholders cannot spontaneously join the networks (without the invitation of a member).

In the *maturity stage*, new entrants (irrespective of the inviting entity) have established relationships with each other. Interactions, flows of information and knowledge and learning processes are at their peak. The density of the network is high (see Figure 3). The network no longer functions according to a mode of exploration, but rather according to a mode of exploitation. It is no longer seeking radical innovation, but it confines itself to incremental improvements. It should be noted that at this stage, in certain cases of planned innovation networks, the initiating agent (in particular, if it is a public agent) may withdraw from the network or reduce its involvement. There is then a shift from a vertical PSIN to a distributed or horizontal PSIN.

In the *decline stage*, the network disappears, having accomplished its mission(s) or because the solution it proposes is no longer suitable or has been supplanted by competing, better solutions or even because what was initially an innovation network is transformed into a simple service delivery network.

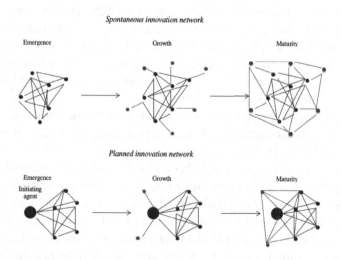

FIG. 3 – The life cycle of spontaneous and planned innovation networks.

2.4 THE INTEGRATION OF THE NETWORK IN SPACE (THE GEOGRAPHY OF PSINs)

PSINs and especially PSINSIs are initially local innovation networks. They organize collaborations on a municipality, neighbourhood or other small scale. This geographical characteristic is of course closely linked to the nature of the innovation that is carried out by the network and the way it is produced (innovation that aims to solve concrete social problems in the immediate living environment of individuals, innovation that involves the people concerned by the problem in the collaboration). PSINs and PSINSIs seem to require proximity, even if the use of ICTs (Internet, social media) somewhat lessens this requirement.

However, there appear to be differences in spatial constraints depending on the type of PSIN considered. After all, spontaneous PSINs are more likely to be proximity networks than planned PSINs. As Green *et al.* (2013, p. 123) note "since the spontaneous network (S1) emerges due to some sort of external pressure and the resulting shared interest among a specified group of actors (for example, from the same industry or region) there is a high probability that many of the participating actors already know each other". Planned PSINs, especially when they are planned by public agents, are less subject to geographical constraints. Depending on the nature of the problem to be solved, the public agent may invite agents located anywhere throughout the national territory or even from abroad.

Furthermore, some complex problems can neither be solved by a single actor nor on a single geographical scale (in this case a local scale). These are problems that, even if they manifest locally, arise in regional, national or international terms. This applies, for example, to migrant and refugee issues or environmental issues. Some PSINs may therefore be considered at higher spatial/geographical levels than the local level.

From the point of view of the spatial dynamics of networks, the behaviours of PSINs (as structural arrangements established to develop an innovation) should not be confused with those of production/distribution networks in charge of the more routine delivery of the innovative solution, once the PSIN has been developed. In the latter case, the network can spread geographically through replication/duplication by other actors, franchising, new legal forms, etc.

2.5 ASSESSING NETWORK PERFORMANCE

The last characteristic of networks that we address is, as it should be, their performance. PSINs are innovation networks, and therefore their performance is closely linked to the success of the innovation for which they were formed. However, as we shall see later, the success of a PSIN cannot be reduced to the success of the public service innovation (PSI) it carries out. A PSIN may create value and be, in a way, a success, even if the PSI is a failure. This paradox refers to how success and performance are defined and assessed.

Our proposal is to define the success of a PSIN (its performance) by its *ability to create value*. But though value is systematically designated as the ultimate goal of any socio-economic activity, it also poses thorny definition problems. This is why many studies devoted to value creation address value as a postulate. For our part, we view value as a multi-faceted category that can fit into different "worlds" (systems), which reflect different dimensions of performance, and which are not independent of each other, in that they have complementary or conflictual relationships.

2.5.1 The worlds of value

To address the notion of value, we propose to rely, freely speaking (that is to say, by using it as a simple heuristic tool), on a conventionalist approach of socio-economic activities, which distinguishes different forms of legitimacy, different registers of justification or categories (or worlds) of "worth" (Boltanski and Thévenot, 1991). We distinguish the following different worlds (systems of definition, legitimization and measurement) of value: 1) the market and financial world, 2) the industrial and technical world, 3) the relational or domestic world, 4) the social-civic world, 5) the opinion/reputation world, 6) the creation/inspiration/innovation world. The last five worlds mentioned can be said to reflect the different dimensions of value-in-use and value-in-context (Figure 4).

In the industrial and technical world, the main criteria for defining and evaluating outputs (products or services) are volumes, traffic and technical operations. The industrial and technical value is measured by the quality, reliability and functionality of the new product or service.

In the market and financial world, the output is envisaged in terms of monetary and financial value and operations. Market value does not directly apply to social innovation and innovation in public services. PSI (including social innovations) cannot be evaluated by the usual market mechanisms (economic success, profit made by the innovator). Nevertheless, in this type of innovation, the market value is not absent. It is present indirectly, if not in terms of prices (which are irrelevant), at least in terms of costs. It is also present indirectly in the very objective of some social innovations and the corresponding PSINs: for example, social innovations and PSINs aiming to re-introduce long-term job seekers into the labour market, in other words, to provide them with income, PSINs focused on social innovations aimed at saving energy or preserving the environment or health, and so on.

The social-civic world and social-civic value assess results in terms of fairness, justice, inclusion, social solidarity especially with respect to disadvantaged people and environmental protection. Social-civic value is essential for social innovation, and even more so if it occurs in public services. It should be noted that social-civic value is not synonymous with public value. Indeed, in our analysis, public value is an all-encompassing category, which includes all the other dimensions of value discussed here.

The relational or domestic world values interpersonal relationships, empathy and trust relationships reinforced over time, and places a strong focus on the quality of relationships when assessing output. The relational or domestic value reflects the (geographical and human) proximity to the user/citizen.

The world of reputation and reputational value are based on the brand image of an organization, community or territory. When, through social innovation, a given organizational form (a company, or a PSIN or a PSINSI) contributes to the health and well-being of its employees or citizens, to the future of the planet, etc., it (co-)creates reputational value.

The world of innovation values creativity, inspiration, experimentation and knowledge. Feller (1981) considers innovation in the public sector as "conspicuous production". The idea is that, in a field where it is difficult to measure performance, innovation values the public agent and makes his/her public service activity visible. However, a PSIN can generate so-called creative/innovative value, even if the innovation that it is supposed to develop is a failure from the point of view of other dimensions of value (in particular industrial and technical value and market and financial value). After all, the formation and existence of the network give a positive and rewarding image (an innovative, creative image) of the community or the organization that implements it. These communities or organizations are viewed as dynamic, resilient, enterprising and creative. Even if it is not based on the same drivers, creative/innovative value appears here, in its ultimate result, to be closely related to reputational value.

This discussion of value raises a number of interesting questions.

- The first is the distinction between *value* and *value added*. After all, there is a temptation to apply the concept of value added to all the concepts of value mentioned above (civic value added, domestic value added, etc.). But in reality, this concept has a strong industrial connotation (the value added is the difference between production and intermediate consumption), which reduces its transposition to the other dimensions of value to a metaphorical dimension.

- The literature on value (especially in the context of the so-called Service Dominant Logic, as we have already noted) is concerned with how value is created and especially co-created. The question that should be asked is whether the different conceptions of value have identical relations with the process of co-creation. For example, it can be asked whether, because they reflect a certain intensity of real links (fidelity) or virtual/emotional links (empathy) between the citizen and the public agent, relational and domestic value and social-civic value are not more likely to be co-created than industrial value.

2.5.2 From the various worlds of value
to the various concepts of performance

Different concepts of performance are associated with these different worlds/concepts of value: industrial and technical performance, market and financial performance, domestic or relational performance, social-civic performance, reputational performance and innovation performance. The industrial and technical performance of the PSIN can be measured, for example, in terms of efficiency and productivity associated with innovation, in terms of volume and sustainability of the jobs created or in terms of economic development (especially at the local level). Civic, relational, reputational and innovation performances can also be somehow quantified (Djellal and Gallouj, 2013), perhaps by measuring the time spent in a given relationship within a given value world, or by measuring some elementary activities undertaken within the relationship or associated with it. For example, indicators of relational performance include better user satisfaction and less user turn-over; the amount of time devoted to vulnerable users is an indicator of social-civic performance; the number of innovative solutions introduced or diffused and scaled up is an indicator of innovation performance, and so on.

2.5.3 Interactions between different worlds of value/performance

These different concepts of value and corresponding performance are not, of course, independent of each other (see Figure 4). They can complement and reinforce or compete and conflict with each other (in the latter case, the creation of one form of value leads to the destruction of another form).

For example, the (co)creation of industrial and technical value (and performance) positively affects market and financial value (and performance). Similarly, an improvement in relational performance (reflected, for example, by an increase in user loyalty) can have a positive influence on market performance. As we have already pointed out, an improvement in creative/innovative performance positively affects reputation performance.

These different types of performance may also be negatively related, as they may conflict with each other. For example, good civic performance (a significant amount of time given to users in difficulty) may worsen productivity (technical performance). Likewise, an improvement in civic performance worsens market performance. In general, social and civic value and performance are most often at odds with market and financial value and performance and industrial and technical value and performance.

These interactions between the different concepts of value and performance are closely related to the interactions between the different institutional logics that we discussed above (§ 2.2).

FIG. 4 – The different dimensions of public value and their interactions.

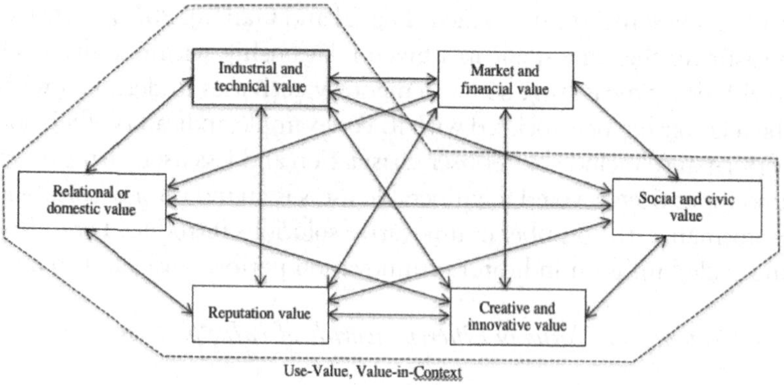

CONCLUSION

This structural arrangement that we call "Public service innovation network" (PSIN) is a new form of expression of innovation networks which takes seriously innovation in public services or in public service, the participation of citizens and third sector organizations and the intangible forms of innovation (invisible innovation). After all, PSINs mobilize a diversity of public and private agents, especially citizens, collaborating to co-create value by co-producing innovations in the field of public services (sector) or public service (function), whatever the nature of the innovation. PSINs may simultaneously be considered as forms of innovation, innovation organizational modes, instruments for public policy (especially at local level) and palliative solutions for deprived and weakened public services. They occupy an important place within the New Public Governance paradigm.

We have attempted in this work to understand what distinguishes PSINs from other innovation networks and especially traditional innovation networks (TINs) and public-private innovation networks in services (PPINSs). We have tried to define and characterize PSINs, by examining, first of all, a number of structural variables: the nature of the actors involved and their interactions, and the forms and modalities of the innovation carried out by the network. We then shifted the analysis towards dynamic variables, describing the modes of emergence and functioning of the networks, and their integration in time and in space. The ultimate goal of PSINs being the co-creation of value, we finally introduced a typology of the worlds of value, which makes it possible to consider a plurality of (competing or complementary) performance principles at work in PSINs.

Although PSINs are increasingly taken seriously in contemporary economies, efforts are nevertheless needed to theoretically reinforce this concept. After all, the literature is dominated by case studies and by a concept of PSINs (in particular when they focus on social innovations) as temporary curative arrangements (aimed at overcoming the temporary failure of public services). One way to reinforce the theoretical basis of PSINs might be, not only to analyse them autonomously, but to explicitly include them in the mapping and discussion of innovation systems (whether local, regional, national, social or sectoral).

This work was undertaken within the EU-funded COVAL project [770356]: "Understanding value co-creation in public services for transforming European public administrations", H2020 project 2017-2020.

BIBLIOGRAPHY

AGGER A. and HEDENSTED LUND D. (2017), "Collaborative Innovation in the Public Sector – New Perspectives on the Role of Citizens?", *Scandinavian Journal of Public Administration*, vol. 21, n° 3, p. 17-37.

AGRANOFF R. (2007), *Managing within Networks: Adding Value to Public Organizations*, Washington, DC, Georgetown University Press.

ALFORD J. (2014), "The multiple facets of co-production: Building on the work of Elinor Ostrom", *Public Management Review*, vol. 16, n° 3, p. 299-316.

ANSELL C. and TORFING J. (2014), *Public Innovation through Collaboration and Design*, Oxon and New York, Routledge.

ANSELL C. and GASH A. (2007), "Collaborative governance in theory and practice", *Journal of Public Administration Research and Theory*, vol. 18, n° 4, p. 543-571.

ATKINSON R. (1999), "Discourses of partnership and empowerment in contemporary British urban regeneration", *Urban Studies*, vol. 36, n° 1, p. 59-72.

BARABASI A.L. and ALBERT R. (1999), "Emergence of Scaling in random Networks", *Science*, vol. 286, n° 5439, p. 509-512.

BASTIAT F. (1848), *Selected Essays on Political Economy*, Princeton, NJ, D. Van Nordstrand.

BATTILANA J., LEE M. (2014), "Advancing research on hybrid organizing –Insights from the study of social enterprises", *Academy of Management Annals*, vol. 8, n° 1, p. 397-441.

BEKKERS V., EDELENBOS J., NEDERHAND J., STEIJN B., TUMMERS L. and VOORBERG W. (2014), "The Social Innovation Perspective in the Public Sector: Co-creation, Self-organization and Meta-Governance", in BEKKERS V., EDELENBOS J. and STEIJN B. (eds), *Innovation in the public sector: linking capacity and leadership*, Basingstoke, Palgrave MacMillan, p. 223-243.

BESHAROV M.L. and SMITH W.K. (2014) "Multiple institutional logics in organizations: explaining their varied nature and implications", *Academy of Management Review*, vol. 39, n° 3, p. 364-381.

BILLIS D. (2010), "Towards a theory of hybrid organizations", in BILLIS D. (ed.), *Hybrid Organizations and the Third Sector. Challenges for Practice, Theory and Policy*, Basingstoke, Palgrave Macmillan, p. 46-49.

BLAND T., BRUK B., KIM D. and LEE K. T., (2010), "Enhancing Public Sector Innovation: Examining the Network-Innovation Relationship", *The Innovation Journal: The Public Sector Innovation Journal*, vol. 15, n° 3, p. 1-25.

BOLTANSKI L., THÉVENOT L. (1991), *De la justification. Les économies de la grandeur*, Paris, Gallimard.

BOMMERT B. (2010), "Collaborative innovation in the public sector", *International Public Management Review*, vol. 11, n° 1, p. 15-33.

BOVAIRD T. (2007), "Beyond engagement and participation: User and community coproduction of public services", *Public Administration Review*, vol. 67, n° 5, p. 846-860.

BOVAIRD T. and LOEFFLER E. (2012), "From engagement to co-production: How users and communities contribute to public services", in PESTOFF V., BRANDSEN T. and VERSCHUERE B. (eds), *New Public Governance, the Third Sector and Co-production*, London, Routledge, p. 35-60.

CALLON M. (1986), "Éléments pour une sociologie de la traduction. La domestication des coquilles Saint-Jacques dans la Baie de Saint-Brieuc", *L'Année sociologique*, n° 36, p. 169-208.

CARPINI M.X.D., COOK F. and JACOBS L.R. (2004), "Public Deliberation, Discursive Participation, and Citizen Engagement: A Review of the Empirical Literature", *Annual Review of Political Science*, vol. 7, n° 1, p. 315-344.

DESMARCHELIER B., DJELLAL F. GALLOUJ F. (2019a), "Innovation in public services in the light of public administration paradigms and service innovation perspectives", *European Review of Services Economics and Management*, p. 91-120, 2019-2, n° 8, p. 91-120.

DESMARCHELIER B., DJELLAL F. GALLOUJ F. (2019b), "Towards a servitization of innovation networks: a mapping", *Public Management Review, https://doi.org/10.1080/14719037.2019.1637012* (retrieved on March 3, 2020).

DOZ Y.L., OLK P.M. SMITH RING P. (2000), "Formation process of R-D consortia: which path to take? where does it lead?" *Strategic Management Journal*, vol. 21, n° 3, p. 239-266.

EDVARDSSON B., TRONVOLL B. and WITELL L. (2018), "An ecosystem perspective on service innovation", in GALLOUJ F., DJELLAL F. (eds), *A Research Agenda for Service Innovation*, Cheltenham, UK, Northampton (MA), USA, Edward Elgar Publishers, p. 85-102.

EGGERS B., SINGH S. (2009), *The Public Innovators Playbook*, Washington, DC, Harvard Kennedy School of Government.

EIGLIER P. and LANGEARD E. (1987), *Servuction, le marketing des services*, Paris, Editions Mac Graw Hill.

FORREST S., JONES T. (1994), "Modeling complex adaptive systems with echo", in STONER R.J. and YU X.H. (eds), *Complex systems: mechanisms of adaptation*, Amsterdam, IOS Press.

FRANKE N., SHAH S. (2003), "How communities support innovative activities: an exploration of assistance and sharing among end-users", *Research Policy*, vol. 32, n° 1, p. 157-178.

FRIEDLAND R., ALFORD R.R. (1991), "Bringing society back in: symbols, practices, and institutional contradictions", in POWELL W.W., DIMAGGIO P.J. (eds), *The New Institutionalism in Organizational Analysis*, Chicago, University of Chicago Press, p. 232-263.

FUGLSANG L. (2010), "Bricolage and invisible innovation in public service innovation", *Journal of Innovation Economics*, vol. 1, n° 5, p. 67-87.

FUGLSANG L. and SORENSEN F. (2011), "The balance between bricolage and innovation: management dilemmas in sustainable public innovation", *Service Industries Journal*, vol. 31, n° 4, p. 581-595.

FUNG A. (2003), "Thinking about Empowered Participatory Governance", in FUNG A. and WRIGHT E.O. (eds), *Deepening democracy: Institutional innovations in empowered participatory governance*, London and New York, Verso, p. 3-44.

GAGON C., KLEIN J.-L. (1991), "Le partenariat dans le développement local : tendances actuelles et perspectives de changement social", *Cahiers de Géographie du Québec*, vol. 35, n° 95, p. 239-255.

GALLOUJ F., RUBALCABA L., WINDRUM P. (eds) (2013), *Public-Private Innovation Networks in Services: the dynamics of cooperation in service innovation*, Cheltenham, UK, Northampton (MA), USA, Edward Elgar Publishers.

GALLOUJ F., SAVONA M. (2009), "Innovation in services: a review of the debate and perspectives for a research agenda", *The Journal of Evolutionary Economics*, vol. 19, n° 2, p. 149-172

GALLOUJ F., WEINSTEIN O. (1997), "Innovation in Services", *Research Policy*, vol. 26, n° 4-5, p. 537-556.

GEBAUER H., JOHNSON M., ENQUIST B. (2010), "Value co-creation as a determinant of success in public transport services: a study of the Swiss federal railway operator (SBB)", *Managing Service Quality*, vol. 20, n° 6, p. 511-530.

GRANOVETTER M. (1973), "The strength of weak ties", *American Journal of Sociology*, vol. 78, n° 6, p. 1360-1380.

GREEN L., PYKA A., SCHÖN B. (2013), "A life cycle-based taxonomy of innovation networks – with a focus on public-private collaboration", in GALLOUJ F., RUBALCABA L., WINDRUM P. (eds), *Public-Private Innovation Networks in Services: the dynamics of cooperation in service innovation*, Cheltenham and Northampton, MA: Edward Elgar Publisher, p. 113-135.

HARDYMAN W., DAUNT K., KITCHENER M. (2015), "Value co-creation through patient engagement in health care: a micro-level approach and research agenda", *Public Management Review*, vol. 17, n° 1, p. 90-107.

HARTLEY J. (2005, "Innovation in governance and public services: Past and present", *Public Money and Management*, vol. 25, n° 1, January, p. 27-34.

HIRSCHMAN A.O. (1970), *Exit, voice and Loyalty. Responses to decline in firms, organizations and States*, Cambridge (MA) and London, England, Harvard University Press.

HOLLAND J.H. MILLER J.H. (1991), "Artificial Adaptive Agents in Economic Theory", *American Economic Review*, vol. 81, n° 2, p. 365-370.

KEAST R., BROWN K. and MANDELL M. (2007), "Getting the right mix; unpacking integration meanings and strategies", *International Public Management Journal*, vol. 10, n° 1, p. 9-33.

LEVITT B. and MARCH J.G. (1988), "Organizational Learning", *Annual Review of Sociology*, vol. 14, n° 2, p. 318-340.

LOEFFLER E. (2009), *Opportunities and challenges for innovative service delivery*, OECD-CRC, June, Paris.

LUSCH R., VARGO S. (2006), "Service-Dominant Logic: reactions, reflections and refinements", *Marketing Theory*, vol. 6, n° 3, p. 281-288.

MARTIN B. (2015), *Twenty challenges for innovation studies*, SPRU Working Paper Series, SWPS 2015-30, November.

NEWMAN M.E.J. (2003), "The Structure and Function of Complex Networks", *SIAM Review*, vol. 45, n° 2, p. 167-256.

O'LEARY R. and BINGHAM L.B. (eds) (2009), *The Collaborative Public Manager*, Washington, DC, Georgetown University Press.

OECD (2014), *Together for Better Public Services*, Directorate for Public Governance and Territorial Development, Paris, OECD.

PESTOFF V. (2009), "Towards a paradigm of democratic participation: Citizen Participation and Co-Production of Personal Social Services in Sweden", *Annals of Public and Cooperative Economics*, vol. 80, n° 2, p. 197-224.

PESTOFF V., BRANDSEN T. (2008), *Co-production. The third sector and the delivery of public services*, London and New York, Routledge.

PESTOFF V., BRANDSEN T. and VERSCHUERE B. (2012), *New Public Governance, the Third Sector, and Co-Production*, London and New York, Routledge.

PESTOFF V., OSBORNE S.P. and BRANDSEN T. (2006), "Patterns of co-production in public services: Some concluding thoughts", *Public Management Review*, vol. 8, n° 4, p. 591-595.

POLITT C., BOUCKAERT G., LOFFLER E. (2006), *Making quality sustainable: co-design, co-decide, co-produce, co-evaluate"*, Scientific rapporteurs, 4QZ Conference.

PRIGOGINE I., STENGERS I. (1984), *Order out of Chaos: man's new dialogue with nature*, New York, Bantam New Age Books.

PYKA A., SCHÖN A. (2009), *Taxonomy of innovation, cooperation and networks in service industries*, ServPPIN project, European Commission.

PYKA A., WINDRUM P. (2000), *The self-organisation of innovation networks*, Eighth International Joseph A. Schumpeter Society Conference, Manchester, United Kingdom, 28th June-1st July.

RASHMAN L. and HARTLEY J. (2002), "Leading and learning? Knowledge transfer in the Beacon Council Scheme", *Public Administration*, vol. 80, n° 2, p. 523-542.

ROBERTS N. C. and KING P. J. (1996), *Transforming Public Policy: Dynamics of Policy Entrepreneurship and Innovation*, San Francisco, CA, Jossey-Bass.

SANGER M.B., LEVIN M.A. (1992), "Using Old Stuff in New Ways: Innovation as a Case of Evolutionary Tinkering", *Journal of Policy Analysis and Management*, vol. 11, n° 1, p. 88-115

SAY J.-B. (1803), *Traité d'économie politique*, [1821] *A treatise on the political Economy*, Boston, Wells and Lilly.

SCHÖN B., PYKA A. (2009), "A taxonomy of innovation networks", *FZID discussion papers*, n° 42-2012, Univ. Hohenheim, Forschungszentrum Innovation und Dienstleistung, Stuttgart.

SICILIA M., GUARINI E., SANCINO A., ANDREANI M., RUFFINI R. (2016), "Public services management and co-production in multi-level governance settings", *International Review of Administrative Sciences*, vol. 82, n° 1, p. 8-27.

SIRIANNI C. (2009), *Investing in Democracy. Engaging citizens in Collaborative Governance*, Washington DC, Brookings Inst. Pr.

SØRENSEN E. and TORFING J. (2010), "Collaborative Innovation in the Public Sector: An Analytical Framework", *Working paper n° 1/2010*, Research project Collaborative Innovation in the Public Sector (CLIPS) funded by the Danish Strategic Research Council, Roskilde: Roskilde Universitet.

SØRENSEN E. and TORFING J. (2013), *Enhancing Social Innovation by Rethinking Collaboration, Leadership and Public Governance*, Paper presented at NESTA Social Frontiers, London, United Kingdom.

STYHRE A. (2009), "Tinkering with material resources: Operating under ambiguous conditions in rock construction work", *The Learning Organization*, vol. 16, n° 5, p. 386-397.

SUNDBO J. (2009), *Public-private networks and service innovation in knowledge intensive services: a report of European case studies*, ServPPIN project, WP5, October.

THORNTON P.H., OCASIO W. (1999), "Institutional logics and the historical contingency of power in organizations: Executive succession in the higher education publishing industry, 1958–1990", *American Journal of Sociology*, vol. 105, n° 3, p. 801-843.

THORNTON P.H., OCASIO W., LOUNSBURY M. (2012), *The Institutional Logics Perspective: A New Approach to Culture, Structure, and Process*, Oxford University Press, London.

TOIVONEN M. (2010), "Different types of innovation processes in services and their organisational implications", in GALLOUJ F., DJELLAL F. (eds), *The handbook of innovation and services*, Cheltenham, UK and Northampton, MA, USA, Edward Elgar, p. 221-249.

TOIVONEN M., TUOMINEN T., BRAX S. (2007), "Innovation process interlinked with the process of service delivery: a management challenge in KIBS", *Economies et Sociétés, série EGS*, n° 8/3/2007, p. 355-384.

TUOMI I. (2002), "The future of knowledge management", *Lifelong Learning in Europe*, vol. 7, n° 2, p. 69-79.

VICKERS I., LYONA F., SEPULVEDAA L., MCMULLIN C. (2017), "Service innovation and multiple institutional logics: The case of hybrid social enterprise providers of health and wellbeing", *Research Policy*, vol. 46, n° 10, p. 1755-1768.

VOLTAN A., DE FUENTES C. (2017), Managing multiple logics in partnerships for scaling social innovation, *European Journal of Innovation Management*, vol. 19, n° 4, p. 446-467.

VON BERTALANFFY L. (1968), *The quest for a general system theory*, New York, George Braziller.

VON HIPPEL E. (1986), "Lead Users: A Source of Novel Product Concepts", *Management Science*, vol. 32, n° 7, p. 791-805.

VOORBERG W., BEKKERS V., TUMMERS L. (2015), "A systematic review of co-production and co-creation: embarking on the social innovation journey", *Public Management Review*, vol. 17, n° 9, p. 1333-1357.

WINDRUM P., SCHARTINGER D., RUBALCABA L., GALLOUJ F., TOIVONEN M. (2016), "The Co-Creation of Multi-Agent Social Innovations: A Bridge Between Service and Social Innovation Research", *European Journal of Innovation Management*, vol. 19, n° 2, May, p. 150-166.

DEBATES AND VIEWPOINTS

SERVICE INNOVATION IN HISTORICAL PERSPECTIVE

The case of "platforming"

Gilles PACHÉ
CRET-LOG, Aix Marseille
University

INTRODUCTION

The question linked to the universalist or culturalist nature of management tools and approaches is very old. This is also the case in economics, with the seminal work of Rostow (1960/1990) who tried to identify a standard model of the stages of economic growth, independently of any institutional context. Logistical services do not escape the temptation of universalism, i.e. the application of the same organizational framework of product flows, also independently of any institutional context. Since the 1980s, the implementation of platforms by large retailers has thus become widespread throughout Europe. The policy of "platforming" has led them to abandon direct supplies of their stores from manufacturing factories. This policy has spread to all large retailers in a homogeneous manner, which allows many academics to conclude that "platforming" is a universal service model. It is possible here to refer to *circulation norms*, in the sense of Colin (1982), which are imposed on companies in the management of their supply chains. We will show how circulation norms provide an original insight into the implementation of service innovations that are prominent in contemporary supply chains.

Historians report on situations in which "platforming" was at the origin of logistical performances, some of which led to the success of projects that were fatal for humanity (like the triangular trade). The interest of the approach is to investigate historical phenomena in order to better understand the contemporary dynamics of some innovation ecosystems within logistical services, which sometimes lead to excesses of what Bauman (2007) calls "liquid times". The methodology of this viewpoint is based on the analysis of secondary data from research conducted by historians on the above-mentioned phenomena, identifying more specifically the designing and delivering of innovative logistical services in their works. The purpose of the contribution is to underline that circulation norms are not linked to the managerial revolution that began in the second half of the 20th century. On the contrary, they appear very early on as a true service innovation. Through three, sometimes dramatic, historical examples (the triangular trade, the Armenian genocide, the Overlord operation), we will describe the existence of highly structured "platforming" processes, which today serve as a reference to the famous hub-and-spokes model. The three historical examples finally enable us to identify a "service-based archetype" that indicates how networks for logistical innovation were created in the past.

The focus on service innovation from "platforming" processes, as suggested in the viewpoint, is in line with the critical analysis conducted by Gallouj *et al.* (2003). Indeed, even if "platforming" processes are based on the technical system of hub-and-spokes, they correspond to a radically new approach of interface management between supply and demand, resulting in a strong reduction of transaction costs. According to Gallouj *et al.* (2003), it is important to break from this narrow vision of service innovation, which has long been synonymous, in the dominant economic streams, with the adoption of technical systems of industrial origin. The main issue was then to assess the impact of innovation on different variables such as employment, skills or work organization. Although it remains important to understand the purely technical dimensions of service innovations, it is only possible to analyze the resulting change in interactivity and coordination between actors, e.g. within a supply chain.

1. AN OVERVIEW ON "PLATFORMING" PROCESSES

The massification logic on which "platforming" is based has been known and studied for many years. They are at the origin of a model of "space radialisation" which has deeply reorganized the shape of contemporary supply chains. Monnoyer and Zuliani (2007) have clearly underlined the structuring power of these radialisation practices by relying on the case of Airbus, which famous A380 aircraft production network (and associated services) extends over a larger scale. One of the most emblematic configurations of "platforming" is undoubtedly the hub-and-spokes model, which originated in the air transport and express courier industries (Lumsden *et al.*, 1999; Bowen Jr., 2012). It means that the location of a shipping unit, for example a factory, is close to a structuring axis, itself connected to a focal point for grouping and then splitting, towards another structuring axis on which the destination unit is located, for example a store (see Figure 1).

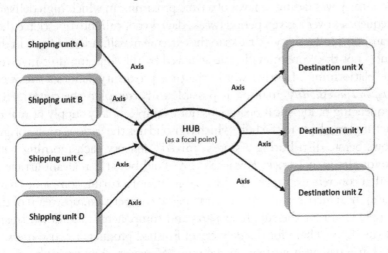

FIG. 1 – Hub-and-spokes model.

The hub-and-spokes model was designed by Frederick W. Smith in the early 1970s. While he was a student at Yale University, he wrote a dissertation in which he presented a business plan for a company in order to be capable of delivering a package within 24 hours from any shipping unit in the USA. At the time, air freight transport was divided between passenger airline companies. For these companies, parcel delivery remained a marginal activity and the logistics service quality was poor. Using operations research tools, Frederick W. Smith imagined the creation of a specific fleet of aircraft, based on a hub through which parcels transited before leaving for their destination units. The advantages of this type of network are numerous: fewer routes and aircrafts, shorter lead times, optimized aircraft loads and lower costs (Mason *et al.*, 1997). Drawing directly from his dissertation, Frederick W. Smith created in 1971 an air transport company: Federal Express, renamed FedEx in 1994. After two years of testing, he bought 14 Falcon 20, chose Memphis as a hub and launched his business serving 25 American cities. His experience in Vietnam with the US Army, accustomed to integrating air and ground transport, gave him the clever idea of parking his trucks on the runways of airports to accelerate transshipments prior to delivery.

In the Frederick W. Smith fresh perspective, the notion of spatial proximity was fading in favor of a time proximity in which high delivery frequencies over a given period (week, day) do not call into question either transport productivity - thanks to the extreme massification of flows in the hub - nor the economies of scale achieved by the shipping unit involved in "platforming". In other words, the time proximity defines a *maximum temporal accessibility*, making it possible to better plan the coordinated sequencing of logistical operations, for example a daily supply of manufactured products to the hub, which consolidates the various multi-origin flows before distributing a store's "mixed" delivery each morning with no (or almost no) stock. Kasarda's (1999) old but still relevant article is full of concrete examples in which large manufacturing companies have set up near airport hubs to win time-based competition, upstream of the supply chain for the supply of parts and components, and downstream of the supply chain for the delivery of finished products to customers.

Little has been written on the topic. However, the geography of the structuring axes - or radial axes - determines industrial and logistical investment decisions. However, it is both the connection to grouping platforms and the coordination of flows within "platforming" that directly conditions the logistics service quality provided to destination units (Khorheh and

Moisiadis, 2015), and consequently the market shares that shipping units can hope to obtain. The battle over speed between FedEx (the innovator), DHL and UPS (the followers), for example, is a testimony to these stakes, especially since consumers who order online, in direct relation to logistics performance of companies, can express their dissatisfaction with the failure to meet delivery windows. It would be a mistake to believe that "platforming" is just a recent service innovation linked to the acceleration of flows in a just-in-time economy. On the contrary, history shows that "platforming" has been at the origin of logistics performance, some of which have unfortunately enabled the success of tragic projects for Humanity.

2. THE TRIANGULAR TRADE CASE

Triangular trade, which took place from the 16th to the 19th century, consisted in supplying Europe with products from the American colonies, and in return providing them with the labor needed to operate the plantations, based on a proven economic model (Grenouilleau, 2018). The key resources of each country were as follows: (1) for Europe, clothes, wheat, jewelry, pearls, alcohol and weapons; (2) for Africa, slaves, mostly prisoners of war and mostly the result of tribal conflicts; (3) for the Americas, sugar, coffee, cocoa, indigo, cotton, tobacco, etc. In other words, it is above all a question of trading and getting rich. Stein (1979) was thus able to identify 500 families who had fitted out 2,800 ships bound for Africa in Nantes, Bordeaux, La Rochelle, Le Havre and Saint-Malo in order to transport labor to the Colonies of America, buy raw materials there and then export them to Europe to make a comfortable profit. For that purpose, a process of "platforming" was initiated to organize the grouping, transport and distribution of slaves as efficiently as possible (Fulconis et al., 2017).

It has been demonstrated by historians that inter-tribal conflicts, razzias, customary law and offences have fuelled the sources of supply of slaves in Africa (Coquery-Vidrovitch, 2016). The razzias are legally organized by sultans to supply traders with African captives for their exporting. Far from wanting to suppress a trade from which they took profit, these sultans only thought of imposing transit taxes on the caravans along the different "spokes". To become more efficient, African slave traders will increasingly need sophisticated logistical means, and to have more weapons and horses - a guarantee of power - they will be forced to sell more captives by engaging in wars against neighboring kingdoms. Other tribal chiefs also organized *razzias* and sold men for beef, weapons and clothes. In this tragedy, therefore, it must be recognized that there was collaboration by native potentates who cared little about the destination of their compatriots.

Captives from the hinterland, the indigenous "suppliers" must have had strong relays and relationships, as well as porters for barter products. The supply networks, although they extended from the Senegambia to present-day Angola, were in fact limited to a few sites that acted as genuine switching units in which grouping operations and transitory "storage" of slaves were carried out. These sites were in fact the real hubs of the triangular trade: Juda in Benin (now Ouidah) and Lagos in Nigeria, which centralized nearly 60% of the supply, but also Loango in Congo and Luanda in Angola (see Figure 2). For each of the European countries involved in triangular trade, the counters played their role of *concentrator* perfectly. Once grouped together, the slaves would then have been ready to face the crossing of the Atlantic Ocean before being distributed and then sold in the Colonies of America for those who would have survived the terrible journey.

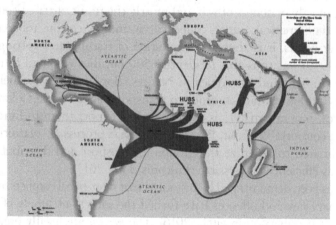

FIG. 2 – "Platforming" in the slave trade.
Source: Adapted from Eltis and Richardson (2015).

3. THE ARMENIAN GENOCIDE CASE

Even if for some historians, the first (colonial) genocide of the 20th century was that of the Hereros and Namas in present-day Namibia, perpetrated by German colonial troops from 1904 onwards, and leading to the deaths of 85,000 people, the Armenian genocide of 1915 is the one that has left the most lasting impression, both in the horror of the exactions committed and in the rigorous nature of its implacable organization. The approximate, but generally accepted, death toll is 1.5 million (Mouradian, 2013). The origins of the Armenian genocide are now well known. Prey to revolts by Christian subjects in the north of the Ottoman Empire (vast territories were lost during the Balkan wars), it collapsed at the turn of the 20th century. In 1908, a movement of young army officers ("Young Turks") seized power. They entered the war alongside Germany in 1914. After a disastrous campaign against Russian forces in the Caucasus, they were defeated at the Battle of Sarikemish. The Armenians of the region were then accused of siding with the Russians, and the Young Turks took advantage of this to present them as a real threat to the State.

The deportation of Armenians from Eastern Anatolia was methodically managed. With the exception of the Armenians in Constantinople, who were protected by foreign embassies and communities, Armenians in urban centers were kept away to prevent their elimination in the cities from causing disorder. Convoys were therefore organized along the roads, which acted as "spokes", and most of them placed in concentration camps for four months, demonstrating the speed of the deportation resulting from their rigorous planning. Of the 1.2 million deportees, approximately 600,000 died on the roads. The survivors of the deportation were distributed to about 20 camps, divided into three main axes: the first axis follows the Baghdad railway line; the second axis follows the Islayie-Alep route; and the third axis follows the Euphrates line. As from October 1915 a new main phase of the genocide begins, that of the extermination of the internees in the camps in Syria and Mesopotamia, which still led to the death of 300,000 to 400,000 Armenians.

In reference to the methodical organization of the deportation process, scheduled from the Spring of 1915 onwards, Bloxham (2003) does not hesitate to speak of a real "logistical" issue driven by the Young Turks to resolve the Armenian question. This death logistics was supervised by civilian and military officials and was accompanied by a systematic campaign of mass massacres, as stated above. Hewsen (2001) has proposed a historical atlas that provides a detailed picture of how the movement of Armenians took place until their deaths. It shows that a true process of "platforming" was explicitly set up by the Young Turks through different "relegation zones" within the Ottoman Empire. These are presented as places for grouping families from which deportation routes to the concentration camps were organized, which can be likened here to the radial axes of the hub-and-spokes model (see Figure 3).

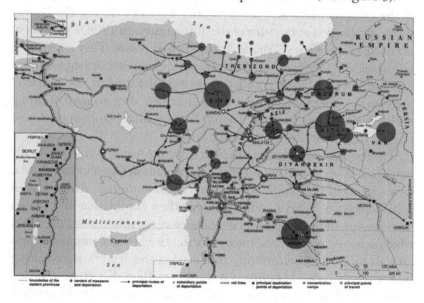

FIG. 3 – Armenian genocide: routes of deportation acting as "spokes" and centers of massacre/deportation acting as "hubs".
Source: Armenian National Institute, Washington DC.

4. THE OVERLORD OPERATION CASE

Military logistics has been a continuous source of service innovations to optimize the support of troops in combat and to defend possessed or conquered territories. Thus, Colin (2013) was able to highlight how the French Royal Navy forged, in the 17th and 18th centuries, an efficient tool to counter the powerful British Navy, relying on what would later become *archetypes of logistical services* in terms of procurement from a network of global suppliers, the development of nomenclatures and production ranges, but also the construction of warehouses to ensure optimal stock availability. The turning point in the evolution of logistics took place during World War II, and more specifically during the Overlord operation. Beyond the extremely meticulous preparations, we may say that the success of the Overlord operation is largely based on a large-scale "platforming" process.

Unlike the Germans, who failed in their will to invade the United Kingdom for lack of meticulous preparation of operations, the Allies decided to plan with extreme rigor the logistics accompanying the liberation of the Nazi-occupied European Continent. Thus, the many logistical facilities necessary for the success of the Overlord operation were put in place, both in terms of storage and transport, in particular with the creation of artificial ports equipped with handling equipment, towed from England and anchored in front of the Normandy beaches, and depots located in the South of England, themselves replenished by depots on the East coast of the USA. The Allies were also to devise a remarkably efficient system for concentrating the flows, based on the model of future air transport hubs, by choosing a gathering point for the invasion fleet in the middle of the English Channel on the eve of D-Day (humorously called "Piccadilly Circus"). From there, the Allies would reach the famous Normandy beaches *via* four channels (as "radial axes") previously secured (see Figure 4).

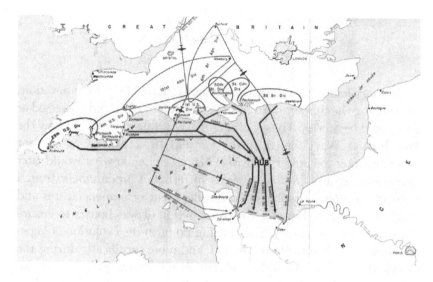

FIG. 4 – "Platforming" in the Overlord operation.
Source: Adapted from Harrison (2012).

Even today, the Overlord operation is still considered the most important military logistics achievement in modern history. We also know
how essential it was in the birth of a management approach that spread,
from the 1950s onwards, to all industrial and commercial companies,
capable thanks to it of freeing themselves from spatial and temporal
constraints to conquer increasingly globalized consumer markets. For
a long time confined to an instrumental vision favoring the analysis
of tools dedicated to the management of materials flows, logistics will
gradually develop service innovations that contribute to the collective
value creation (or co-creation). The origins of logistics, marked by the
contributions of military discipline, explain why the emergence of an
organizational vision has not always been easy, even if it is now a reality,
both for practitioners and researchers.

CONCLUSION

This viewpoint presented three examples of "platforming" from modern history. Many other cases could have been mobilized with a more or less similar conclusion. During Antiquity, for instance, the transport and storage of grain for the supply of Rome required a complex supply chain. The interruption of maritime shipping during the winter months thus required the products to be stored in suitable places, from hinterland regions to the sea and from the sea to hinterland regions, for redistribution. As a result, early hubs have been implemented in Africa, Asia Minor and on the margins of Italy itself. Another example is that of spices, frankincense and myrrh, transported in the ancient world over long distances to customers located in the Mediterranean, crossing the Arabian Peninsula on camels. Hull (2008) explicitly refers to supply chains based on a hub-and-spokes model with spokes that are totally secure given the value of the products.

In other words, there is limited novelty in many contemporary managerial practices, which simply update, with the help of disruptive technologies, old but sometimes proven approaches. After all, the accounting documents used in 4500 BC, intended for the various stakeholders, attest to the fact that managerial thinking is very old. Logistical organizations do not escape the presence of these distant roots, and they can be found today in many management models. In particular, it is clear that "platforming" has a high degree of generalization, which explains its dissemination within many business networks, where hubs are crucial for their operation and the implementation of a dynamic of spatial diffusion. More generally, hubs play the role of accelerators in the development of growth of an exponential nature, as can be the case today with the Internet. They thus constitute a radical innovation of service, the in-depth study of which is more than ever indispensable.

REFERENCES

BAUMAN Z. (2007), *Liquid times: living in an age of uncertainty*, Malden (MA), Polity Press.

BLOXHAM D. (2003), "The Armenian genocide of 1915-1916: cumulative radicalization and the development of a destruction policy", *Past & Present*, n° 181 (November), p. 141-191.

BOWEN JR. J. (2012), "A spatial analysis of FedEx and UPS: hubs, spokes, and network structure", *Journal of Transport Geography*, vol. 24, n° 10, p. 419-431.

COLIN J. (1982), "Réseaux de circulation des marchandises, réseaux de circulation de l'information", *Bulletin de l'IDATE*, n° 7, p. 99-109.

COLIN J. (2013), "Les prémices de la logistique: l'organisation des marines de guerre en France du XVIIᵉ siècle au XVIIIᵉ siècle", *in* FABBE-COSTES N., and PACHÉ G. (Eds.), *La logistique: une approche innovante des organisations*, Aix-en-Provence, Presses Universitaires de Provence, p. 219-230.

COQUERY-VIDROVITCH C. (2016), *Petite histoire de l'Afrique: l'Afrique au Sud du Sahara, de la préhistoire à nos jours*, Paris, La Découverte.

D'ESTE C. (1983/2004), *Decision in Normandy*, London, Penguin Books.

DJELLAL F., GALLOUJ C., and GALLOUJ F. (2003), "L'innovation dans les services en France: un bilan (1999-2002)", *Economies & Sociétés*, Série Economie et Gestion des Services, n° 5, p. 1979-1999.

ELTIS D., and RICHARDSON D. (2015), *Atlas of the Transatlantic slave trade*, New Haven (CT), Yale University Press.

FULCONIS F., GODBILLE T., and PACHÉ G. (2017), "Organization of Transatlantic slave trade: a global supply chain perspective", *in* HEMPEL K., DUEDAHL P., and POULSEN B. (Eds), *Reforms and resources*, Aalborg, Aalborg University Press, p. 73-108.

GRENOUILLEAU O. (2018), *La traite des Noirs*, Paris, Presses Universitaires de France, 3ʳᵈ ed.

HARRISON G. (2012), *Cross-channel attack: US Army in World War II-The European theater of operations*, Atlanta (GA), Whitman Publishing.

HEWSEN R. (2001), *Armenia: a historical atlas*, Chicago (IL), University of Chicago Press.

HULL B. (2008), "Frankincense, myrrh, and spices: the oldest global supply chain?", *Journal of Macromarketing*, vol. 28, n° 3, p. 275-288.

KASARDA J. (1999), "Time-based competition and industrial location in the fast century", *Real Estate Issues*, vol. 23, n° 4, p. 24-29.

KHORHEH M.-A., and MOISIADIS F. (2015), "Investigating opportunities and challenges of consolidation in hub-and-spoke logistics networks", *Australian Academy of Business & Economics Review*, vol. 1, n° 2, p. 120-134.

MASON R., McKENNEY J., CARLSON W., and COPELAND D. (1997), "Absolutely, positively operations research: the Federal Express story", *Interfaces*, vol. 27, n° 2, p. 17-36.

MONNOYER M.-C., and ZULIANI J.-M. (2007), "The decentralisation of Airbus production and services", *The Service Industries Journal*, vol. 27, n° 3, p. 251-262.

MOURADIAN C. (2013), *L'Arménie*, Paris, Presses Universitaires de France, 5th ed.

ROSTOW W.-W. (1960/1990), *The stages of economic growth: a non-communist manifesto*, Cambridge (MA), Cambridge University Press.

STEIN R. (1979), *The French slave trade in the Eighteenth century: an old regime business*, Madison (WN), Wisconsin University Press.

ABSTRACTS/RÉSUMÉS

Takeshi TAKENAKA, Hiroshi NISHIKOORI, Nariaki NISHINO, Kentaro WATANABE, "Re-design of service systems based on employee satisfaction, customer satisfaction and labour productivity"

This study uses standardized indicators of employee satisfaction (ES), customer satisfaction (CS), and productivity to assess existing services and to identify service eco-systems that simultaneously realize appropriate values for customers, employees, and service providers. First, results are obtained using standardized ES and CS from comparison of industries and companies. Then a theoretical service model is constructed from a game theoretic viewpoint according to empirical analysis of data. Based on the service model, a computer simulation is conducted to test possible service models that have been redesigned in terms of pay structure.

Keywords: employee satisfaction, service system, simulation, pay structure, service engineering.

Takeshi TAKENAKA, Hiroshi NISHIKOORI, Nariaki NISHINO, Kentaro WATANABE, « Reconception des systèmes de services fondée sur la satisfaction des employés, la satisfaction des clients et la productivité du travail »

Cette étude utilise des indicateurs normalisés de satisfaction des employés (SE), de satisfaction des clients (SC) et de productivité pour évaluer les services existants et pour identifier les écosystèmes de services qui réalisent simultanément des valeurs appropriées pour les clients, les employés et les fournisseurs de services. Tout d'abord, les résultats sont obtenus en utilisant des indicateurs de SE et SC standardisés à partir de la comparaison des industries et des entreprises. Ensuite, un modèle théorique de service est construit d'un point de vue de théorie des jeux selon une analyse empirique des données. Sur la base de ce modèle de service, une simulation informatique est réalisée pour tester les modèles de service possibles qui ont été reconçus en termes de structure salariale.

Mots-clés : satisfaction des employés, système de service, simulation, structure salariale, ingénierie du service.

Juan Carlos ZAGACETA-GARCÍA, "Service firm innovation. Disaggregated sectoral classification analysis for Mexico"

This article is devoted to innovation in services in Mexico. It is based on data from service firms surveys within the 2004 and 2009 economic censuses. These surveys cover all types of innovation, including product and service, processes, organisation, and external relationship innovations. The analysis also captures innovation at branch level, therefore going beyond conventional studies that focus on sector level. We compare results using technological trajectories from the Soete-Miozzo taxonomy (1990). Survey results indicate that though all sectors are innovating, degrees of innovation differ in line with the sector's intrinsic singularities.

Keywords: service innovation, technological change, developing countries, Mexico, censuses.

Juan Carlos ZAGACETA-GARCÍA, « Innovation dans les entreprises de services. L'analyse d'une classification sectorielle désagrégée dans le cas du Mexique »

Cet article est consacré à l'innovation dans les services au Mexique. Il s'appuie sur des données provenant d'enquêtes sur les entreprises de services réalisées dans le cadre des recensements économiques de 2004 et 2009. Ces enquêtes couvrent tous les types d'innovation, y compris les innovations en matière de produits et de services, de processus, d'organisation et de relations extérieures. L'analyse aborde également l'innovation au niveau des branches, allant ainsi au-delà des études conventionnelles qui se concentrent sur le niveau sectoriel. Nous comparons les résultats en utilisant les trajectoires technologiques de la taxonomie de Soete-Miozzo (1990). Les résultats de l'enquête indiquent que si tous les secteurs innovent, les degrés d'innovation diffèrent en fonction des singularités intrinsèques du secteur considéré.

Mots-clés : innovation dans les services, changement technologique, pays en développement, Mexique, recensements.

Leonel CORONA-TREVIÑO, "Challenges for service innovation in developing countries. The cases of Mexico and Latin America"

Following the methodology of two prospective studies, one by Martin (2016) and the other by Djellal and Gallouj (2016), this article's proposed agenda comprises 22 challenges faced by studies of innovation and service innovation in the context of Mexico and across Latin America. Highlighting certain specific economic and social problems in Mexico and across Latin

America, it presents a review of the evolution of innovation thinking. Four scenarios have been designed, towards which economies may evolve, depending on how the challenges posed are taken up: 1) Regional development and inclusive growth, 2) Social and economic polarization, 3) Regional disparity with income distribution, 4) Regional development and income inequality.

Keywords: innovation, service innovation, challenges, Mexico, Latin America.

Leonel CORONA-TREVIÑO, « Les défis pour l'innovation dans les services dans les pays en développement. Les cas du Mexique et de l'Amérique latine »

Cet article s'inspire de la méthodologie de deux études prospectives, l'une de Martin (2016) et l'autre de Djellal et Gallouj (2016), pour proposer un agenda de recherche qui comprend 22 défis posés aux études sur l'innovation et les services, dans le contexte du Mexique et de l'Amérique latine. Il met en lumière certains problèmes économiques et sociaux spécifiques au Mexique et à l'Amérique latine et rend compte de l'évolution de la réflexion sur l'innovation. En fonction de la manière dont les défis posés sont relevés, quatre scénarios sont proposés, vers lesquels les économies peuvent évoluer : 1) Développement régional et croissance inclusive, 2) Polarisation sociale et économique, 3) Disparité régionale avec distribution des revenus, 4) Développement régional et inégalité des revenus.

Mots-clés : innovation, innovation de service, défis, Mexique, Amérique latine.

Magali DUBOSSON, Emmanuel FRAGNIÈRE, Anne-Sylvaine HÉRITIER, Samuele MEIER, Charles WAINWRIGHT, "Fostering 'co-socialization' between patient and nurse to mitigate the risks of digitalizing health care services"

The digitalization of services has also affected the practice of hospital care, particularly among nurses. In this study, we applied the focus group method with an exploratory aim among practicing students in nursing to see if the digitalization of administrative processes in hospitals was having an impact on their usual operating modes for treating patients. The collected data shows a disconnection between the difficulties evoked by the nursing staff in regard to exercising their profession and the digitalization of processes. Following these observations, we propose a new theoretical model based on the SECI (socialization, externalization, combination, internalization) knowledge creation model. As the patient is co-producer of the service, our conceptual model consists of coupling the "SECI loop" of the patient with the "SECI loop" of the nurse at the level of the socialization stage.

Keywords: explicit and tacit knowledge, focus group, frontliners, socialization, work process, digitalization.

Magali DUBOSSON, Emmanuel FRAGNIÈRE, Anne-Sylvaine HÉRITIER, Samuele MEIER, Charles WAINWRIGHT, « Favoriser la "co-socialisation" entre le patient et l'infirmière pour atténuer les risques de la numérisation des services de santé »

La numérisation des services a également affecté la pratique des soins hospitaliers. Ici, nous appliquons la méthode des groupes de discussion dans un but exploratoire auprès d'étudiants praticiens en soins infirmiers afin de voir si la numérisation des processus administratifs dans les hôpitaux a un impact sur leurs modes de fonctionnement habituels pour le traitement des patients. Les données recueillies montrent une déconnexion entre les difficultés évoquées par le personnel infirmier dans l'exercice de leur profession et la numérisation des processus. Suite à ces observations, nous proposons un nouveau modèle théorique basé sur le modèle de création de connaissances SECI (socialisation, externalisation, combinaison, internalisation). Notre modèle conceptuel consiste à coupler la « boucle SECI » du patient avec la « boucle SECI » du soignant au niveau de l'étape de socialisation.

Mots-clés: connaissances explicites et tacites, groupe de discussion, travailleurs de première ligne, socialisation, processus de travail, numérisation.

Benoît DESMARCHELIER, Faridah DJELLAL, Faïz GALLOUJ, "Public service innovation networks (PSINs). An instrument for collaborative innovation and value co-creation in public service(s)"

This article is devoted to a new network form that is developing within the New Public Governance paradigm, namely "Public Service Innovation Networks" (PSINs). PSINs are multi-agent collaborative arrangements that develop within public service(s), spontaneously or at the instigation of local, national or European public policies. They mobilize a variable number of public and private agents, especially citizens, to co-produce innovations and ultimately contribute to value co-creation. Based on a review of the literature and on empirical work carried out under two European funded projects, this article aims to deepen the definition and description of PSINs, especially in comparison with other known network forms, and to examine in particular how PSINs are formed and function to co-create, more or less efficiently, value in public service(s) through innovation.

Keywords: public service, network, innovation, value, co-creation, co-production, collaboration.

Benoît DESMARCHELIER, Faridah DJELLAL, Faïz GALLOUJ, « Les réseaux d'innovation de service public (RISP). Un instrument d'innovation collaborative et de co-création de valeur dans le(s) service(s) public(s) »

Cet article est consacré à une forme résilière nouvelle qui se développe dans le cadre de la nouvelle gouvernance publique : les « Réseaux d'Innovation de Service Public » (RISP). Les RISP sont des dispositifs collaboratifs multi-agents qui se développent au sein des services publics, de manière spontanée ou à l'instigation des politiques publiques. Ils mobilisent un nombre variable d'agents publics et privés, en particulier des citoyens, afin de co-produire des innovations et in fine contribuer à la co-création de valeur. Sur la base d'un bilan de la littérature et de travaux empiriques réalisés dans le cadre de deux contrats européens, cet article vise à approfondir la définition et la description des RISP, en comparaison d'autres formes résilières, et à examiner la manière ils se forment et fonctionnent pour co-créer, de manière plus ou moins efficace, de la valeur à travers l'innovation.

Mots-clés : service public, réseau, innovation, valeur, co-création, co-production, collaboration.

Gilles PACHÉ, "Service innovation in historical perspective. The case of 'platforming'"

This viewpoint focuses on "platforming" as a major service innovation, which importance is now recognized in the organization of contemporary supply chains. On a technical level, "plat-forming" is based on the hub-and-spokes model, widely used in air transport, but also in retail logistics. Three historical examples show that the origins of "platforming" can be traced back to the often dramatic events that have marked the course of humanity, which puts the real originality of this service innovation into perspective.

Keywords: history, hub-and-spokes model, innovation, platforming, supply chain.

Gilles PACHÉ, « Innovation de service dans une perspective historique. Le cas de la "plateformisation" »

Le point de vue s'intéresse à la « plateformisation » en tant qu'innovation de service majeure, dont l'importance est aujourd'hui reconnue dans l'organisation des chaînes logistiques contemporaines. Sur un plan technique, la « plateformisation » s'appuie sur le modèle hub-and-spokes, largement diffusé en transport aérien, mais aussi en logistique de distribution. Trois exemples historiques indiquent que l'on peut retrouver les origines de la « plateformisation » dans des évènements, souvent dramatiques, qui ont jalonné le cours de l'Humanité, ce qui permet de relativiser l'originalité réelle de cette innovation de service.

Mots-clés : histoire, modèle hub-and-spokes, innovation, plateformisation, chaîne logistique.

Achevé d'imprimer par Corlet Numéric,
Z.A. Charles Tellier, Condé-en-Normandie (Calvados), en octobre 2020
N° d'impression : 168457 - dépôt légal : octobre 2020
Imprimé en France

CLASSIQUES GARNIER

Bulletin d'abonnement revue 2021

European Review of Service Economics and Management /
Revue Européenne d'Économie et Management des Services

2 numéros par an

M., Mme :

Adresse :

Code postal :   Ville :

Pays :

Téléphone :   Fax :

Courriel :

Prix TTC abonnement France, frais de port inclus		Prix HT abonnement étranger, frais de port inclus	
Particulier	Institution	Particulier	Institution
▒ 78 €	▒ 98 €	▒ 90 €	▒ 106 €

Cet abonnement concerne les parutions papier du 1er janvier 2021 au 31 décembre 2021.

Les numéros parus avant le 1er janvier 2021 sont disponibles à l'unité (hors abonnement) sur notre site web.

Modalités de règlement (en euros) :

▒ Par carte bancaire sur notre site web : www.classiques-garnier.com
▒ Par virement bancaire sur le compte :
Banque : Société Générale – BIC : SOGEFRPP
IBAN : FR 76 3000 3018 7700 0208 3910 870
RIB : 30003 01877 00020839108 70
▒ Par chèque à l'ordre de Classiques Garnier

Classiques Garnier
6, rue de la Sorbonne – 75005 Paris – France
Fax : + 33 1 43 54 00 44
Courriel : revues@classiques-garnier.com

mis à jour le 10/09/2020

Abonnez-vous sur notre site web :
www.classiques-garnier.com

Checked Out

An Amelia Feelgood Mystery

Author's Note

This is a work of fiction. Names, characters, businesses, places, events and incidents are either the products of the author's imagination or used in a fictitious manner. Any resemblance to actual persons or animals, living or dead, or actual events is purely coincidental.

Vivaeris, LLC
www.vivaeris.com
Checked Out
©2020 Juliet Chase

Beth McElla
Checked Out, an Amelia Feelgood Mystery
ISBN: 978-1-939361-13-4

For everyone that could use a quirky island to escape to.
Findlater Island is yours to explore.

-Beth

Chapter 1

❡

A wave of deja vu swept over Amelia as she stood at the front of the ferry approaching the dock at Findlater Island. This time, though, she knew what to expect and had dressed more sensibly in loose black linen trousers, a light sweater, and turquoise leather walking sandals. Part of cultivating flair was adapting fashion to the current environment, even if it meant looking a little understated. She felt a tiny bit anxious because she might not have gotten the footwear exactly right as it was starting to rain lightly. On the other hand, today she wasn't walking off the boat, so it didn't really matter that much.

She stood by the door of her silver Subaru, breathing in the damp salty air and thinking about what lay ahead. Almost all of her worldly goods (except her furniture) sat crammed in the back of the vehicle. Her packing style had more to do with making use of available space than neat and tidy boxes. To an outsider, it probably looked a lot like those cars you see on the freeway when new college kids leave home for the first time. A fitting image because she felt poised on the cusp of an entirely new life.

Internally, she was a mixture of excitement about starting this next chapter and mild panic at how far off course she had drifted from her intended ten-year plan. She didn't have any more time to dwell on it though as the deckhands got busy tossing ropes thicker than her arms and securing the giant boat to the comparatively small dock. She quickly got back into her car and fastened her seatbelt. Her hands nervously gripped the steering wheel, waiting for the all-important signal to start the engine. The people who would be walking off first stood mashed in between the cars and along the edges of the deck ramps, eager to get on with their plans for the day. It was hard to believe only a few short weeks had passed since she'd first come to this remote island.

And now she apparently owned half of it. As far as Amelia could tell, only a handful of people were aware of that, but it was a small community, and gossip likely spread fast. She was uncomfortable with how she imagined the locals might react. And she didn't feel rich. Her bank account said she definitely wasn't wealthy. Of course, she still had no information on where exactly the rents and such went, so finding that out was high on her list of things to organize as soon as she got settled.

The final rope barrier was removed, and the walkers surged off the ferry like marathoners at the starting gun. Within seconds they had scurried out of sight and the motorcycles parked at the front of the boat were revving their engines, waiting for the all-clear signal. Then they too zipped off into the exit lanes of the terminal with a deafening roar.

Finally, it was her turn. Amelia breathed a sigh of relief when her engine turned over on command. She tried her best to navigate the potholes and narrow bits of the gangway, but with two lanes moving simultaneously in close proximity she had limited maneuverability. She had to jerk the wheel left to avoid running into the narrow bit of the gangway, hitting a deep pothole as a consequence. Darn it, this was not a happy start to this next phase of her life as she heard the undercarriage groan under the sudden contact.

As she drove past the lines of cars waiting to board the outbound ferry, her attention was drawn to an older maroon sedan with a woman leaning out the driver's window looking green. She appeared to be in her mid-fifties with a frosted bouffant haircut reminiscent of the 60s. Her hands gripped the steering wheel of the parked car like her life depended on it. Amelia couldn't imagine getting on a boat in that condition, but at least there were other people around that presumably would help if she needed it. Shaking her head in sympathy, Amelia continued following the car in front of her out of the terminal. Eventually, she was clear of the ferry traffic and turning up the steep road leading to the Ravenswood Inn.

Amelia wasn't too sure what to expect at the hotel this time. True, it hadn't been very long since she'd checked out and gone back to the mainland, but law enforcement had been busy in the interim. More than thirty island residents had been arrested on various charges, mostly tied to drug smuggling. She had no way of finding out how many of them had made bail and returned to the island, but she knew Ralph wasn't one of them.

The local news channels seemed fascinated with his double life of crime. So Amelia was aware that the feds and the state were fighting over the murder vs his drug cartel affiliation and who got to take him to court first. He was sitting in a nearby federal prison while they decided. Her involvement in the takedown had been kept quiet, so she was reasonably confident that the locals didn't plan to meet her with pitchforks. She was still somewhat nervous however that she might have missed something. And she wasn't sure if the hotel had managed to find replacements for any of the staff that, like Ralph, were no longer employable.

Arriving at the inn a few minutes later, she found the small guest parking lot right across the road from the main entrance, tucked behind a stand of evergreen trees. She parked and got out with a sigh of relief. Extricating her overnight case, she decided the rest could wait until she figured out a few things about her stay on the island. She wasn't planning on living at the inn any longer than necessary. For starters, having to run into the village for food three times a day got on her nerves. Plus, she didn't want to eat up the profits by occupying a room that a paying customer would want over the busy summer months. She paused for a moment to admire her own serious-minded businesswoman thinking and to take a few deep breaths of evergreen-scented air. The near-constant high humidity kept the perfumed air refreshing. One step at a time, she reminded herself as she wheeled the case awkwardly over the gravel and across the road towards the front door of the inn. The no vacancy sign was lit, but otherwise, everything appeared as she remembered it.

A familiar smile greeted her from the occupant of the sisal welcome mat by the door. Sadie woofed and got up to sniff at Amelia's suitcase. Amelia rubbed the base of the dog's ears and smiled back. "Sadie! What are you doing here? Who are you staying with now?"

Not surprisingly, the shaggy gray dog didn't answer directly, but turned and trotted through the door when Amelia held it open. She kept going through the small lobby and down the hall towards the staircase. Amelia smiled after her wistfully. She'd missed the dog's company while she'd been in Seattle. Sadie was a major part of the Findlater community and a completely free agent. She was not cut out for condo living in the city. Still, it raised Amelia's spirits to see her friend so soon after arriving. Hopefully, she'd see her again out and about.

Nobody stood behind the front desk. When she'd talked to Becky about her return, she hadn't been able to specify exactly what day she'd arrive as she still had some legal documents that needed to be signed before she left the city. Becky had promised her that a room would be waiting and that everyone was glad she was coming back. Besides Becky, Amelia couldn't imagine who was left to feel that way. She wasn't so attached that she really cared, although she might have been ignoring the image of one glowering island resident in particular that kept coming to mind.

❦

Surveying the tiny hotel lobby, Amelia concluded that not much had changed: same oak reception desk, same seascape oil painting, same ugly blue carpet. Someone had switched the flowers for a huge bundle of heavily scented purple lilacs. The scent lingered in the air, promising all the joys of a quiet weekend in the country.

But no big sign proclaimed 'first murder on the island happened here!' That would *probably* be bad for business. And she didn't know for a fact it was the very first murder, just that it was the only one anyone could remember. The low crime rate was part of why there was no law enforcement on the island. Despite the big drug bust, there still wasn't a plan for any. The general feeling of the community appeared to be that all the bad guys had been caught and there was no further need for police. The fact that the island was still 'lost in the fold' of the map between two counties who saw it as more of a budget liability than a tax asset didn't help.

When still nobody had come to find out if anyone waited in the lobby, Amelia reluctantly reached out and dinged the silver bell on the desk. It made a tinny gulping sound, as if it hadn't been used in a really long time.

After several more minutes, Amelia was getting annoyed when a square woman with gray curls and a gray housekeeping smock over a purple-flowered blouse appeared from the back room. She seemed surprised to see Amelia standing there, so maybe she hadn't heard the bell at all. "Oh! I'm sorry ma'am, we're fully booked. You might try one of the B&Bs in the village."

"I'm Amelia Feelgood, you should have a room waiting for me."

"No, no. I'm sure we're fully booked."

"Can you have someone check, please? Becky told me she had everything ready." Amelia eyed the woman in the smock. She didn't look like someone who knew her way around the hotel's computer system. Not that Amelia could do any better.

"Oh, Becky. But, she's..." the woman paused with her mouth open as if unsure how much she should say.

"Yes? Becky's what?"

"At an appointment." The woman concluded rather lamely.

"Is there anyone else that can help? I'd like to get settled in and go find some lunch."

"I'll... I'll just see." The woman turned and headed back the way she'd come. A few minutes later a slim middle-aged man with dark skin and large brown eyes entered, inclining his head politely. "Ms. Feelgood? My utmost apologies for keeping you waiting."

Amelia peered at the brass name tag pinned to his navy blue vest. She was approaching the age of needing reading glasses but refused to try any out, for fear that it would somehow push her over some invisible threshold from which she couldn't return. "Oh! You're Mr. Jain. I've heard so much about you!"

He inclined his head again with a slight smile. "Indeed, and I have heard much of you. Thank you for returning me to this hotel."

Amelia wanted to ask about his wife but didn't know enough to be confident that the woman was still alive, which might be awkward. "Mr. Jain, Becky assured me that there would be a room waiting for me?"

"Yes, of course. Things are very busy now, so it's not the best room, but I think you'll find it very comfortable." He handed over a plastic swipe card. "It's one of the few downstairs rooms, so you'll need to go around the side and then in through the lower entrance."

"Oh, I wasn't aware the inn had any downstairs guest rooms. Well, that sounds nice."

Mr. Jain gave her a small, tight smile and inclined his head. "Do you need help with your bags?"

"No, I'm good, thanks. I'll only be staying a few days while I figure things out on the island. Do you know anything about who Sadie is staying with? I was surprised to see her at the door."

"Sadie? No, I haven't seen her for a few months. Perhaps she's here to see you?"

Amelia smiled half-heartedly, perplexed. "Okay, thanks again." She turned and went back out the front door. Then she realized Mr. Jain hadn't said whether to go right or left around the building. She supposed it didn't matter too much. She knew the path to the left led to the golf cart coral and the Dumpsters. She might as well explore the path to the right this time. She wheeled her small weekend case behind her but had to stop and pause every time the small wheels caught a rut in the old pavement. It twisted her wrist and gradually peeled away her confidence about being here at all. Had she made a mistake?

She could have turned everything over to an attorney and fled to France as she'd originally planned. But something about the island, and its quirky inhabitants, had made her want to finalize things herself. Explore a little further before she left the Pacific Northwest behind her forever. And make sure she had no regrets about leaving.

The path around the side of the hotel led down a slight slope, and about midway, she found an informal wooden door with a screen door attached. A small sign affixed to the wall said Ground Floor Rooms. The door wasn't locked, so Amelia pulled it open and picked her case up to maneuver it over the sill. A narrow hallway with an even uglier indoor-outdoor carpet in gray and red greeted her.

Pervading the space was a musty, mildewy odor that someone had tried to mask with lemon air freshener and a loud noise like an industrial vacuum cleaner. Amelia quickly found the cause of the noise as the first door she passed was open to the hotel's laundry. Giant silver tumble dryers were spinning with masses of white linens showing through the round glass doors.

Turning the corner, she saw three more doors with brass number plates. It was easy to see which one belonged to her because Sadie sat patiently in front of the one at the end. "Clearly I didn't need to go outside then?" She asked the dog who, only grinned at her in response. Amelia unlocked the door, not sure what to expect in this rather unglamorous part of the hotel. "Okay, it could be worse." She told the dog. It was clearly a room of last resort. But it was private. And the small windows sat so high up on the wall that it would be difficult for anyone to look in. Particularly because the deep shade visible outside suggested that the windows were actually looking out on the area beneath the first-floor deck.

The room itself gave off a comfortable vibe despite its basement location. An old-fashioned dark-wood spool bed was positioned in the corner and covered with a red and white patchwork quilt. A wing chair upholstered in faded blue brocade had been placed by a small tea table against the wall beneath the windows. The rest of the space was occupied by a bureau with a flat-screen TV perched on top. It was cozy, and right now that was good enough. Sadie swished by and jumped up on the bed while Amelia pulled her case through, letting the door swing shut behind her, and sat down in the chair to take stock.

Chapter 2

❦

Sitting quietly for a few minutes was a new thing for Amelia, and she wasn't entirely comfortable with it. She had been trying to practice mindfulness for the last few weeks but always got distracted and then ended up irritated. Somehow it was a little easier to concentrate on Findlater Island, or maybe it was the cute way Sadie gazed up at her with her nose tucked under her paws.

Done with her attempts to reconnect with the universe, she pulled her bullet journal out of her over-sized turquoise purse and considered the list she'd made over the last week. Obviously, she needed lunch and some food for Sadie, but also on the agenda was a trip to the post office and the bank. The funny part of finding out someone has transferred hundreds of properties into your name (without you knowing) is that absolutely nobody has a form for that. She'd managed to extract the name of the bank where funds were deposited from Becky over the phone, but the bank itself refused to do any business with her except in person. Amelia strongly suspected this was a stalling tactic because they didn't sound like they had a plan once she arrived.

She wasn't sure if everything was held in some kind of corporation. All she knew is that the county assessor had her name down as the owner of six pages' worth of properties and thought she should pay the property taxes. She had no idea how she was supposed to prove she was the owner, but the ball had to start rolling from somewhere.

Luckily, she'd been able to rent out her condo for the summer to a visiting grad student planning to do insightful demographic studies of every coffee shop in the greater Seattle area. And then cross-reference them with New York when he returned in the Fall. It sounded like just the sort of thing he would get a federal grant for because really, nobody needed to understand this, did they? But he'd seemed quite dedicated and even more caffeinated when she'd talked to him.

Amelia was happy that she'd have a little extra income to tide things over while she figured out her island situation. She also wanted to get started on a real hobby. She'd gotten yet another lecture from her doctor, who she worked hard to avoid, about lowering her blood pressure. Now that she didn't have to work for the very dead Tony Lyle, she was reasonably confident that a few minor lifestyle changes would make the difference. At least that's what she told the doctor. Inside, she wasn't so sure that her need to take charge and organize the world could be changed. Sitting still made her more stressed, not less. Either way, she'd promised to explore relaxation and on the top of her list was some kind of social hobby where she would meet people, maybe have a glass of wine and let her hair down. The last was purely figurative as she'd sneaked in a quick visit to the magical scissors of Catrine and her sleek bob now cut a sharp angle just below her earlobes.

Closing her notebook, Amelia contemplated Sadie. It was getting too warm to leave a dog in a closed car. And anyway, her car was stuffed to the gills with all her worldly belongings (except the furniture which the grad student was making use of.) So perhaps she should consider one more trip to the village in a golf cart for old time's sake. No time like the present. Sighing, she got to her feet and glanced over at the dog. "You coming?" Sadie leapt off the bed like she'd been coiled waiting for the signal, which was so not true because she'd been snoring only five seconds ago.

Without a word, Sadie led Amelia out of the rabbit warren of basement corridors and up a small flight of stairs that opened into the main hallway that led to reception. Why hadn't Mr. Jain showed her that entrance? Had it been too complicated to explain? Amelia shrugged and followed Sadie out of the hotel and around to the golf carts. She noted in passing that once again nobody was in the lobby.

Only one golf cart remained, and it gave the impression that someone had difficulty parking it because the front was slightly bashed in where it had met with a larger, harder object. Sadie jumped into her usual position on the passenger side as if Amelia had never left the island. There was some comfort in that. Amelia backed up the cart cautiously, and they headed into the village. She kept the speed low, not that it could go very fast anyway, but there were several groups of tourists out walking on the side of the road which someone had deemed too rural for sidewalks. The tourists seemed unaffected by the light mist that still hung in the air.

Amelia and Sadie cruised past the small cluster of medieval buildings the locals called the annex because they were the leftover imported structures that didn't make it into the original reconstructed village plan.

Other than the influx of tourists, everything there was pretty much the same. The road, which wasn't much more than a quiet country lane, was lined with tall evergreens, leathery salal bushes, and the ever-present and obnoxious blackberries. The thick prickly vines now reached out over the pavement thanks to the first of several growth spurts. Amelia wondered if a roadworks department existed on the island to cut them back or if it was up to the most annoyed person to start whacking them.

Almost immediately her question was answered when they had to stop for a woman in an orange vest holding a stop sign. And they waited, and they waited until finally an amazing machine in faded orange paint rolled slowing along the road, cutting off any vegetation that met its metal jaws. It resulted in an oddly flat hedge, but it sat well back from the street and wouldn't endanger any passing pedestrians. Sadie seemed unimpressed and took advantage of the wait to stretch out on the bench seat. She whined softly until Amelia reached over and rubbed her tummy.

❧

It took a couple of trips around the outskirts of the village before Amelia finally found the right side street that led to the post office. It was the most unusual post office she'd ever seen and like nothing the federal government would ever condone.

It was entirely too adorable. No wonder it was technically private, operating with a handshake agreement from the normal system. Housed in an eighteenth-century French dovecote — like a small squat tower that was still perfectly proportioned, it was constructed out of warm honey-colored stone. The conical roof was covered in slate tiles and had a sweet little weather vane on the tip-top. Inside, the wall pockets, originally meant to house the birds, had been converted to mail slots with elegant tiny glass doors. A narrow library ladder had been added on a track for people to reach the ones higher up. In the middle of the room, a round library desk sat with an antique iron chandelier suspended overhead.

A bored-looking young man with a dark cowlick looked over the top of his wire glasses at her but didn't say a word.

"Hi," Amelia started with her friendliest voice. She'd decided to turn over a new leaf on the island and be more friendly. "I need to figure out how to get the mail for several properties delivered to me — that is the mail for the owner, not any occupants."

"Do you have some ID?"

She handed over her passport, driver's license, social security card, and her health insurance card. She'd thought ahead on this one and had everything together, not being sure what people would want to see.

He immediately handed back the health insurance card and then perused the other three. "What property are you referring to?"

"Well, it's most of the island."

The young man's face twisted into a confused scowl. Amelia tried again. "For example, Ravenswood Inn is one of them. Where does the tax statement get delivered? Or how about the pub two streets over, where does its tax statement go?"

"Uh. I wouldn't know that. You'd have to ask the county where they send it."

And that it turned out pretty much exhausted the amount of niceness Amelia had set aside. Grinding her teeth, she turned to leave and then had a sudden light bulb inspiration. "Just a minute." She told the young man who gave her a look that he couldn't care less and went back to whatever he was scrolling through on his phone. Amelia dug her phone out of her purse, having remembered that Becky had bookmarked the county site for her. Maybe the address was in there. A few clicks and a little research later and she had it. She'd spot-checked a few other of the properties, but it seemed like most if not all the mail got delivered to P.O. Box 9872. She glanced around the round building. It did not look like there was more than four hundred mail slots here, certainly not close to a thousand. She waited for the young man to look up again. "It's box 9872. Does that help?"

"Well, it means it's being forwarded. Anything that starts with a nine isn't a real box, it's a placeholder for a forwarding address."

"Okay. Well, how do I go about getting it unforwarded and delivered to me? And can I find out where the mail is being forwarded to?"

He rolled his eyes and sighed like he was a teenager being asked to clean up his room. Amelia wondered if he ever had to do any work here. It didn't look like too much mail came in based on the mail slots she could see easily. He pulled a slim laptop out of a drawer and opened it up. "That box is registered to Tony Lyle. Do you have something legal saying you can make changes to his account?"

"He's dead. Will this do?" She dug out her ace in a hole. Her attorney friend Darnell had drafted her some kind of legal document, she didn't even know what it was called, but it basically said she owned the property listed and any accounts or correspondence attached to them belonged to her. It was all official and notarized and signed by ten people, and it appeared really, really impressive. She also had a copy of Tony's death certificate, which was a little more commonplace. The post office guy frowned outright, confused by the paperwork, and like he would go out of his way not to have to call someone. Amelia held her breath to see which way he would swing.

Laziness won out as he started typing, pausing only long enough to ask her where she wanted the mail sent. That was a bit of a conundrum as she still wasn't sure where she would be staying, even for the rest of the summer. "Can I get a mailbox here, a real one?"

"Sure. 227 is free. He gestured about midway up the wall to the left. It's three hundred dollars for the year."

Amelia gasped. "That's highway robbery!"

He shrugged. "We're private."

"Wait, who owns the post office?" Amelia asked suspiciously.

"Unh..." he typed some more on the laptop before pausing and looking at her with wide eyes. "Um, you do." He sat up straighter and tried to smile slightly.

Amelia's return smile was not at all kind. "Great, so you can wave the fee?"

He gulped. "Yes, ma'am."

"And the mail that's already been forwarded? Where did that go?"

His fingers moved over the keyboard, much quicker and more efficiently than he'd been working before. "To an accountant in Seattle, it looks like. I'll just jot that information down for you." And he did, handing her a piece of notepaper with the relevant contact details for a Jan Smiles, CPA.

Satisfied with conquering one step of her game plan, Amelia got the keys for her new mailbox and turned to leave. Only then noticing a community bulletin board by the door that was covered in small posters and fliers. Someone offered reiki healing, someone else chickens. The community theater was putting on an Ibsen play (Amelia loathed Ibsen with a passion only Ibsen himself could appreciate) and another notice for a book club meeting that evening. At six o'clock at Cheryl's house, and it gave an address. Amelia felt her shoulders relax. Book club! It was one of the hobbies on her list and she could get started tonight. And in someone's cozy living room! So much nicer and relaxed than a room at the library or a community center. She could take a bottle of wine. She put the address and time into her phone and headed out with a new spring in her step, ignoring the young man at the desk. She wondered what kind of books they read.

Chapter 3

❧

Amelia's enthusiasm for life was restored by the fantasy of finding a circle of friends with whom to discuss the joys of books and island life. She'd never belonged to a book club, despite yearning for years. Once upon a time, there had been a neighbor that was big into it and had even suggested Amelia might like to join. But she 'had to discuss it with the group first'. The neighbor, Ashley, had never brought it up again, so Amelia had assumed she'd been voted down or they didn't want new people.

Still, she'd been more than a little envious when Ashley would pass her in the hall on her way out with a couple of bottles of Cabernet under her arm. It was the camaraderie that she envied the most. Once she'd stopped lugging the unread book of high-brow poetry around with her in college, she'd discovered that she actually liked reading. These days her tastes were decidedly binary. On the one hand, she loved a bit of good non-fiction research, like her book of hobbies for busy women, or something on the communication of plants and trees. Occasionally she would discuss these with a coworker or an acquaintance, but most people seemed bored at the thought of learning anything voluntarily.

Her other reading though, she kept to herself. About five years ago, Amelia had discovered trashy romances. Despite being over thirty, the thought of what her mother would say if she found out about these books made her sweat slightly. Thank god for the anonymity of e-books. But she was pretty sure she didn't want to discuss these in book club. They were her delicious secret and it would take a lot of trust to share it.

She and Sadie departed the post office on a high. The skies had cleared and now puffy white clouds decorated a clear blue sky without a hint of rain anywhere but the still-wet grass. Amelia felt that she'd made good progress on her task list while Sadie seemed happy to once again have the breeze blowing her floppy ears. Amelia parked the golf cart as close to the market green as possible. The farmer's market and craft fair bustled with life, even busier than it had been a few weeks ago. She headed towards the medieval market cross, brought over from a small English village in Northumberland that had made the debatable choice to modernize in 1928. Mr. Evans had been happy to purchase it for a song and ship it to the US where he'd reassembled it as part of his reconstructed village on Findlater Island. Amelia knew all this because it was written on a plaque staked into the ground right in front of it. The structure was lovely, but somewhat out of place in this part of the world. But, just like it had been in its original home in England, it formed the center point of this village with all amenities spreading out from it.

When she'd been here last, Amelia had found herself eating most of her meals out at the pub, which proudly displayed the antique sign for The Hanged Man despite being known officially as Joe's Bar & Grill. Still, it wasn't the only restaurant option. One of her many resolutions for a semi-permanent life on the island consisted of trying out a few more of the establishments. Even though the fried comfort food of the pub called to her seductively, she decided to try the tiny Thai place on the opposite side of the green. Thai-later, was housed in the basement floor (the sign said garden level) of an adorable Georgian townhouse. Since Georgian townhouses weren't typically freestanding in their original environment, this one seemed oddly orphaned in its new locale. It sat sandwiched between a medieval guildhall with an overhanging second story and a Victorian arts and crafts bungalow — that was the bizarre architectural charm of Findlater.

The stress of the structure's separation from its original neighbors showed in the fairly new bricks that made up the sides of the building. They'd been painted white like the facade, but they stood out all the same. The bow windows in the front displayed the wares of a jewelry store. Amelia couldn't help but pause to peruse the selection and drool briefly over an opal and gold bracelet. Perhaps when her bank balance was significantly healthier, she would be able to indulge herself a little. She let herself be enticed with visions of being decked out in a 1920s flapper dress bedecked with jewels as she walked slowly over to the below-street access to the restaurant.

The black cast-iron gate that led to the lower level was propped open with an attractive rock. Amelia headed down the small flight of stairs and then paused to regard Sadie, who had stuck close to her once they left the golf cart. "I don't think you can come inside, Sadie. Do you want me to meet you somewhere?" She wasn't sure how she expected the dog to respond to that, but it now felt uncomfortable to talk with her any differently than she would to a person.

Sadie regarded her quizzically for a second and then kept going down the stairs. Amelia followed her and then saw a floral pet bed tucked in the shadowed corner of the tiny courtyard under the stairs with a bowl of water. It was clean and dry, without a dead leaf to be seen anywhere. Sadie was already curled up with one front paw stretched out over the edge of the bed. Amelia rolled her eyes in disbelief that she hadn't anticipated that Sadie knew what she was doing.

She opened the door to the restaurant and found herself in a charming, tiny Asian palace. It wasn't fancy exactly, but every surface was covered with something decorative. Potted bamboo grew in the corners, and an aquarium with decorative fantail goldfish made up the base of the counter. The air was filled with scents of sesame and other spices. Two tiny cafe tables with matching stools made up the seating, but both were occupied by young families trying hard to get their children to eat something they didn't recognize from the grocery store freezer aisle. Amelia headed to the counter where she saw a pile of menus and studied her options. An Asian woman smiled and waved from the kitchen area. The menu consisted of noodle dishes and grilled meat dishes, but a small section at the bottom had her smiling broadly. Banh mi were Amelia's lunch weakness. When done right, the Vietnamese sandwiches made from a crispy French baguette combined with spicy pickled vegetables and filling were divine. When things didn't go so great, it was often a soft subway roll with too many raw carrots and bland filling. There was never any way to really know in advance. The majority of people that filled out online restaurant reviews appeared in Amelia's opinion to have no appreciation for this original fusion experience at all. It would be miraculous if this tiny restaurant on Findlater could achieve banh mi greatness, but she had to know, one way or the other. The woman in the kitchen took her plastic gloves off and came through the glittery beaded curtain. "Ready?" she asked with a smile.

"Yes! I'll have the pork banh mi to go, please." She handed over a five-dollar bill and then dropped her change in the glass tip jar by the register.

The woman inclined her head politely in acknowledgment and went back to the kitchen area. "Will be just a minute."

Amelia swiveled to take in the rest of the establishment, never letting her eyes rest for very long in one place. It was absolutely crammed with good luck symbols and icons from several cultures.

"Ma'am?"

She turned to accept a tubular package wrapped neatly in white butcher paper. She could feel her mouth salivating at the thought of what she might be about to experience.

"And this is for Sadie." With both hands extended, the woman handed Amelia a smaller package, also wrapped in white paper.

"How did you...?"

"Sadie is very special. She has a good heart." She bowed slightly and headed back to the kitchen.

Amelia took both packages and pushed the door outwards with her elbow. The aromas wafting up from the bag were enough to make her stomach growl. Sadie glanced up from the dog bed under the stairs and started thwapping her tail gently.

"Well, I guess we both have lunch now, huh? Does that mean you found a good place to eat it too?" She didn't wait to see what Sadie had in mind, but started heading back up the short flight of stairs to the street. Sadie came up behind her and waited patiently.

Perusing the busy market full of white tents, she searched for a possible lunch spot, but nothing looked too inviting. Then she spotted a couple getting up from a low garden wall farther down the street and started legging it before anyone else could grab it. The spot was perfect. Lovely flowers behind and plenty of people watching while they ate, and still out of the way of most of the traffic.

Amelia sat down on the low stone wall and set her sandwich aside to unwrap Sadie's gift. It was a beautifully presented rice cake with chicken and barbecued pork slices arranged with some small curls of carrot. Sadie's ears perked and her mouth opened in a smile, so Amelia lowered the entire paper with contents down to the sidewalk. She wasn't sure how to break it into smaller pieces, but Sadie seemed quite familiar with this dish and devoured it quickly and easily. Amelia grabbed the butcher's paper after the dog had licked it clean before it could blow away and folded it under her hip.

Biting into her own sandwich, she closed her eyes in bliss. This was one of the good ones. The bread was crunchy on the outside and the filling perfectly spiced, balancing with the pickled vegetables. Thin slices of jalapeno pepper meant no two bites tasted exactly the same. French fries at the pub were suddenly not quite as appealing as they'd been an hour ago. She tried to eat slowly so as to savor her lunch, but all too soon she was dusting the crumbs off her lap and looking for a trash can to dispose of the paper.

Trash dealt with, she paused briefly in a quiet corner of the village green to get her phone out of her bag and check messages. There were none. She shouldn't be surprised. She wasn't very outgoing, and so her social circle hadn't extended very far beyond work. Since she's been so summarily (and illegally) forced out of her job, none of her former coworkers had yet felt the urge to stay in touch. She couldn't blame them, they weren't likely to be very secure in their jobs after that either.

Still, it was a little unnerving to realize that not much of anyone was concerned with her whereabouts. Sadie whined gently then, and Amelia smiled wryly. Well, Sadie cared. And quite frankly, she was a better person than most of the humans Amelia had met. "Right, let's make sure the world is still standing, Sadie, and then we'll get back to it." She checked her favorite local news site. Other than habit, she wasn't sure why she felt compelled to do this. She opened it occasionally for weather or juicy scandal updates, but nothing routine. Whatever prompted it, she was still shocked when she saw the leading headline. 'Woman Found Dead in Car on Ferry' She furiously clicked on the link — somehow she knew. There wasn't much in the article. Apparently, it had only happened or been discovered a few hours ago, but updates were promised. There was no mention of Findlater Island or which ferry it happened on.

"Who was she and who wanted her dead?" Amelia muttered to herself. And did that mean there was a killer loose on this small remote island, the one with absolutely no law enforcement? And how was Amelia going to find all that out before the killer struck again? Now that she owned most of it, she was beginning to think of it as her island. And now it was under threat, assuming there had actually been a murder, of course.

Chapter 4

❦

Amelia's brain wouldn't let go of the puzzle of the dead woman or an equally pressing sense of impending doom. Which might be a little ridiculous because even if it was true, and the deceased had come from Findlater this morning, it was hardly proof of foul play. Nor did it become truly Amelia's problem, even if she was murdered. By dying on the way to the mainland, the woman was sure to be in the hands of a proper medical investigation and that made it none of Amelia's business. And yet... she couldn't help but be slightly more aware of her periphery. Sadie seemed unconcerned with everything except why they were standing still on the sidewalk. Resolving to let things lie until further details emerged, Amelia headed back into the thick of the village, determined to tackle the bank before she stopped at one of the three wine stores to get ready for her very first book club meeting.

The bank, not-so-creatively named Findlater Community Bank, was housed in a renovated carriage house, on the last street of the English section before the village transitioned to a smaller area of German/Swiss chalets and square towers. Like the post office, it wasn't very busy inside, so Amelia walked right up to the single teller. "My name is Amelia Feelgood. I'd like to meet with a manager about some accounts that need to be transferred to my name."

The woman dressed like a retired schoolteacher regarded Amelia as if she'd asked for all the money in the till to be put in a reusable shopping bag. "Um. That's not possible right now."

"Okaaay, any particular reason?"

"Well, the manager isn't here today."

"And there's only one?" Amelia tried not to let her impatience show in her voice.

"Well, normally there's two but Misty, that's Ms. Green, is out on maternity leave."

Amelia was momentarily sidetracked at the thought of someone being named Misty Green and almost cracked a joke, but something stopped her.

"And there's no one else that can help me?"

"Not without all the approved paperwork. Donna should be back in a week."

"A week! What happens if there's an emergency?"

"Like what?" The teller looked genuinely baffled.

"Um, well..."

"Exactly. Ms. Kline left on the ferry this morning to go see friends on the mainland. She'll be coming back on the boat next week."

Island time... Island time... Amelia counseled herself for patience. Seven days weren't going to make that much difference. And in that time maybe she could clear up some of the other property matters that would make this transaction go a little faster.

"Is it possible to make an appointment with her now for when she's back?"

"Um, no. I don't have access to her calendar, but if you call next Friday, I'm sure someone will be able to set something up."

"Okay, thanks." Amelia wasn't completely sincere. She wasn't happy at all, but it was hardly this poor teller's fault. She headed back out into the bright sunlight, collecting Sadie from where she waited in the shade, and drove over to the third wine store, the one she hadn't gone in on her previous visit. This one claimed to have local vintages, all the new small breweries and wineries that had sprung up on both sides of the mountains as well as gins flavored with regional ingredients and the like. A lovely brass cowbell donged when she opened the door, and Amelia's head swiveled up to admire it. The old tarnished metal suggested it was authentic and had come from Switzerland, not China; she'd have to look into one of those for the hotel. A man wearing a crisp black apron nodded to her from the counter but didn't swoop in to interrupt her browsing. Their online presence hadn't lied. They had all kinds of quirky wines, from mountain huckleberry to dry rhubarb that was a lovely pink color. She settled on a relatively neutral white wine from eastern Washington for book club but couldn't resist trying one of the really out-there flavors for herself. She walked back and forth, trying to decide. Finally, with a quick toss of eenie meenie minie mo, she picked up the bottle of salmonberry wine and headed to the register.

"Ever had this before?" the man asked her, holding the bottle she'd finally picked out.

"No, why?"

"It's… different. Let me know if you like it and I can recommend some other things to try."

"Thanks!" Feeling ever so slightly a little more local than when she'd entered the shop, Amelia left the store with her purchases and decided it was time to finalize her preparations for book club. She and Sadie headed back to the golf cart. Dropping the wine carefully into the small space back behind the seats, Amelia only then remembered that they still needed to stop at the tiny overpriced grocery store to get some basic supplies and Sadie's food. It was on the way back to the hotel, so she opted to drive the short distance rather than walk. She parked again a minute later but Sadie didn't make a move to leave her seat so Amelia headed in. Grabbing a small red plastic basket by the door, she quickly loaded up on dog food, treats, and a few snacks for herself. Remembering at the last minute that she didn't have a corkscrew for the wine, she found one of those too and grimaced at the price. "Ten dollars! For that piece of crap?" But unopened wine was undrinkable wine so reluctantly she put it in the basket. Maybe she should stick to wine in the box from now on. No opener required. It hurt even worse because somewhere in her car were at least two bottle openers. It was simply that she would have to completely unpack it in order to find them and that made paying ten dollars for a third slightly more attractive.

⌘

Back at the hotel, Sadie set herself up for the evening in the middle of the full-size bed while Amelia opened her weekend case to consider her wardrobe options. She supposed she could keep what she had on, but she felt a little warm and worn after traveling all day, so a shower and fresh clothes seemed preferable for everyone concerned. She pulled a lime-green linen jumper that she always wore with a white tee underneath. The color always made her feel bold, and the baggy expanse of fabric made good camouflage for her slightly square body. Setting everything on a chair, she headed into the bathroom. It didn't feature the sparkly glass tile extravaganza she'd experienced in the guest room upstairs. This bathroom with its tiny black-and-white tiles must have been installed in the 1920s and never updated. It epitomized quaint. It was thoroughly charming. The shower had only a drizzle of water.

She sighed and did the best she could. But it was not the immersive experience she'd been hoping for. Amelia dressed and fished out a treat for Sadie and then checked the time on her phone. She still had three hours before book club. Should she have dinner before? But then, if they had food, she'd feel rude for turning it down. But if they didn't, she might expire from hunger before it was over. Such a conundrum. She got out the box of cookies she'd gotten for emergencies. Then she regarded herself in the mirror. She looked... plain. Had she left her sense of style in the big city?

Panicked, she flicked through the side pockets of her case until she unearthed a peach scarf. Then she stood in front of the mirror again and tried different ways of wearing it until she found one that she thought said, *this scarf suddenly appeared around my neck like this, and I took no effort with it whatsoever.*

Turning on the TV, which someone had left on the local news channel out of Seattle, she stood transfixed. The newscasters were discussing the dead woman on the ferry. Only now they identified her as fifty-five-year-old Donna Kline and said her death was still under investigation. "Don't tell me she's the bank manager!" she gasped at the TV.

They didn't; they switched to sports, leaving Amelia hanging onto why a woman who had died on a ferry had the same name as someone who had left on a ferry on the same day. There never seemed to be any such thing as coincidences.

She sat down on the edge of the bed, crossing her legs comfortably and waiting to see if they would come back with more details. While they rattled through the latest baseball scores, she checked her phone for the address listed for the book club. "Oh!" she exclaimed loudly enough to make Sadie lift her head. She was going to the same building as the Thai place with the Vietnamese sandwiches. It must be on one of the upper floors. At least she knew where it was and how to get there. She wasn't crazy about having to park farther away, which seemed likely given the traffic around the farmers' market. Now that it was staying light later, people probably lingered over the crocheted placemats at the market more than they did earlier in the year.

She ditzed around the room nervously waiting for time to pass. She played with Sadie, checked for her non-existent messages a few more times, read her horoscope (Libra), and flipped channels after the news never came back to the dead woman.

Finally, the time to leave arrived, and she realized she was anxious. Amelia wasn't entirely sure that the mean girls from high school hadn't grown up to join book clubs. Even though she remained confident that she'd never gone to school with any of these women, some stereotypes really seemed to fit. She found a short-sleeve white cardigan in her case and grabbed her purse. Sadie elected to stay in the room.

Outside of the inn, Amelia had to decide between her car and the golf cart. Rain pinged down from the leaden sky, so she opted for the Subaru. Eyeing all of her possessions smooshed against the windows redoubled her resolve to find some place to live. She was desperate to unpack. She drove slowly into the village, just in case any random tourists popped into the road. Most of them seemed to have gone back to their rooms or wherever they were staying. The rain turned a little heavier, and she turned up the windshield wipers.

Amelia congratulated herself on making the right choice. If she'd taken the golf cart, she'd be soaked through by now. The rain worked in her favor too because by the time she got to the center of the village, the craft fair was packing up quickly. She smiled with satisfaction when she pulled into a parking space just a couple of doors down from the Georgian townhouse with the restaurant and the book club. Maybe if they didn't have food at the meeting, she would have a few minutes to nip down and get another sandwich. She salivated at the thought. Almost hoping she would have an excuse.

She checked the clock on her dash before getting out of the car. When she was excited about something, she tended to be early. And enough overheard conversations about how irritating others found this, particularly if they were the ones setting the arrival time had made her self-conscious about it. She didn't want to piss anyone off until she had confidence they wouldn't be friends. But in that situation, she wouldn't be excited, and she, therefore, wouldn't be early. Or come at all, in most cases.

When she deemed enough minutes had passed to not appear too

overly eager, she got out and locked the car. Then she had to unlock it again because she'd forgotten to retrieve the bottle of wine she'd stashed under the passenger seat. Bottle in hand, she looped her purse over her arm and visualized herself as her former neighbor headed off to meet her besties at book club. It was enough to carry her through the front door and up the three flights of stairs to the top floor. Her confidence started to evaporate slightly when she raised her hand to knock on the white door with elaborate moldings. But she did it anyway.

Chapter 5

An almost spherical woman opened the door with a wide grin. She had one of those faces that seem to automatically make even the grumpiest person smile. Her dark hair dipped to her shoulders in fat curls, framing equally dark eyes and deep dimples. She wore an extra-large, loose, red t-shirt that said *Librarians do it digitally* and a long flowered skirt that ended just above her bare feet. Amelia's mind was still preoccupied with the t-shirt so it took her a few seconds to get out, "I'm Amelia, I'm here for book club?"

"You're in the right place! I'm Cheryl, come in and meet everyone. I think a few more are still coming."

Amelia tried to hand her the bottle of wine but Cheryl was already bouncing into the room so Amelia followed meekly behind. The apartment took up one half of the top floor of the building and flowed in a long rectangle. The windows at the front of the facade making up one wall of the living room and then one room stacked behind the other from the dining room, kitchen, and then two small bedrooms at the back. She got all this from the enthusiastic pointing of Cheryl as she stood in the entrance to the small kitchen. She finally took the bottle of wine from Amelia and handed her a glass of red wine in exchange. Amelia sipped cautiously as she stood and surveyed the room. Cheryl's taste was clearly eclectic. This top floor must have originally been storage and servants' quarters because there wasn't a flat ceiling anywhere that Amelia could see. Everything was angled and dipping here and there to maximize the floor space without too much thought for architecture. Cheryl had draped bits and pieces of artwork, floral wreaths, interesting textiles, and some African beads wherever there seemed to be room. The colors were bright and random. The overall effect evoked a charming bohemian hideaway with a faint scent of sandalwood.

For the book club meeting, Amelia had been expecting a circle of straight-back chairs for some reason. But the women already there were lounging on the sofa, a nearby ottoman, and window seats tucked into the deep sills at the front of the house.

She turned back to Cheryl, gesturing toward her shirt. "I thought I'd already met the librarian?"

Cheryl laughed. "Oh, you mean Pearl at the public library? Yeah, she's a hoot. Absolutely hates book clubs, by the way, so you'll never find her here. I work at the Findlater Archives. Technically, I'm an archivist, but they don't have any good t-shirts for that, and I haven't been able to think of one to make my own."

"Oh! I didn't know there was an archive. Does that have something to do with Mr. Evans?"

"Yeah, it's all his sales slips and correspondence. It's housed in a barn on the far side of town so unless you know it's there you could go right past it and never have a clue. Never seems to be a problem with the eager beaver grad students, though. They can find the place in the dark. Sometimes I wish they'd get a life."

Amelia didn't have any ideas on what to say to that. Cheryl didn't seem angry, just more matter of fact about her job than Amelia would have expected from something so academic. She smiled as politely as she could manage and went to claim the unoccupied window seat. She gave a general wave around the room. "Hi, I'm Amelia."

They chimed in quietly with first names only. Dana was a blond fifty-something in jeans and a fitted t-shirt, Laura was a mousy woman about the same age with dark hair wearing a floral print shirt dress, and Alyssa was in her thirties with a boyish figure and hair swept back in a tight ponytail. One of them added, "Kristi should be here in a minute and Donna won't be here this week."

"For once we don't have to watch her constantly dunking that silly tea bag all evening."

Amelia couldn't see who had made the rather snide remark, but there was a generally restrained titter around the room.

"Am I the only new person?" She interjected.

"Well, so far. But then we'll see who shows." It was Dana that said that, Amelia was pretty sure. They were all lightly chatting, but it seemed to Amelia that the woman called Laura hung back from the conversation. She was the one seated on the other window seat, farther away from the main seating area. Cheryl came back into the room with a platter of cheese and crackers, which she placed down on the coffee table. "So Amelia, are you new to the island?"

"Um, yes. I haven't really settled in yet, but I'll be here for the foreseeable future."

Cheryl and Dana exchanged glances. With a light laugh, Dana asked, "What she really wants to know is are you single?"

"Um, yes? But I'm not looking to date anyone right now."

Cheryl burst into giggles. "Oh, if you could see your face! It's no big deal, but it's a small island. There aren't too many singles over twenty-five. There's a bit of a rotation. The single guys always go for the new girls first, then the recently divorced or split up, and then the cycle continues. Laura here is with Stan and Kristi is married to Ivar, but Dana, Alyssa, and I are single. Don't be surprised if you suddenly meet," she held her fingers up in air quotes, "some single guys in their thirties and forties in the next week or so. And darn it, I thought this might be my time to get with Carl. But you're totally his type."

"Oh. Well, I'm not really looking to get involved with anyone."

Dana rolled her eyes. "That's what we say too but come January when you haven't been off the island for four months and it's too miserable to be outside, we all sing a different tune."

At this point, Amelia really, really wanted to ask if any of them knew Gus, but if they didn't, she didn't want to throw fresh meat to the lions so she bit her lip.

A knock thumped happily on the door and Cheryl disappeared to open it, coming back with a woman that exuded healthy body confidence. Cheryl did the formalities. "Amelia, this is Kristi, she's a yoga instructor. Kristi, this is Amelia. I'm sorry, what business are you in, Amelia? I forgot to ask."

"Investments at the moment, I recently left a job in Communications though."

"Okaaay, well I think everyone is here unless we get any more newcomers. Anyone else need more wine?"

❧

"Amelia, I promise we're not always this crazy." Cheryl gave a friendly smile as she topped off wine glasses. Amelia gave a tight smile in response. She wasn't feeling this group yet, but maybe she was being unfair due to unreasonably high expectations of how good book club would be. "So um, what book are you guys reading?"

Looks were exchanged around the room. "We're still finishing War and Peace. We've been on it for six months." Dana chimed in dryly.

"Oh, wow. That's intense. I'm not sure what I was expecting, but Tolstoy wasn't it."

"No worries, we didn't expect it either. It was initiated as the default tiebreaker if we couldn't agree on anything else. And hence the notice in the post office for new members."

"So... you haven't found a new book to read in six months?"

"Not that we could agree on, but Donna promised that she has something juicy, and there's a new release from Kelan James out next week."

"I've heard of him, doesn't he write science fiction?"

"Normally, but apparently he's branching out to more literary fiction under a pen name. He used to live here you know."

"Really?"

"Yeah, out at that Three Bears Cottage in the woods. Nobody knows why he left. That was probably about a year ago, now."

And Gus had bought the cottage when he moved here. What had he said before? Something about having been on the island for about six months, so that made sense.

The quiet one, Laura, spoke up. "Well, Donna isn't here. I think we should read something that's out now so we can all check the reviews. I think that Nora Roberts one I suggested last time would be lovely."

Dana glared daggers at Laura. "That again, Laura? Don't you have enough romance with good old Stan?"

"We're fine, thank you. Stan takes very good care of me. I don't see a problem with having a little more romance in the world." Amelia heard her continue with a mutter under her breath, "might do you some good."

Dana rolled her eyes rather aggressively and crossed one leg over the other, high up on her thigh. "Well, if we're not going with Donna's suggestion, I think we should read something non-fiction and relevant. I found one on interracial conflict in the badlands of South Dakota."

There was a stunned silence for a minute before Alyssa spoke up gently. "Not sure the bookstore can get enough copies of that in time, yeah?"

"You know I'm always open to trying e-books, guys. It would give us a lot more options." Cheryl interjected cheerfully from the deep corner of the velvet sofa.

Dana shuddered. "No. Just no. I need the feel of a real book in my hands."

"Okay then, War and Peace again?" this from Kristi whose eyes had lost their sparkle.

It wasn't lost on Amelia that so far nobody had actually discussed Tolstoy's epic novel. She couldn't point fingers. She'd never read it either. She leaned over towards Laura on the other window seat and asked quietly, "Is anyone actually reading it?"

Laura gave a little nervous twitch at being conversed with directly, but then she smiled slightly and shook her head. "I don't think so. I sure haven't."

An uncomfortable silence descended on the group, just as a black and white cat wandered into the room. It did a loose circuit of the room, sliding under the outstretched hands and sniffing any plates within reach. Amelia extended a hand low to the ground, but the feline moved past without pausing. She sat back up straight.

The conversation drifted to what was going on at the local elementary school where Alyssa was a first-grade teacher. Then Kristi interrupted from the armchair where she'd been absently fiddling with her phone. "Oh my god, you guys! Donna's dead." Her wide eyes were shocked and unfocused.

"What?" erupted as a group response.

"Scott just texted me from the pub. Everyone's talking about it. She was found dead on the ferry. Oh, my god."

"But what happened? She wasn't old, and she was healthy. Well, sort of. As much as any of us, anyway." That from Alyssa.

"They don't know yet. Investigations are ongoing." Kristi responded as the now official purveyor of news, even though everyone had their phones out and nearby. "You don't suppose..."

"What?" Cheryl prompted.

"... that it had something to do with Phil? I mean, he didn't seem that upset when they broke up last week, but I don't think it was his idea."

"Hmmm, doubt it. He's already seeing Denise." Cheryl contributed.

"From the hair salon? But isn't she going out with Antonio?"

Laura squeaked from the window.

"Split. He's nosing around Lucia, now that she's back for the summer."

Amelia's head was spinning. How did they keep all these relationships straight? Maybe someone had a chart? Like fantasy football brackets?

"Ivar wants to head home. I hope you guys don't mind but I'm just... wow." Kristi stood up and took her wineglass into the kitchen.

"Yeah, I guess, me too." Alyssa got up and followed her, and pretty soon Amelia was at the door saying goodbye to Cheryl. "Thanks for having me. It was interesting and your place is lovely."

"Aw, thanks! Please come back next time. I promise this isn't normal." The cat sat with all four paws together at Cheryl's feet, giving the uncomfortable impression of a witch's familiar.

Amelia gave a non-committal nod. She didn't want to pretend to read War and Peace for the next year, but on the other hand, they seemed like interesting women despite some of the angry undercurrents between a few of them. She'd wait and see how things developed.

Chapter 6

Exiting the townhouse, Amelia paused for a second on the elegant front steps. She was still hungry after only having two crackers and a piece of cheese. There had been plenty more food prepped in the kitchen, but it seemed rude to stay for that when clearly the party was breaking up. If one could call book club a party. But maybe that was appropriate when the book club never got around to actually discussing the book.

She peered over the railing at the little Thai place on the lowest level. The lights were out, and all indications were it was closed. The pub it would have to be then. The sunlight was beginning to fade into dusk. She made her way down the steps and carefully maneuvered through the empty white tents erected on the green for the regular weekend farmer's market and craft fair. As she came through to the far side, she could see groups of people gathered outside the pub talking.

Hmmm. Might be a night for takeout. She didn't want to get drawn into deep mournful discussions about a woman she'd never met. Unless of course, they were useful somehow. Maybe if she saw anyone she knew she would sit down for a bit, but otherwise heading back to her hotel room with dinner seemed like the best idea.

She studied the group of people clustered outside the pub entrance. Nope. She didn't know any of them. She pulled open the heavy oak door and peered into the dim interior. It was loud inside.

If people were talking about Donna, they weren't too depressed about it. She scanned the tables quickly and didn't see any familiar faces, so she made her way to the cash register. Maybe she should try something different this time? The woman manning the till was clearly busy, but she gave Amelia a friendly nod as she ran the credit card for a family of four. Amelia helped herself to a menu from the stack and considered her options. She wasn't in the mood for fish or a burger. She submitted to her inner child, absolutely not the one in charge of her health. "Can I get a double order of mushroom lasagna to go? Oh, and a patty for Sadie?"

"You've got Sadie now? I was wondering where that dog had got to. Sure thing, might be a minute. We're super busy tonight."

"No problem, what's going on?" Amelia asked as casually as she could manage.

"Graduation week at the high school. Grandparents and other relatives come in from all over. It's a big deal."

"Ah." She stepped back to allow a big group to reach the counter. Looking around, it seemed that most everyone was in family groups with teenagers in tow. No Gus. Should she drive out to his place to say hi? Probably not. It wasn't like she could pretend to be on her way to anywhere way out there, and they hadn't really reached the friend stage. He might not be on the island anymore anyway if he'd been here undercover for the drug bust. She would have to wait and see. Really.

"Here you go, hon." A carryout bag was placed in her hands. Amelia smiled weakly in thanks and squeezed her way out through the people waiting for a table to open up. Outside again on the sidewalk, she breathed in a sigh of relief. She unapologetically didn't care for crowds. The last of the light had faded away while she was inside. She faced the green and the entrance point that she'd come from, but now she could only see the pale shapes of the tents in the dim streetlights. The tent pegs and bits and pieces left about were completely invisible, so she opted to walk around on the sidewalk back to her car. She did not have time to deal with a broken ankle. As she strolled, she listened in on the few conversations around her. She had no idea Findlater got so busy in the summer, but the place was bustling.

The couple in front of her were talking about what to do over the weekend. "We should go check out the antique shops and the thrift stores. People here probably don't even know what things are worth. We might find real treasure."

The man responded, "Where do you think they get their merchandise? It's probably all brought in containers from the east coast. Come on Darlene, we came here to get away from shopping and the city. I want to go fishing."

Darlene sighed with a dramatic pause. "Fine. But you owe me a nice dinner out with no complaining."

He leaned over and kissed her temple, and they continued on in harmony.

Amelia smirked, glad her days were hers to decide, even if they became a little lonely here and there. But then her ears tuned in to the people behind her who were being much more careful about being overheard. "Donna was a total cow. She deserved what she got."

"Shhh. What if someone heard you?"

"Oh, please. Who wouldn't think that? Bet they find some irregularities at the bank when someone finally looks."

"What do you mean? Like what?"

"Funds missing from donation accounts. And well... I shouldn't say anything, but when my grandpa died, his watch wasn't in the safe deposit box. But Fiona found it in a pawnshop in Seattle the week after."

"That doesn't mean..."

"No, but when I asked around, other people were missing things they expected to find in the boxes and didn't. It's not like there's proof, other than Granddad's watch, but it's odd. Always small things, but worth a few hundred dollars at a minimum. Nobody's missing trinkets or paperwork, and it's always people that have died recently."

Amelia was dying to turn around and ask questions in the worst way, but she forced herself to gaze ahead and keep to her normal pace. The spot where she needed to turn the corner was coming up soon.

"So how did you know it was his watch?"

"It was engraved on the inside back cover with his name and birth date. She probably didn't check there."

"Think it happened to anyone recently?"

"Dunno. But you remember that old guy who used to pan for gold under the bridge?"

"Yeah, what about him? Ivan something, wasn't it?"

"He died a month ago, kept all his gold bits in the bank, and he'd been collecting for over fifty years. His great-grandson is here taking care of stuff. Heard he's big on the MMA circuit in California."

Amelia strained her ears, but their voices were drifting as if they'd turned away. She risked a quick look over her shoulder as she turned left towards her car. She saw the silhouettes of two medium-sized men who had crossed the street to go up behind the bank. Interesting that she wasn't the only one who immediately thought the woman had been murdered. Although their theory seemed like so much fantasy.

She was lost in thought when she unlocked her car. And she stood there before getting in for several minutes, thinking about what she'd overheard. Then something brushed her ankles, and she squealed loudly, only to see it was a cat that had rushed by and up the steps of the nearby building where a door was being held open. When her heart slowed down a little, she got in and hit the lock button. Then she drove cautiously back to the inn, keeping an eye out for rogue tourists, deer, and any murderers that might still be lurking in the blackberry brambles.

What did an MMA fighter look like, anyway? She had a sudden vision of Bruce Lee taking vengeance on the island. But surely someone that physical would kill more violently? Still, that didn't mean he didn't do it. Maybe someone at the inn had some idea of this guy's name.

❧

Amelia parked back under the dense evergreens at the inn's guest parking lot, setting the emergency brake with a sense of accomplishment. There were no streetlights here, so she had to sort of feel her way from the car to the entrance of the hotel. She'd meant to grab some clothes and things out of the back of her car, but with only the dim interior light, which was mostly blocked by stuff, it didn't seem worth the hassle. Something important might get dropped and lost in the gravel. She had her dinner in the still-warm sack and a bottle of wine waiting in her room. It would have to do.

When she opened the lobby door to the electronic-sounding ding dong, she remembered that she wanted to get a cowbell for the door instead. It slipped her mind though when Becky came bustling through from the back.

"Oh! Ms. Feelgood! You're here. It's good to see you again." Becky seemed slightly nervous, but perhaps it was simply because of their shared past. Amelia couldn't be sure.

"It's good to see you too, Becky. How are things? I saw you convinced Mr. Jain to come back. Is that working out okay?"

"He didn't need much convincing. But yeah. His wife died a couple of months ago and the bank gave him a bad time about the loan he had to take out, so he was grateful for the work." Amelia was suddenly glad she hadn't asked Mr. Jain how his wife was doing. And what was his first name, anyway? Nobody ever seemed to call him anything but 'Mr.'.

"So everything's back to normal?"

"Umm. Well. That might be pushing it, but I think we're getting there."

"Oh, you might be someone who would know. I overhead something in the village. Something about a young man being on the island who's the descendant of some old guy who used to do gold panning around here. Do you have any idea who that might be?"

"No idea," Becky said a little too quickly. She sort of gulped a breath before adding, "the old guy was Ivar Magnusson. Why?"

"Just curious."

"Everything okay with your room? I'm sorry we had to put you in the basement. But everything else was booked, and you said to focus on profits..."

"Absolutely right. And Sadie and I are fine. She showed me how to get there from the entrance under the stairs."

"Really? Even I find that one hard to navigate."

Amelia smiled and ended the conversation with "Good night, I'll probably see you sometime tomorrow."

"Good night, Ms. Feelgood." Becky turned and went back into the old kitchen where the staff tended to hang out. The lobby was the least welcoming room in the entire inn from what Amelia could see, which seemed highly ironic.

She took the rapidly cooling bag of food and retraced her steps down under the stairs, down a dingy corridor, and around the corner by the furnace room to the door with the brass number plate. When she unlocked it, Sadie met her with a wagging tail at the door, intent on leaving. Amelia sighed and set the food down on the console holding the TV and then followed the dog down the other corridor to the exterior door. Sadie waited impatiently for her to open it and then zipped under the trees. A minute later she returned, looking more relaxed and ready to go back to the room. By the time Amelia opened the take out box of lasagna, it was lukewarm at best. Tomorrow she would start tackling more permanent living arrangements.

Chapter 7

✃

When she awoke on Saturday, Amelia had to blink a few times and consider whether it was really morning. Only dim light filtered through the windows high on the wall of the hotel room, and they didn't lead to open sky, anyway. She pulled her phone off the nightstand and discovered it was in fact already 7:20 am. Sadie groaned and rolled over on the far corner of the bed she'd claimed as her own. There wasn't anything they had to get up for, but Amelia didn't see any point in being lazy. She needed breakfast, a more permanent place to live, and to figure out what happened to Donna, the banker lady. All pretty much in that order.

She got up and took a shower. When she returned to the main part of the room, Sadie hadn't moved a muscle. Amelia checked to make sure she was still alive and was greeted with one amber eye opening. Then it shut again. Amelia got dressed and then opened the small drawer in the nightstand where she'd stashed the dog treats. Sadie was instantly alert and stuffed her nose well into the drawer.

They headed out together to conquer the day. It took almost twenty minutes to re-arrange the things she'd crammed into the front passenger seat to the back of the car so that there was room for Sadie. But once that was done, Sadie hopped in and curled up on the seat like she'd always been there. Feeling optimistic about her residential issues, Amelia drove her car into the village for breakfast. There didn't seem to be too many choices besides the pub and

Vegi Heaven for the most important meal of the day, but that was okay as not many people appeared to be early risers on the island. She wasn't in the mood for spelt pancakes, but it was nice to know they were an option. If nothing else, she enjoyed the guilt of eating bacon and eggs a little more. And generally, the menu at the pub was more suited to her sensibilities.

It was still cool enough to leave Sadie in the car while she went in, but she rolled down the windows a bit and parked in a shady spot just in case it warmed up suddenly. Then she eagerly headed in and indulged in French toast with bacon and maple syrup. She caught up on her lists in her journal, including the one for book club. It was odd that they could never decide on a book to read. But maybe they weren't the only book club in town. Although she'd quite liked Cheryl, and Alyssa seemed okay. There was no reason she couldn't see them at other social events, was there? There were only a few other people in the pub so far and none of them were doing anything particularly interesting, so Amelia ended up eating fairly fast. She had another cup of coffee to stretch things out a bit, but it was mostly because she wasn't entirely sure what to do next.

Finally, when she couldn't take the inactivity anymore, she paid and headed back out to the car. She'd thought and thought about how to solve the issue of the property she owned and where to live. She'd ultimately decided to start with the real-estate agent she'd seen in the windmill when she'd met Seth the computer guy the last time she'd been on the island. It took a few wrong turns and readjustments before she found the right side street that led to the unusual building. Since there was only one business per floor, it was simply a matter of climbing until she found them. Seth and his computers occupied the top and the fabric store took up the ground level. Unfortunately, none of them were open yet as it was still only 8:30 so she let Sadie out of the car and they played fetch with a small stick in the parking lot. Sadie then plopped herself down, panting under a fig tree in a giant earthenware pot in the small garden that surrounded the hexagonal structure.

Seth pulled up in a battered old red Toyota. When he saw her waiting by the front door, he paused several feet back. "Oh um, hey? You here to see me?"

"No, not this time. Do you know when the real-estate office opens?"

"Whenever Rich gets here. He's usually in by nine I think."

"Okay. I guess I'll wait here then."

He nodded and unlocked the door, propping it open with the attached doorstop. Amelia had a sneaking suspicion he didn't remember who she was, but really, did he need to? Now that she had her laptop from home, she wasn't too likely to require his services again. Hopefully.

Instead, she thought about what books she would want to read if she were running her own book club. Which she really, really didn't want to do. She absolutely wasn't interested in discussing her nonfiction reading. It was interesting, and she enjoyed it, but she loved the learning for the sake of it. She didn't need anyone validating her hero worship of Amelia Earhart. As for her other books, no way was she going to sit around and listen to people discuss steamy romances. But on the other hand, if they happened to mention an author or title that she hadn't heard of before, she'd be all ears.

It was at that point that a man in a tailored suit walked up to the door. Amelia could feel herself blushing as if he now knew what she read. "Are you Rich?"

"Yes, am I the lucky guy you're waiting for?"

His swarm was light for a salesman, but still present. Amelia's blush and her smile faded. "Maybe, I'm more likely to be a headache. Are you free to discuss this in your office?"

"Of course, of course." He led the way inside and up almost all of the gazillion stairs to the floor just below Seth's computer den. He unlocked the office door, flicked on some lights, and went behind the single desk in the room. He gestured to the guest chair at the front. "Now, how can I help you?"

"What do you know about the rental properties on the island formerly belonging to people named Lyle?"

"Quite a bit, actually. I manage the base leases for the portfolio."

Amelia's smile returned and lit her face like the sun through a stained-glass window. "Oooh, that is good news."

"Really? Are you looking to rent long term? There are several available properties..."

"Ummm. Not exactly. I'm the new owner."

"You're Amelia Feelgood?" his mouth hung open, and he leaned back in his chair.

"Yes. Why are you surprised?" She was genuinely curious, as she couldn't remember ever engendering this much of a shocked reaction in a man before. At least not on the first day.

"Well, I guess I expected someone more..." His eyes drifted to the window, never a good sign in her experience.

"More?" she prompted.

"More old." He finished lamely.

Right. Amelia didn't buy that, but she supposed it didn't matter all that much. She got back to business.

"Well, that's okay then. Firstly, you mentioned unoccupied residences. I'd like to take one for myself for the indefinite future. Can you show me what's available?"

"Of course. Let me go over them with you here and then I can take you to see the ones you're most interested in." He pulled up a spreadsheet on his laptop that he retrieved from the bottom drawer and added a couple of filters. "So you have a range of options. There's of course Mariposa. We rent that out by the week, but it's currently not booked. Then there's one two-bedroom property in Schinn's landing, there's a 17th-century English cottage on the outskirts of the village, a second-floor Georgian flat on the green, and a smaller flat at the top of one of the medieval things in the

German section. But I should warn you about the one in the landing, people keep complaining about the lack of hot water. We don't have the most dedicated plumbers on the island, so..."

Amelia nodded thoughtfully. That one was definitely out. "What's Mariposa? I've never heard of that before."

"It was Mr. Evan's private residence."

"But didn't he live in the mansion in the woods?"

"Sure, as a young man. That was his father's and grandfather's place. Mariposa is the place he had built in the 30s on the edge of the cliff for all his high-flying parties. Very Art Deco. It's huge, with twenty bedrooms and a full ballroom. We usually rent it out two or three times a year, sometimes to a Hollywood swank, but more often an all-inclusive wedding. It rents for $40,000 a week, which makes up for all the time it sits empty. But it's yours if you want it."

"Um, no, I think I can pass on that, but I'd love to see it sometime. I'll pass on the cold water place too, but if we could see the other three?"

"No problem. I should mention that only the Georgian flat has screens on the windows so if you're at all worried about bugs in the summer you should bear that in mind. Do you want to go now?"

"Why not? You don't mind if Sadie comes along too, do you?" It was clear that he did mind, but that he wasn't going to piss off his most important client by saying so. His thin lips were forced into a smile when he responded, "No problem."

༄

Despite the superior functionality of the Georgian flat (tall ceilings, modern kitchen) and the sweet charm of the German medieval apartment (hand-painted cupboards) Amelia fell in love with the English thatched cottage. A dark red climbing rose bloomed over the dark beam that ran across the top of the door. The walls were thick, probably a couple of feet, and that created deep window sills perfect for a fat vanilla candle or a vase of flowers. She couldn't stop smiling as she toured the tidy little property. There were two decent sized bedrooms upstairs. The layout suggested that there had been more originally, but someone had decided to modernize to more substantial proportions with en suite bathrooms. She wondered if Mr. Evans was even now rolling over in his grave because someone messed with the authenticity of no plumbing. Downstairs held the open kitchen and living room, a mudroom with a small washroom, and that was the entire house. It was perfect. The happier she got, the more Rich started to look depressed. Finally, she called him on it. "Is there something wrong? Is this the highest paying property or something?"

"No, no. In fact, it's empty because most people get tired of bending over to come in the front door."

"Oh, well, that's not a problem for me." Amelia felt smug about her height for the first time ever.

Rich didn't respond, so Amelia asked again. "So why are you looking, um... not exactly happy about things?"

"Nothing, just getting hungry for lunch. So is this the one you want?"

"Yeah. Pretty sure this is it. And Sadie likes it."

"Okay then. Well, let's go back to the office and I'll mark it occupied and give you the keys."

"Great! Oooh, I'm so excited to have my own place. Do you think you might have some time next week to go over the other aspects of the business with me? I'm sure it's all in good hands, but I'd like to understand it so I don't accidentally mess anything up." The last bit she added to pacify his ego. Or an implied threat that she would make something bad happen if he didn't clue in her on what she owned. Either way, it worked as he nodded and held the front door open for her as they left.

Back at the windmill, Amelia trudged up the stairs one last time to get the keys. It was amazing that nothing on the island seemed to have elevators. Of course, if they did, there probably wouldn't be a repairman out for months when they broke, but still. She was going to have amazingly fit legs if this kept up. Puffing slightly as she sat back down in the guest chair at Rich's desk, she thought of one more critical question. "What do I do about furniture?"

"Well, if you're not bringing your own, then I suggest you contact Scott Templeton." He handed her a card. "He runs an IKEA shopping service. You pick out what you want from the catalog, he goes over to the mainland and collects it, brings it back on the ferry, and here's the best part, puts it together."

"For a fee, I'm assuming."

"Sure, but probably less than paying shipping charges if you bought everything online or in a mainland store. He's one of your tenants, so you could probably cut a deal. Let me know so I can mark it in the books." That sounded like a great way to mess up the accounting, but until she had things sorted at the bank, that might be her only choice.

Rich opened his top drawer and pulled out a set of keys. Handing them to her, he said, "Congratulations on your new home. I'm sure you'll love it."

"Thanks!" and she got up to leave. She was still puzzled about why he seemed so unenthusiastic about it, he'd really tried to upsell the Georgian flat that was two buildings down from Cheryl's place. But while lovely, with big rooms and high ceilings, it had felt a little cold and formal.

She was thoughtful as she headed back down and collected Sadie from under the fig tree. She hadn't wanted to come inside, maybe because of all the stairs. They got back in the car, but before Amelia turned the key, she got out her cell phone and scrolled through the contacts. She was operating from almost pure instinct. She hit call next to a number and waited and waited through the rings. "Harrison." A gruff voice finally answered.

"Sheriff? It's Amelia Feelgood."

"I know. I have you saved under Troublesome Civilian."

"Really?" She was tickled pink.

"No. You're under F."

"For Findlater or Feelgood?"

"Sure. Now, why are you calling? Please don't tell me you've got another body."

"No. Not exactly. I think you may have one." Her voice was gleeful.

"Definitely not. No spare deads around here."

"The woman who died on the ferry. She came from here."

"Did she? Still not my problem. They took her off in Seattle. She was alive when she got on the ferry. That makes it a city, county, or state problem, but since it's a different county, it's definitely not my problem."

"But you talk, right? I want to know what she died of. I'm pretty sure I saw her in the ferry line as I was coming on the island, and she didn't look good. Which probably means whatever killed her, happened here. So sooner or later it will be your problem."

"I'm refiling you under D for do not answer."

Amelia smiled, she had his attention even it was unwilling. "Look at it this way. Get me a little information and maybe I can solve everything before you have to do any work. Or spend any money."

There was a long pause and then a sigh. "I'll call you back. Don't wait up."

She did a little dance in her seat. But talking to him had made her think of Gus, who she still hadn't seen around. Maybe she should take a quick drive out that way. She didn't have to go down his driveway or anything. It would just be a scenic tour to go to the end of the road and see where it connected up with the inn's cottages.

Chapter 8

❧

It was almost dinner time when Amelia slipped her phone back in her purse after metaphorically twisting the sheriff's arm. She and Sadie both needed food, but she wasn't in the mood for either takeout or sitting in a restaurant for an hour. She had house keys now, though, so in just a few days she could be in her own place fixing a meal in the kitchen. With that in mind, she decided to stop by the tiny grocery and get cleaning supplies. She'd find something that would work for supper without needing a stove or microwave.

Pulling into the parking lot that had exactly three spaces, she rolled all the windows down so Sadie would be comfortable and hurried inside the store. She grabbed a small cart and aggressively steered it to the aisle that had a little bit of everything, including cleaning supplies. The only other person in the store, a slow-moving man with a bad comb-over, glared at her but went around the corner to another aisle. Amelia ignored him and loaded up on paper towels, all-natural essential oil cleaners, and basic white shelf liner.

There was something to be said for being presented with only one or two choices; shopping went much faster. She got Sadie some more treats and then considered her own meal options. Nothing was exactly enticing.

Finally, out of desperation, she picked out a sub sandwich, opting for the one that had been made that morning instead of the day before (it was turkey, cream cheese, and cucumber) and a bottle of grapefruit juice. On impulse, she added a small bag of vinegar potato chips and headed for the register. She spotted bad-comb-over guy still lingering in the canned goods aisle.

While the clerk scanned her items and slowly moved them into a paper bag, Amelia noticed that a sign had been fixed to the small counter announcing that a fund had been set up at the bank to support Donna's family due to the tragedy. "Did she have much family?" she asked the clerk.

"Hmm? Who?"

Amelia pointed at the sign.

"Oh, not much. An elderly mother and a nephew, I think. One of her friends came by with that, not really the sort of thing you can say no to, not when it's an islander."

Amelia just nodded and collected her bag. Bad comb-over guy still hadn't made it to the register. Exactly what did he find so fascinating in the aisles that had so little to choose from? Shaking her head in disbelief, Amelia hurried back to Sadie.

Back at the car, she had to rearrange yet a few more things to make room for her purchases in the back seat, and then they were headed back to the hotel. She was starting to get worried that something was going to be squished beyond repair, and if it turned out to be her favorite French straw summer hat, she was going to be upset. Tomorrow she would give the cottage a good cleaning and unload the car. Even if she didn't have furniture to put in the house yet, at least she would be able to see out the car windows.

Driving back through the village towards the hotel, Amelia pretended to herself that she wasn't looking, but she knew she was scanning the pedestrians as she drove by. She still hadn't seen hide nor hair of Gus. It wasn't any of her business where he was or if he was coming back; she reminded herself. Maybe she'd stop by his house tomorrow after unloading the car. Then, if it was unoccupied, or for sale, she could put him out of her mind and focus on getting her business interests organized. She still couldn't believe she was now some kind of property baron. She needed to start being responsible about her portfolio and start evaluating whether or not she was selling up.

Despite her lecture to herself, she couldn't stop scanning faces as she continued driving through the village, which is why she noticed two familiar-looking women stepping out of the bookshop. One of them was Dana, and she thought the other was Kristi, but the woman stood at an angle and it was a little hard to tell. They were both dressed in dark yoga pants with expensive-looking patterned sports tops. Dana's was blue and purple and the other woman's green and aqua. They both had the hard-won figures of women not afraid to be seen on a public street in Lycra. Amelia envied that confidence, but only briefly.

The women continued standing on the sidewalk, talking as Amelia drove slowly past. Dana's hands were making gestures towards the shop, but then they stopped talking and went in opposite directions. Amelia's eyes followed the hand gestures towards anonymous arms in the bow window, changing out the display. Everything was being set up to feature one book, from multiple copies of the hardback to enormous posters of the cover. The title was Endless Night. She made a mental note to look it up on the Internet as soon as she was back in her room. The bookstore sure seemed to be making a big deal of it.

It was a few more hours before Amelia remembered to check up on that book. When they got back to her basement hotel room, Sadie wanted her dinner, insistently barking at the bag Amelia had placed on the small table until a dish was placed before her. Amelia decided she might as well eat then too and found a nature program on sloths that kept her mildly entertained while she ate the rather tasteless sandwich. There was an unexpected coziness to the small room in the basement. She supposed it might have something to do with the lack of traffic in the hallway. And unlike her last stay, she was quite certain nobody was trying to look in her windows, not unless they wanted to crawl under the deck and that would be fairly obvious.

Only after she took a shower and got tucked up in bed, did she remember she still had research to do. Sadie groaned and put a paw over her eyes. So Amelia turned off the lamp by the bed and used only the light from her phone. A long drawn-out sigh came from the stretched-out dog before she started snoring gently from her position on the far corner of the bed. Amelia wondered how she ever thought she could go back to living in Seattle without her new best friend. She forced her thoughts from that short-lived mistake. She had work to do and a big moving day tomorrow.

Unfortunately, Endless Night was a fairly popular title, so it took some maneuvering with search filters before she found what she was looking for. The advertising proclaimed it the future best seller of the year, a break-out novel based on a true story by Bryan Sinclair; the story of a young man's quest to learn his origins on picturesque Findlater Island. The cover was monochrome in tones of amber through almost black. A solitary figure of a man stood on an isolated beach facing towards an island not far from the shore. The blurb hinted at dark and sinister secrets. It was to be released tomorrow. Amelia hesitated for only an instant before placing a pre-order for the ebook. This way it would automatically download to her phone overnight and she wouldn't have to remember to go back. There was something about this book that was relevant to the book club. Had this been the book Donna planned to recommend? And if it had been, did it have anything to do with her death?

She went back and checked some of the other links. There were a few well-placed mentions that Bryan Sinclair was rumored to be Kelan James. The speculation seemed more advantageous than purely speculative, and Amelia's experience in communications told her this was likely quite intentional, drawing on James's fame and fabricating intrigue.

She would sort it all out in the morning. She attached her phone to the charger and rolled over. "Night, Sadie." She called out into the darkness before settling down for sleep.

Chapter 9

ℰↄ

In the dim light of the subterranean room, Amelia's eyes popped open with excitement. It's moving day! She thought before anything else. Finally, she could unload her car and then get back to some semblance of a normal life. Maybe. Certainly, she'd be able to drive into the village to buy groceries and put them in the car without rearranging all her worldly possessions. There was just something about Findlater that made her yearn to be a more established member of the community. With a surge of excitement, she got out of bed and headed into the bathroom. Sadie lifted her head briefly as Amelia passed and then collapsed again with a groan. As Amelia brushed her teeth with unusual vigor, she wondered if Sadie also got herself to the groomers just like she took herself to the vet. She'd have to inquire because if not, Sadie was getting a bath in the very near future.

Sadie must have sensed Amelia's thoughts because she rolled over on her back and stuck all four legs straight in the air, making it clear that she would be hard to move if the mood didn't strike her. Somehow Amelia knew that whenever she designated bath day, Sadie was going to be next to impossible to find. She got dressed briskly, forsaking most of her signature flair for common sense when dealing with dirt. She fed Sadie and then they headed out to the car, this time leaving the hotel via the downstairs exit so Sadie could pee under the tall trees on their way.

She got Sadie settled into the passenger seat and then ducked inside the lobby to check out. It was an awkwardly simple process since clearly she wasn't paying to use something she already owned. So it consisted mostly of handing over the key and wishing the young woman (one Amelia had never seen before) a nice day.

With the justification of a hard day's work ahead, Amelia decided to stop at the pub for a big breakfast on the way to the cottage. It was still early, so most of the tables sat empty, but she enjoyed what little people watching was on offer. She filled up on a large spinach and goat cheese omelet. With hash browns. And sourdough toast that she spread liberally with the homemade raspberry jam currently on the tables in pretty glass jars. It was genius marketing; she realized when she strode up to the register to pay and found that the jam was also on sale for ten dollars a jar. She bought two.

A man was coming in just as she approached the big oak door to leave. He stepped back and held it open for her. Such politeness warranted a second look as far as Amelia was concerned. And then she almost stopped in her tracks to stare. If she'd been a casting director in Hollywood, she'd have made up a movie just to feature this man. He had white-blond hair in a short stylish cut and the palest blue eyes she'd ever seen. Combined with bronzed skin, his overall appearance was eerie and very striking. On top of that, he was a specimen of peak physical fitness. He'd have stood out anywhere but here on the middle-aged tourist paradise of Findlater, he was a god.

His polite "Ma'am" jerked Amelia back to reality. If this wasn't the mixed martial arts star she'd heard about, she'd eat her hat. She opened her mouth to ask, but then realized that questioning a total stranger before they've had their breakfast might not go over as well as she wanted. So she replied with "Thanks!" and headed back to the car.

She'd been reluctant to leave the windows open with all her stuff in the car, so she thought she'd agreed with Sadie that the dog would wait by the door of the pub for her. When Amelia looked around, Sadie was nowhere to be seen. She called for her a few times, "Sadie?" but no floofy, wagging tail appeared. Even though Sadie was known to be a free agent, Amelia was hesitant to head to the cottage without her. She hesitantly walked down the block, looking between the buildings for any sign of the dog. Unsure where to look next, she turned around, her shoulders slumping, and headed back. Moving didn't sound like quite as much fun without a supportive assistant. But when she got back to her car, parked a few spots down from the pub, Sadie waited by the passenger door, panting slightly with her tongue hanging out.

"Where did you go, Sadie?"

Sadie just jerked her eyes to the door and back again.

Amelia took the hint and unlocked the car. Once Sadie was settled, she headed around to the driver's side and they set off for the cottage. Her new house wasn't technically very far away when measured by a ruler on the map. However, Mr. Evans must have adapted the science of brain folds to cram more buildings into his recreated village by using squiggly little lanes that curved hither and yon. Which meant that it still took her twenty minutes to drive there. She had high hopes she'd be able to scrape a few minutes off that as she got used to where to turn. But then again, the clueless tourists who stepped into roads without looking had to be factored in as well.

She signed in exasperation as yet another middle-aged woman stepped off the curb without looking for traffic, presumably to get a better shot on her phone of the medieval stable — proclaimed in all the brochures to have once been the inspiration for something or other in Shakespeare. Amelia eased her foot off the brake as the woman continued walking down the middle of the road, thankfully behind the car, and proceeded on towards the cottage.

Out of nowhere, she heard sirens coming up fast behind her and hurriedly hit the brakes once again. Habit had her edging the car to the right, but as she did so her gaze was locked in the rear-view mirror because how could there be emergency vehicles on an island with no hospital and no police? Frowning, she continued to look back up the road until an ancient ambulance from the seventies or even older came trundling down the road that led to the ferry dock, its lights and sirens still blazing. Amelia couldn't see who was in it, of course, but she added finding out to her mental to-do list.

☙

Amelia and Sadie pulled up next to the rough-hewn granite curb in front of their new home. The small house was even cuter than Amelia remembered from her first visit. The climbing rose draped over the door was dripping with crimson blooms against the warm stone of the house. It had a lovely lemony scent that made her think leaving the front door open for a while wouldn't be such a bad thing. The remnants of a cottage garden peeked out from among the weeds along the base of the walls. The whole package was adorably quaint. Amelia took a deep breath as she inserted the massive brass key in the lock of the paneled oak door and twisted. It opened easily and Sadie bounded through into the entry. Amelia paused just inside the doorway, taking it all in. Her new home. For as long as she wanted, whether or not she ever made it to France.

For the first time, enough doubt crept in over her long-held plans to relocate to Europe for her to actually notice and acknowledge it. She hadn't lost her interest in maintaining her sense of flair (or sharing it with the world) but perhaps she could do that here, at least for a while. Perhaps she would even soon be able to afford to take a trip to France to see if it did actually meet her expectations before moving permanently.

She stepped farther into the open kitchen/living room and shut the door behind her. She would need to fetch the cleaning supplies from the car, but first, she wanted to reacquaint herself with the house. Let it sink into her bones as her home. Amelia wandered through the small cottage, admiring the way the morning light caught the spiderwebs and dust, making them sparkle.

Sadie came bouncing back in to find her and then stayed close to her ankles as she headed up the stairs to the bedrooms with the deeply slanted ceilings. Looking in the bathrooms as a homeowner instead of a guest revealed just what a deep cleaning they needed. When she opened one of the built-in wardrobes in the back room, the one overlooking the small garden, she was surprised to find a folding mattress. She set it out in the hallway until she could decide what to do with it. There were no other signs of habitation. The house had clearly sat empty for quite some time. Which seemed odd given the number of tourists wandering around the village.

Amelia went back down the stairs and out to the car. She pulled the bags of household cleaners (all-natural, ethically sourced with essential oils) and paper towels out of the car. Sadie followed her out and decided to do a thorough inspection of the garden. Amelia decided she might as well leave the front door open and let some of the fresh air and rose scent circulate. She climbed the stairs again, figuring she would move the dust from the top to the bottom and then out. But after an hour of dusting and scrubbing, she was sneezing pretty badly.

Perhaps she needed a cup of English tea to go with her English cottage and English cottage garden. She was pretty sure her electric kettle was located relatively near a door in her car. And she had purchased a new box of imported tea at the store, so in theory, this would be an easy job.

The water was just coming to a boil in the kettle when a "Hello!" rang out from near the front door with forced cheer. Amelia moved away from the counter until she could see the door, but the bright light coming from behind meant she couldn't make out the figure standing there. The person moved forward a few feet, and that's when Amelia recognized Dana.

"Oh! Dana, right?"

"Yes, that's right. And you're Amelia?"

"Exactly. I was just making some tea. Would you like some?"

"Oh no, I don't have time to stop. Rich mentioned someone was moving in today. My garden backs up to yours, so I wanted to swing by and say welcome to the neighborhood."

Amelia knew she had a cynical streak a mile wide. She didn't think women like Dana ever did anything that didn't serve themselves in some capacity. It was doubtful she ever issued a 'welcome' that didn't come with a major serving of information gathering.

"Oh, that's so kind of you. How do you know Rich?" Two could play at this game, she figured.

She thought Dana twitched slightly.

"In the winter, you'll discover what a small island it really is. Are you staying past the summer?" Dana inquired, her voice dripping with girlish sweetness.

"My plans are totally up in the air until I see where things stand here," Amelia responded cheerfully.

"Rich was telling me you're the new landlord."

Amelia shrugged. There was no point in denying it, but she didn't have to elaborate either. She sipped her tea. "Are you sure you don't want some tea? I could use an excuse to not go back to cleaning." Her hint lay heavy in the air.

"No, I've gone off tea for the moment. Did you hear Laura was taken to the mainland because of poisoning? People are saying she got something wrong in her herbal tea mix." Dana shuddered in a way that came across as superficial. She seemed to sense that if she lingered Amelia was going to ask more questions because she was suddenly moving quickly towards the door. "I'll leave you to it. I need to get to yoga class, anyway. Do stop by if you need anything."

Amelia smiled and waved, strongly suspecting (but not caring) that her smile was coming across as more of a smirk. It often did.

Chapter 10

೮৲

By lunchtime, Amelia was sore from scrubbing and congested from all the dust. The upstairs now felt habitable, barely. While she cleaned, she considered the little information bomb Dana had dropped about Laura. Had she been poisoned? Was it related to Donna's death? Now that she thought about it, Donna's green face in the ferry line might easily have been from poisoning. And really, how many other ways were there to die that slowly?

Through the small window in what she'd determined would be her bedroom, she could see Sadie stretched out under an old apple tree in the small garden, tail and paws twitching ever so slightly. It was time for lunch. The last thing she wanted to do right now was cook and then have more cleaning up to do. Now that she lived on the outskirts of the village, she could walk to get something to eat, leaving the unpacking of the car until later. And... Sadie could now be left to her own devices. Amelia took a bowl of water out to the garden, sacrificing a crystal trifle dish, at least temporarily. She figured Sadie deserved the best, and besides; it was the first suitable thing she found in the car. The universe clearly meant it to be a dog bowl today.

Sadie looked up briefly when Amelia came outside but closed her eyes again, snuggling into the long grass and ferns where she was stretched out. Amelia took that to mean Sadie wasn't interested in coming with her, so she went back through the house and locked up. It was only when she stood on the stoop under the climbing rose that she realized she didn't have a particular destination in mind.

So she pulled out her phone to check her options. There was a German beer garden that was closest (in the Germanic architecture section, naturally) but the fish and chips place was calling her name. Suddenly she craved flaky cod and thick steak fries smothered in ketchup. She rechecked the directions and headed out.

The fish and chip shop consisted of little more than a serving window opening on the sidewalk about three blocks over. But Amelia had only to follow the delicious fried aroma she picked up from two blocks away to find it. Not surprisingly, there was a line. She shifted her weight impatiently while a rather pudgy couple, clearly vacationers, she thought to herself with the disdain of someone who'd lived on the island for less than a week, debated the merits of mushy peas with the teenager attempting to take their order. Finally settling on one order with and one without, they paid and moved over to the side. Amelia let out an audible breath of relief as the line advanced forward. Everyone ignored her.

Although it felt like an hour, only ten minutes had elapsed by the time she was holding a paper basket brimming with crispy deep-fried fish and golden strips of potato. Her stomach rumbled in anticipation. She looked around for where she could sit, but there was nothing suitable. The shop next door was a butcher and the one on the other side sold blown glass knicknacs — neither required chairs for their customers to shop. She followed the couple that had been in front of her in line down the street. They looked like they might be locals or at least frequent visitors. Sure enough, they turned the corner at the next intersection. As she continued trailing them, Amelia spotted a small pocket park with a grassy knoll and a couple of half-sized picnic tables. The couple she'd been following took one, and she sat down on the other. They eyed her a little warily, so Amelia took out her phone to show she wasn't going to engage them in unwanted conversation. She stuck the end of a fat fry in her mouth and only then remembered that the e-book should have downloaded in the middle of the night.

She quickly pulled up her e-book app on the phone. There it was! She clicked it with fierce eagerness and started reading as soon as it opened to page one. Three pages in, she remembered she was also here to eat and diverted her gaze long enough to spread tartar sauce and ketchup in the appropriate places. She went back to the book, absently moving food to her mouth every couple of pages.

Endless Night told the story of a boy and then a teenager whose mother had an affair with a married man. The mother hadn't known the man was already married, and her life and mental health tumbled out of control when she found out she was pregnant. The boy, the result of the affair, grows up knowing all of this. When he turns eighteen and is aged out of the foster care system, he heads out into the world determined to seek answers and some form of retribution. He arrives on Findlater Island, on the trail of his biological father. That same day he meets a sixteen-year-old girl who offers to show him the island.

"Uh-oh," Amelia said under her breath. She glanced down at the almost empty basket and selected one last fry. Then she started skimming the pages, reading for clues rather than plot. The boy quickly figures out that the girl is his half-sister, but he doesn't share the news with her. Instead, he milks her growing attraction to him, even pretending to be younger than his actual age to attend the local high school. All with the intention of getting close to the man who betrayed his mother. Intentional literary irony? Amelia wondered to herself and kept swiping pages. The young man avoids intimacy with the girl by playing the gentleman card, which drives her even deeper into first love.

The app says she's read about 65% of the book, so Amelia wasn't too surprised when the big embarrassing reveal took place shortly thereafter. The girl is crushed, betrayed by her first love and by her father's sins being unmasked. The men in her life and the author don't seem overly concerned over this, but Amelia grinds her teeth in sympathetic anger. It hit her then. If she felt this angry reading a fictional account, was it enough to drive someone to murder if the story was true? And if it was true, who was the girl?

Had it been Donna? But then who would want her dead unless she had another side to the story? But then she'd been the one with the new exciting book to share at book club, perhaps this book. Or had she been about to propose something else as a decoy? Or... Amelia's mind was spinning with possibilities. Had Donna known who the characters were based on and threatened to tell?

Amelia put her phone away and gathered up her trash, surprised to see that the park was now empty. She checked her phone again. She'd been sitting there for over an hour. And now she had more questions than ever. Perhaps there were still some clues in Gus's house. After all, that was rumored to be the residence of the man who'd written the book, whether under a pen name or not. Perhaps she would take a trip out there this afternoon. Then Amelia realized she would need to unpack the car first unless she wanted Gus to see her looking like someone who lived out of their car. No, definitely not, she decided. She strode back towards the cottage briskly, with renewed purpose.

❧

Intent to get the car cleaned out enough to drive out to Gus's place to investigate Amelia created an efficient process with that goal in mind. She left the front door open and all the car doors ajar. She opted not to put anything away but instead create a landing zone in one corner of the living room. She paused briefly with her hands on her hips when Sadie wandered back inside and started snuffling through the growing pile of stuff. Then she got back to work hauling her things in. It seemed like double the amount of what she'd put in the car in the first place. Perhaps because she didn't have any furniture. She was going to have to do something about that. Tomorrow.

When she pulled the last stray sock out of the back seat, she waved it over her head unconsciously as she stretched her arms. Now she needed a shower. She glanced at the clock on the stove as she went into the kitchen area to wash her hands. 6:15 already? She'd better hurry. Thankfully, it was staying light out longer and longer, but there were limits. While she didn't think Gus kept normal hours, arriving on his doorstep too late would send entirely the wrong message.

She found her carefully packed bag with summer separates and opened it on the living room floor. Should she go with a skirt or pants? A skirt might look too dressy, but then it was almost full summer... Then she remembered her striped shirt dress in the suit bag and dragged it out from under a box of kitchen utensils. Holding it up, she tugged on a few of the creases and decided it would have to do. She headed upstairs to take a shower but was distracted on the way. Halfway up the stairs was a small arched window that overlooked the back corner of the garden, an odd angle that probably meant more in the house's original location. There had been some movement that caught her eye as she came up the stairs. She peered through the ancient wavy glass, trying to make out what it was. Only then did she notice the small bronze latch on the window frame. She unhooked it and opened the window. She didn't see anything moving, but now she could hear talking. A man and a woman. Both voices sounded familiar, but it took a few minutes to place them. They were talking softly just on the other side of the trees.

"We can't keep doing this here! He'll find out, smell something, or come home early."

"I'll find us a new place, I promise. Give me a few days."

"Why did you have to show her the cottage, anyway? It's not like she doesn't own other places to live."

"And how would it have looked when she found out it was empty and I didn't show it to her?"

The voices faded as they moved further away, but Amelia was pretty sure she'd been listening to Dana and Rich. Were they having an affair? And they had been meeting in her little cottage? Her nose wrinkled as she passed the folding mattress leaning against the wall in the hallway. Ewww! First thing tomorrow, she was putting gloves on and hauling that out to the trash.

She showered quickly and dressed, glad to see that the steam from the shower had relaxed at least a few of the wrinkles in her dress. Downstairs, she fed Sadie and made herself a cheese sandwich to eat while she drove. Sadie once again opted to remain behind.

Driving through the heart of the village, Amelia almost pulled into a parking space when she passed the fully dressed window of the bookstore. Endless Night was everywhere, and she noticed a stream of people leaving the bookstore with a hardback copy in hand. Maybe tomorrow when they weren't so busy she would stop in and find out what they knew. She kept driving, glancing in her rearview mirror to see if she'd held up traffic. She had, but only for a block as nobody was interested in going beyond the village. She sighed to herself as she drove into the perpetually dark forest. It sent a slight shiver down her spine and made her think of Hansel and Gretel heading into the woods. On the other hand, people had such a tendency to gather like sheep. Deep in her bones, she knew that someone had strayed outside of those lines and that's why Donna was dead.

Slowing down to make the turn at the fancifully carved sign for the Three Bears Cottage, peppered by Gus with red and white 'No Trespassing' signs, Amelia tensed in anticipation of what she might learn. But first, she was going to have to convince him to let her look through his house.

Chapter 11

❧

The driveway to Gus's cottage was of course unoccupied. Amelia hadn't expected anything different. Even if he was in residence, she was sure he would keep his vehicles out of sight. But there was an empty, abandoned feel to the place — like walking into a summer rental after it's been vacant for the winter. She knocked on the cute front door softly. There was no response and no sound of footsteps. If any curtains twitched, they were well out of her peripheral vision. She paused, listening, then knocked again, harder. Still no answer.

Then her phone rang somewhere in the depths of her over-sized pink tote bag that she'd slipped over her shoulder so she could throw it at anyone who attempted to attack her, thus providing a few seconds of distraction. Perhaps she needed a different self-defense strategy or at least a second purse. When she finally fished it out, there was nothing displayed on the caller id. Nothing at all. But the phone was still ringing. "Hello?" she answered tentatively. Not sure if she was going to be greeted by an old school friend or an automatic computerized voice threatening her in Chinese. Those always made her nervous because she wasn't sure what she was missing.

It was neither of those. It was Gus. Who didn't bother with any of the usual salutations but instead started with, "What are you doing standing on my front porch?"

Amelia looked around wildly. Where was he? And it seemed a bit of a stretch to call the tiny thatched turret suspended over the doormat, a porch. "Where are you?" she finally asked, bewildered.

"Amelia, why are you on my porch?"

"I need to check something in your house. Why are you calling me? Can't you come to the door?"

"Not if I'm not there. Which I'm not."

Amelia was busy peering into the nearby windows, trying to figure out where he was positioned.

"Amelia. Are you listening to me?"

"Hmmm? Gus, where are you?"

"Not where I can open the door, that's for sure."

"Then why are you calling me?"

"To find out why you're standing at my front door!" Gus sounded a little aggravated, which Amelia thought was a bit rude as he was the one keeping her waiting.

She was still craning her neck and trying to twist her body to see around the edges of curtains. There was a long-suffering sigh in her ear.

"You might want to check your left earring. The back is about to fall off."

Absently, she put up her left hand to her ear. He was right, and these were her favorite pair. She put her bag down on the stoop and fixed the earring. Then his words finally registered. "How?" She swiveled and looked up in the little hood of thatch. It was so dark and cobwebby up there any number of cameras could be hidden, well, small ones anyway.

"Now you're catching on."

"So you're really not here?" Disappointment bled into her voice.

"No. I can't really talk any longer, Amelia. I'll be back in a couple of weeks."

"Oh, okay." Well, she couldn't break in without him knowing about it, which probably meant nobody else had either, or he'd have said something, wouldn't he? She slowly walked back to her car, trying to think through the mystery that was Gus. But he said he was coming back. So that meant he hadn't gone for good. That was... intriguing, she finally decided.

She would have made up for her disappointment over not searching the little house in the woods with a stop at the bookstore, but when she drove back through the village, they were already closed. She was tired and distracted enough by her conversation with Gus that she missed her turn and ended up driving through a twisted maze of narrow cobblestone streets before she finally found an intersection she recognized. Not very many of the houses had porches or spaces to sit outside, maybe that accounted for the seeming absence of people beyond the main tourist district. Maybe.

She finally pulled up in front of her new home with a sigh of relief. A glass of wine and then bed. That was all she had the capacity to handle right now. Everything else could be sorted out in the morning. She'd already planned to spend the first few nights sleeping on the floor in her bedroom. So she dragged her pile of blankets and pillows up the stairs, arranging them in a basic mattress shape before going back down to open the wine. She was looking forward to camping out.

She hadn't slept on the floor since her one and only sleepover when she was eleven. That hadn't gone particularly well, as she'd informed her new and short-lived friends that their crushes on the newest boy band were infantile and pointless. They'd shunned her after that, but she had enjoyed sleeping on the floor. She paused for a minute to wonder what had happened to those girls. The boy band had only lasted another six months before being ripped apart by a drug scandal, but presumably, the pubescent girls had grown up to lead boring, ordinary lives. Well, she and Sadie would make the most of their sleepover experience this time.

In the morning, Amelia realized the difference between sleeping on the floor as an eleven-year-old and a thirty-ahem-something woman. She groaned as she sat up and felt every joint in her body protest. Furniture moved so far up the list as to almost eclipse the murder in importance. Almost.

Sadie padded over and gave her a few encouraging licks on the face. The dog at least appeared happy to have her helpful human lower down.

"What are we going to do about a bed, Sadie?"

The dog sat abruptly, her tail still sweeping across the broad planks of the hardwood floor. She smiled and woofed suddenly.

Amelia grinned, not having a clue what Sadie was trying to tell her but enjoying the conversation just the same. Slowly she dragged herself to her knees and then stood, doing her best to shake all the cramps out. A hot shower helped bring things back to center, and then for the very first time, she went downstairs and fixed breakfast in her own kitchen on the island. She took her toast and coffee out to the garden where there was a low stone wall and sat down. It was still a little chilly and most of the surfaces were damp with morning dew but the cheerful twitter of birds and sunshine through the new green leaves made up for all of that. Sadie started sniffing under all the bushes. Amelia leaned her head back and just breathed in the peace and quiet. Birds chirped incessantly as they went about gathering their own breakfast. Then she heard a faint metallic squeak.

Amelia watched bemused as a man wearing a dark hoodie slipped between the narrow opening of a small gate in a neighbor's garden and then slithered down the tiny lane between the gardens. Slithered was really the only word for it. He didn't run, but he certainly moved faster than a walk. And he hadn't bothered to close the gate. There was also something about him that seemed familiar. She flipped through her mental catalog of everyone she'd met on the island. The list was growing by the day, but it wasn't yet impossibly long. She paused when she got to Rich, the real-estate agent. She thought back to the man in the alley. It was possible. She certainly couldn't rule it out. Then she glanced over at the garden. Wasn't that Dana's place? Huh.

She finished her coffee and headed inside, slightly daunted by the empty rooms that needed at least a minimum of furniture. On an island without a furniture store.

Just as she walked back into the kitchen, her cell phone rang. Somewhere. It was downstairs, definitely downstairs. That was good because she was too, which should make this easy. She cocked her head to try to pinpoint the direction of the tiny device currently belting out a tinny version of 'Island Girl' which she'd picked as her current default ringtone. That didn't help identify the caller at all or how desperately she should try to find the phone before it switched over to voicemail. A few seconds after it stopped ringing, she located it on the mantle over the giant open fireplace. The voicemail was from Sheriff Harrison, 'Call me' is all he said, not even bothering to rattle off his number. Then again, he was still a little irritated that she had it in the first place. She called him back.

"Screening your calls now, Ms. Feelgood?"

"No. I just moved, and it took me a minute to find my phone. But you probably didn't call me to chat."

"No, probably about it," she heard him mutter under his breath. "You were right. The woman on the ferry was murdered."

Amelia allowed herself a brief thrill of I-so-knew-it-and-I-was-right before stuffing that feeling back where it belonged. After all, murder was nothing to celebrate. "Was she killed on the island?"

"Yes." He sighed heavily. "You were right about that, too. Some kind of plant or herb or something. Probably mixed with other plants and herbs into an herbal tea. At least that's the toxicologist's theory. I don't suppose you've found out anything? No point in denying you've been looking." He warned.

"Nothing about plants or herbs. Although..."

"What?"

"Another woman was taken to the hospital with suspected poisoning. Or at least that's the rumor. Laura something. I'm not sure about her last name."

There was a heavy sigh. "She still alive?"

"As far as I know, but I'm not plugged into the local gossip, and I don't know how true any of that is."

"Fine. Call me if the rumor mill offers up something concrete. If it is related, I'll have to send someone out there."

He probably didn't intend that as a threat, but Amelia took it as one. She needed to solve this case. It was time to stop dallying around with all her other projects.

"I don't suppose you know where Donna was going?"

"When?"

"When she got on the ferry. Where was she headed?"

"Oh, that much I do know. She had an appointment at a local TV studio. Scheduled to do some kind of a spot about small-town island life. Can't see anything too suspicious there."

"Shows what you know about small-town island life." Amelia shot back emphatically. In her bones, she was positive that interview had everything to do with why Donna was dead.

"Any chance you could keep your nose out of this one?"

"Probably not, but on the other hand if you're going to swarm the island with investigators and have it solved by the weekend there won't be much I can stick it into, will there?"

Dead silence met her snarky question. She sighed, "How far down the list is it?"

"Really, really far down. Gang shooting with three dead yesterday." He answered quietly.

"Ah, well, I'll just keep digging and let you know if I find anything significant."

"Try not to get hurt then at least. Gus..."

"Gus, what?" her ears perked up.

"Nothing. Forget I said anything."

"You didn't." She made exasperated faces at the phone.

"Bye, Ms. Feelgood. You know where to find me."

"Bye. And thanks for the information."

They hung up. Amelia stood there in the empty room with a giant pile of stuff in the corner, even more questions buzzing in her head, and pondered.

Chapter 12

༄

A knock on the front door snapped Amelia out of her reverie. Eagerly she headed for the door, pulling it open to find... Cheryl. The bouncy woman who'd hosted the odd book club. Cheryl smiled at her, her curls bobbing next to her round face. This time she was wearing a shirt that said *I write good smut.* Amelia blinked at that and then wondered if she had read anything Cheryl had written. "Do you?" she asked, pointing at Cheryl's chest.

Cheryl's face went blank in confusion, and then she glanced down. Her smile radiated across her entire body like the sun coming up. "My pen name does. Cheryl Robertson writes only serious treatises on the care and handling of old documents, and abstracts on the contents of those old documents. And if you tell my mother anything different, I will kill you."

Amelia took a step back, eyeing Cheryl with the same wariness you might give a large, strange dog, and said, "Okay."

Cheryl stepped into the cottage. "I wanted to stop by and see how you felt about book club and maybe ask a favor." She glanced around the open space devoid of furniture and then more carefully at the pile in the corner. "Forgive me, but I don't see any books in that pile."

Amelia, far more used to judging others than having them notice her long enough to do the same, sensed defensiveness rise in her throat for a few brief seconds. A sensation she didn't much care for. "I have almost everything on my Kindle, although I use my phone more these days. Real books are nice, but they take up too much space in my condo."

"Oh! so you're not staying?"

"For now, I am. A grad student has the condo for the summer. Which is why I don't have any furniture, although that stuff would look very odd in this cottage."

Cheryl smiled again, but this time it was more of a satisfied smirk, as though Amelia had walked right into her verbal trap. "I think I can help you."

"Really? Is there a secret furniture store on the island?"

"Sort of. And you own it. So, here's my proposal. It's supposed to pour down rain all next week."

Amelia nodded but wasn't sure why the topic had suddenly switched from furniture to weather.

Cheryl continued, "And I have forty-five grad students coming for a week-long symposium on archive management. They were planning to camp in the adjacent field."

Amelia was starting to get a glimmer of where Cheryl was headed with this. "And I own something you want to borrow for the week?"

Cheryl grinned, "I knew you had to be one of the smart ones. Exactly. I want to put them up in Mariposa free of charge." She looked a little stressed at her own daring and started talking faster, "in exchange I can get some guys to bring down any of the furniture you want to this place. Mariposa has a little bit of everything, and it's the only place that's big enough for them all. Well, except for one of the hotels but those are all full and quite frankly neither the Center nor the students can afford to pay anything."

Amelia hesitated, "I don't know... I haven't even been up there myself. I can't really be confident of what I'd be agreeing to."

"We can go take a look right now if you like? My neighbor Bessie does some cleaning up there, and she has a key. The island rumor mill is consistent with saying you're the new owner, so there's no trouble there."

Amelia frowned, "What else is the rumor mill saying?"

"Oh, plenty. But it's best not to pay too much attention to it. Just when certain threads start emerging as persistent, there's probably at least a handful of truth behind it."

"What's it saying about Donna?"

Now it was Cheryl's turn to look confused by the change of subject. "Ummm, not much? She sort of showed up at things and threw her weight around. People are a little relieved to have the pressure off. Book club won't be the same without her and her incessant tea bag she kept in her purse," She added cheerfully. "Speaking of which, you never said what you thought of the group?"

Amelia pondered an appropriate reply. "I'm not really that interested in reading War and Peace," she finally admitted.

"Who is? I tell you what, I'll sweeten the pot. Let my students stay at Mariposa and I'll invite you to the real book club."

"There's more than one? How come nobody said anything?"

"It's kept very quiet. The meeting you came to is the decoy club. The one we divert people to that aren't going to fit into the real one."

Amelia felt that same burn of disappointment she'd experienced all those years ago watching her neighbor skip down the hall with her bottle of wine. "What exactly do you read in this club?"

"Nothing. That's the point. We talk about books we've liked and people pick up new authors to try. But it ends up being pretty much all trashy romances."

Amelia's heart swelled with longing and she saw a quick flicker in Cheryl's eye that said she'd picked up on it.

"People read all kinds of things but we only talk about books with romance, sci-fi romance... paranormal romance... steamy romance..." She was pausing between each genre like leading a bear into a cage with treats. Amelia caught herself leaning forward and saw no point in denying her interest. She wanted in that book club.

"I need to see Mariposa before I agree, so if you have time to go now, let's do it. And then if I don't see a problem and the students clean up immaculately when they leave, you bring me furniture, and let me in your smutty book club we'll have a deal."

Cheryl stuck out her hand. "Deal."

Amelia shook it.

❧

Amelia and Cheryl headed out the front door, Sadie having waved her tail politely goodbye from her position in front of the empty fireplace. Amelia took that as the dog, saying she was fine where she was and would see her when she got back. Amelia immediately knew which car belonged to Cheryl. A rusty once-red hatchback that looked like it had seen its last mile five years ago was pulled up tight against the granite curb.

Cheryl laughed, "if you could see your face! Everyone gets that look when they see Desdemona." She finished kindly. "Come on, I want to show you something." She walked to the car and around to the driver's side, then leaned over and popped the hood. Amelia watched her prop it up on that little stick thing and then gingerly walked over to join the other woman. She instinctively took a step back in shock. The working parts of the car gleamed like an immaculate kitchen, some parts were even plated in chrome with brass fittings.

"What? How?" she turned to Cheryl.

"My brother Sven. Every summer he comes here on vacation planning to kick back and do nothing. About three days in, he can't stand it anymore and spends the rest of the time tinkering with Desdemona." She shrugged. "It works out. Sven gets what amounts to a relaxing vacation to him, and I have a car that looks like crap on the outside but has the best running engine on the island."

She took the stick out and dropped the hood back in place.

"Come on. Time's a-wastin'!"

Cheryl settled in behind the wheel while a still shocked Amelia got into the passenger seat. The interior of the car was nowhere near as clean as the engine block. Apparently, Cheryl had an addiction to peanut butter cups. Amelia filed that away for future reference. At least it didn't smell bad.

When the engine started, the car purred like a stroked cat. Cheryl pulled away from the curb like a drag racer, flinging Amelia back in her seat. "You must be glad there aren't any cops on the island, huh?"

Cheryl grinned. "You have no idea. Don't worry though, I'm a safe driver. After all, if I'd ever hit anyone, there would be cops stationed here by now." The car slowed when they got to where tourists were beginning to congregate in front of restaurants and shops. "I swear some of these people leave their brains at home," Cheryl announced out of the blue as they stopped for a couple standing still in the middle of the crosswalk. Amelia just nodded as they watched the drama unfold in front of them. The man wanted to go to the left. (He was gesticulating wildly in that direction.) Both women looked to see what might be attracting his attention and spotted the fish and tackle shop midway down the block. "Un-huh," they said in unison. While the woman, who now appeared to be rethinking her relationship with the man, was tugging on his arm towards one of the five knitting shops in town. It seemed like an unending conflict as old as time until an entire group of Japanese tourists, complete with a petite leader carrying a tall pennant flag, entered the crosswalk and got their phones out to start recording. "They think it's performance art." Cheryl snickered. "There's an exhibition scheduled for later in the week."

"Well, it kind of is," Amelia said in sympathy. The added attention somehow united the man and woman once again and they exited the crosswalk at an angle, making a beeline for the bakery. "It's nice they have something they can agree on."

The Japanese tourists burst out into a flurry of conversation, showing each other their phones. But they kept walking at the urging of their leader with the flag, so Cheryl was able to drive again, and then they were out of the congested center of town.

They settled into a relaxed silence for the ten minutes or so it took to drive through Schinn's Landing and into the woods. When they passed Gus's cottage Amelia broke the silence with studied nonchalance, "Do you know who lives there?"

Cheryl glanced over at the sign covered in no trespassing signs, "No, why?"

"Just wondering. I noticed it when I came to check out the old mansion."

"I heard it was one of the drug lords, but I never met him, or her. Probably go back on the market soon."

"Hmmm."

They kept driving past the old Evans mansion, through the dense dark green of the forest, so thick that bright emerald moss grew down the center of the pavement. This was uncharted territory for Amelia, and she glanced around with interest. The wooded area primarily comprised thick untended trees with an occasional dirt driveway connecting with the paved road at an angle. She couldn't help but wonder why none of them were straight with ninety-degree intersections. Was it so people wouldn't be able to see what was going on?

She saw a deer watching curiously from a patch of brush near the road, but absolutely no signs of people. They must all stay holed up in whatever houses existed at the ends of those driveways. She speculated for a minute on what the odds of being shot would be if she were to say go introduce herself to each and every one. She shivered. Higher than she was willing to risk.

Chapter 13

❧

Despite still purring like a tiger, Cheryl's car slowed to a near crawl as they ascended a steep hill. An old sign, half-buried in overgrown rhododendron bushes, announced *Welcome to Mariposa*. It had a mid-century style to it, and Amelia thought it probably did date back that far. Cheryl cheerfully played tour guide without her even having to ask.

"They tried to make it into a resort in the early sixties, right after Mr. Evans died, but it didn't go over very well. Too far from the village or not enough socialites. Something didn't work, so then it was empty until the late eighties when someone got the bright idea to do weddings. And that's pretty much what it's been ever since. An onsite wedding venue or sometimes a rock star or starlet will rent it for a month or two while they recover from plastic surgery or over-indulging in something. Basically, people with money who don't want to see anyone."

"Anyone I'd know?" That was really for future reference, as Amelia was woefully ignorant of pop culture, but she was as capable as anybody of looking things up on Wikipedia.

"Ummm, Chad Bowman of the Slutty Pumpkins?"

"Never heard of him."

"Most haven't. He looked surprisingly normal without all the makeup. Finally cleaned up his cocaine habit. Or at least for that round. He didn't mix much, but he did go to the pub a time or two. That was about four years ago."

Amelia sat up straighter as the trees began to thin. It was harder to sit upright than you might think when the car was still tilted at a fifteen-degree angle as they climbed the hill. Then it was right in front of her, like a magnificent mirage suddenly appearing on the road. Mariposa. Shangri-La might have been a better choice, Amelia thought to herself. It was an Art Deco masterpiece, but unlike the molded ice cream shapes of Florida, someone had looked to the architecture of the Mediterranean. Onion domes adorned the corners of the staggered layers, and beautiful cobalt blue and turquoise tiles were embedded in the white plaster. "How on earth do they keep it white?" She knew how often the 'white' structures in the city had to be scrubbed down to remove the natural green that Mother Nature preferred in this region. Moss and algae were simply better embraced, in her opinion.

"Every six months," Cheryl said with a smirk. "And guess who's paying for it?"

Amelia groaned. She needed access to those books and fast, or she was going to be lucky to see Paris, Idaho, never mind France.

They got out of the car, their shoes chinking on the finely packed gravel of the circular drive. It brought home just how empty the place currently was as no other noise disturbed the peaceful sounds of nature. Cheryl fished around in her purse and produced a single brass key on a gaudy, rhinestone keyring.

"I thought your neighbor had the key and was meeting us here?"

Cheryl smiled gently, "I knew we'd end up here. Bessie is getting up in years. I figured I'd save her the trip by asking for it before heading to your place."

"And she just gave it to you?" Island security was not what she had gotten used to in the city.

Cheryl shrugged, "Why not? Come on, let's go furniture shopping!"

The front door opened easily, without a single squeak. It was a magnificent masterpiece of bronze and cut glass with a stylized design of gazelles. Two ornate carriage lamps in the shape of pomegranates hung down on either side. Amelia walked slowly inside the former residence of a playboy of the golden era, her eyes wide as she took everything in.

It was faded elegance, there was no doubt about that. But it had a charm and a style of its very own. She could see that it wasn't as it had been when he'd lived there. The walls were now all painted soft neutrals, hardly something that was fashionable in the thirties, and there weren't very many breakable ornaments around, no big vases or elegant knicknacs. The light fixtures all looked original though and the furniture in the downstairs lounges was big and comfortably stuffed but with that purity of line that typified the era. She wanted to keep exploring, but Cheryl pulled on her elbow.

"Come on! You need a place to sleep. You can come back and explore to your heart's content but there are rumors of a ghost so if that freaks you out don't come alone."

"A ghost?" Far from being scared, she was intrigued and wondering if this would be enough to get her friend Darnell here for a visit. He loved a good spooky story, although he'd never admit it to a soul.

"Yes. Mr. Evans himself. It's said he walks the halls just before dawn and makes sure all the pictures are straight. Why he's worried about that now, I have no idea. But that's the story."

"Huh. Doesn't sound very exciting."

"It's Findlater Island. You'd be surprised what passes for exciting around here." Cheryl started up the main staircase, "Come on, I figure we should raid the stuff not already out. It will be easier and most of it's better anyway."

Amelia followed her meekly, curious to see where they were going and wondering why Cheryl seemed so at home. She lost complete track of that thought as she began panting after the fourth flight of stairs. Still gasping for breath, she finally arrived on the topmost landing a few minutes after Cheryl. It was more finished than an attic, but only the central hallway had a full ceiling height.

All the rooms connected to the main arterial had slanted ceilings, clearly more to do with the outside architecture than what would look attractive in each room. The windows ranged from the grand and fanciful round ones at the front of the building overlooking the drive to prosaic ones on the sides and almost invisible slits in the rooms that overlooked the cliff and the ocean beyond.

"Servants' quarters," Cheryl announced cheerfully back in tour guide mode. "This is where they store all the extras now, furniture too fragile to be used downstairs, or too odd for modern tastes and of course in here," She opened the door to a large room at the end of the hall, "is the supply of mattresses."

Amelia peered over her shoulder. Sure enough, ranks of thick mattresses, still in their original plastic casings, sat stacked on their sides. "Why..."

"One of the rock stars got a little rowdy. And by that I mean he took a steak knife to every mattress in the place. Replacements took two weeks to arrive, which caused a problem with the wedding group that was supposed to show up the same day. Ever since then, a backup supply is kept here. It's come in handy more than once."

"So I just take one?"

"They all belong to you, sweetie. They're also all the same, so I'll just have one of the guys grab one when they grab the furniture. They're good quality so..." She pulled the door shut again. "Now, let's start in here. Do you have a basic list of what you're looking for?"

The two of them picked over the attic like little old ladies scouring a thrift shop for hidden treasure. They pulled and nudged the contenders towards the hallway so they'd be easier to retrieve, and then looked over the final selection.

"This will look really nice, I think," Amelia announced with satisfaction.

"Good. Then I'll send a couple of the guys up with a truck

shortly. We should head back so they can get this done before dark."

"Oh! Yes, of course. I guess I'd better figure out where I want it all to go." Amelia was slightly shell-shocked at this unusual method of furnishing her new abode, but she was relieved to have the problem mostly solved.

"So you're good with the grad students staying next week?"

Amelia shrugged. "A deal's a deal. I think it will be fine. This place sounds like it's survived worse."

"It definitely has." Cheryl headed downstairs while Amelia sagged behind her. How was it that the shorter, rounder woman wasn't tired or breathless while she felt like she needed to lie down for a couple of hours? She'd fallen out of her regular exercise routine when she lost her job. She added it to her mental to-do list that was growing uncomfortably long.

She sighed a little as Cheryl locked the door behind them, slipping the key back in her purse. She wanted to explore the magnificent house, to pretend she was a visiting (daring) socialite, probably with a cigarette holder (although she would never, ever smoke of course). Flair had been much more common back then (and appreciated), or at least it seemed that way in the movies.

The drive back down the mountain passed quickly and uneventfully. Cheryl chatted about various people Amelia hadn't met. She found it interesting, but without being able to put a face to the story, she was having trouble keeping people apart in her mind. She carefully glanced down each driveway they passed, trying to see if it was possible to see more coming from this direction. It wasn't really. In a few cases she spotted bicycles that had been left in the drive and she thought she saw movement near Gus's cottage, but it might have been only another deer.

Perhaps it was time to start a project plan for all the things she needed to accomplish on the island. If she set herself deadlines, she was more likely to get things done. And then she remembered the bank and the lack of availability of any manager. Perhaps a plan would only add to her frustration. She could at least start a list. And reward herself with a return trip to Mariposa to wander the halls when she accomplished a major milestone.

"Who keeps the schedule for Mariposa?" she asked Cheryl.

"Hmm? Oh, do you know I'm not too sure. It used to be Mrs. Jain, the wife of the manager at Ravenswood, but since she died, I'm not sure who's taken it on."

Great, one more thing she needed to track down and understand.

"Here you go. Safe and sound!" Cheryl announced as she pulled up in front of the cottage. Amelia blinked. "Thank you for that, and the furniture solution."

"Oh no, thank you. The guys will be by in a few. Don't go anywhere!" And with that, Cheryl peeled away from the curve with an engine rev that had curtains twitching in the nearby houses. Amelia smiled and went back into her adorable and soon to be furnished cottage to start making lists.

Chapter 14

❦

The pretty street remained completely empty. Amelia knew this because she'd been looking up and down it for the last hour. She wanted her furniture. More importantly, she needed to be able to leave the cottage and go into the village for more investigating. And she couldn't do that until Cheryl's 'guys' showed up. She hesitated to call and check up on things because she didn't want to burn her book club bridges just yet. Still, if they weren't here by 4 p.m. she promised herself, she would ask for an update. Sadie projected unconcern, sacked out smack in the middle of the living room floor, doing a realistic impression of a dead dog.

There were a million things she could be doing while she waited. She knew this. And not a single one was as enticing as looking down the street for a truck. When her legs started to tire from standing in one position, she gave in. Making a large cup of tea in the small kitchen, she added a generous spoonful of sugar and some cream. Then she went back outside and made herself comfortable on the small front stoop. Or as comfortable as you can get sitting on uneven cobblestones. Red rose petals drifted down on her head from the vine above, and she sighed with the sheer romantic bliss of it all.

Of course, that was the moment a bangy loud truck turned the corner. It's suspension clearly shot as it rattled over the bumps in the road. Amelia stood up. Was this...? Yes, it was pulling to a stop right in front of her cottage. Her furniture was here! She would sleep in a real bed tonight. If she could find her sheets, that is. She half twisted to go look for them and then realized she needed to direct the unofficial movers.

The two young men that got out of the truck might have been romance cover models. They were in their mid-twenties, chiseled and relaxed in the way only people with idealistic futures and no mortgages can be. Amelia thought about this and realized that actually she met that description now. So why wasn't she relaxed? Oh yeah, she needed to track down a murderer. And then there was the ambiguous matter of Gus, and France, and... she'd relax later.

"Ms. Feelgood?" the first mover asked her standing mid-path, his work gloves in hand.

"Yes, that's me. Do you have my furniture?"

"Got all of it in one go. Yes, ma'am. I'm Ken, and this is Evan. Do you want to show us where you'd like things now and then we'll get it unloaded?"

"Sure."

She led them into the house and noticed Sadie had disappeared. She showed the two young men through the cottage, pointing out where she wanted the bigger pieces. There weren't that many. She hadn't wanted to overcrowd things with too much furniture and figured she could always go back and get a few of the smaller items that she could carry by herself if she needed them later.

They nodded and strode to the truck, opening the rear door with a loud rattle. Amelia made herself comfortable out of the way in the minuscule front yard and admired their flexing biceps as they moved things in. They finished within the hour. As Amelia slipped them a tip, she considered asking them about people in the village, particularly Donna, but ultimately held her tongue. She still wasn't sure how Cheryl fit into the whole picture, and she was sure anything she said to these two would be reported back.

She knew they were on Cheryl's payroll somehow, but she was genuinely grateful for having her problem solved so quickly so she didn't resent giving them the extra money. They smiled and waved goodbye. The truck disappearing back the way it had come with a loud rattle and a grinding of breaks as it turned sharply at the corner.

Inside the cottage again, Amelia realized that it now looked messy. The furniture might be in place, but so was her giant pile she'd unpacked from her car. If she started pulling things off the top, she wouldn't be able to stop until everything was tidy. Or she could head into the village. Her rumbling stomach chose for her. She would go and find some supper and then come back and locate her sheets. Then tomorrow she would split her time between unpacking and investigating. Probably.

She decided dinner would be the standard fare at the pub. It was just easier not to have to think through new options. She'd had enough stimulation for the day, so a basic burger and fries in a familiar environment sounded right. Sadie again opted to stay at the cottage but asked to have her dinner outside under the old apple tree. Amelia got the hint when Sadie picked up the newly acquired steel dog bowl by the rim and took it outside, where she sat under the tree with the bowl between her front paws and smiled. Amelia dutifully brought her food out and put it in the dish. She made a second trip to the yard with a bowl of water. Satisfied the dog was settled for a few hours, she locked up and headed into the village.

The drive into town was relatively quiet. It was still early enough in the evening that tourists were wandering about, but for once they stuck to the sidewalks. The weather continued to be pleasant without being truly glorious, and the scent of lilacs wafted in the air. It was not quite the traditional dinner hour yet, so the pub wasn't particularly busy.

Seated at her favorite corner table, the one tucked back from the front door, Amelia did a quick scan of the dining area before pulling her journal out of her purse. She had a decided sense that she was getting distracted by a lot of interesting but not useful intelligence. It was time to lay things out and figure out what was truly missing. She spotted the first hole in her investigation almost immediately. She still didn't know which TV station Donna was going to when she boarded the ferry. Obviously, she'd never made it to her destination, but where had she been headed? And who would have that information?

She was tapping her pen against her bottom lip, trying to come up with a list when a plate laden with food slipped in front of her. Distracted, she raised her eyes to see Becky.

"Oh!" Her mouth hung open and her pen was suspended in midair, well, attached to her right hand, anyway.

"Everything okay, Ms. Feelgood?"

"Um, yes, of course. I'm just surprised to see you, Becky. How are you? I missed you at the inn when I checked out."

"Oh, you know. Fine, I guess. Sorry, I need to take their order." And she hurried back to the kitchen.

Amelia looked around confused, who's order was she taking in the kitchen? Or had she just been trying to get away? She looked around the pub one more time. It wasn't particularly full, maybe about two-thirds of the tables were occupied. She didn't recognize anyone, but that wasn't saying all that much. She took a large bite of her burger and contemplated while she chewed. Then she returned to her journal, while surreptitiously keeping an eye on Becky's movements. They weren't anything suspicious. She brought food from the kitchen and delivered it, took orders from new customers, and generally acted like a seasoned waitress.

Amelia forced her attention back to the matter of Donna and her final destination. Maybe the sheriff had learned something since they last spoke. It would be challenging to get it out of him, but perhaps if she offered him something in kind... And then there was the teller at the bank. Amelia still thought she knew more than she had shared on that first encounter before everyone found out

Donna was dead. At least she had a good excuse to return to the bank, as it was now obvious to everyone that Donna wouldn't be returning her message.

Local gossip had made it clear that Donna wasn't currently in a romantic relationship either. Gossip could get these things wrong, but what it did prove was there wasn't much point trying to chase that tail without more to go on. Right, she would start with a visit to the bank in the morning, and if that yielded nothing then she would call the sheriff again.

With renewed purpose, she polished off her meal, eager to get back and make up her new bed before nightfall. Becky slipped her check onto the table without pausing as she brought menus to new customers. Amelia sighed and hoped everything was fine with the younger woman. She would add Becky to her list of things she needed to spend time on and hope that nothing catastrophic happened in the main time.

Reluctantly, she closed her journal and slipped it into her bag when she noticed a steady stream of people entering the pub. She wouldn't be able to concentrate if it got noisy and besides before long someone would be leaning on the doorframe staring at her to encourage her to free up the table. She would just get a jump on that and save everyone the awkwardness.

The line at the cash register was moving extremely slowly. Amelia would have resented it, except she wanted to take advantage of the chatty hostess too. While she waited behind a middle-aged couple from out of town who were earnestly inquiring about local knitwear, she kept her gaze moving around the pub. It stalled when she saw that super-fit young man from the other night sitting at the end of the bar. Although his looks might have been arresting the first time around, it was the way his head stayed bent to have a serious whispered conversation with Becky, standing by his side that caught her attention. He glanced up and met Amelia's stare, then said something to Becky who quickly whisked away. The young man with the ice blond hair turned back to his beer like nothing had happened.

"Miss?"

Amelia jerked back to the present. It was her turn at the register.

"Sorry. Hey, do you know anything about that book? The one set here on the island?" She played up the tourist angle, hoping the woman didn't recognize her. It must have worked.

"Oh yes, dear. So exciting! Don't tell anyone, but the author is coming in person this weekend! It's limited space in the bookstore, so try to get there early."

"Really? Wow." Amelia eyed the woman with new respect. She remembered from her marketing days that the 'shhh, don't tell anyone…' line was as old as time and still worked like magic. Still, that was interesting. The man himself was coming to town. She might have missed the small gasp behind her if the room hadn't hit a natural lull in the noise level. She turned ever so slightly to see Laura, the mousy one from the book club, and supposedly in the hospital with poisoning, two people behind her in line. She was pale as a ghost. She rummaged around in her purse as though looking at her wallet, but Amelia was convinced it was a diversion. The pudgy middle-aged man next to her rubbed her shoulders with concern while glaring at Amelia. Interesting. Hadn't someone said Laura, like Donna, was one of the few that had grown up here and stayed? Hmmm. She needed a high-school yearbook STAT.

As she left the pub and walked back to her car, she realized she had quite a few errands to run tomorrow. Luckily, it was a day when the small library was open. There was just a chance that they might have the yearbooks. If not, Cheryl probably knew who would. And she needed to stop by the bank. And at some point, she was going to have to go buy real groceries, not the few small items of a vacationer.

When she got back to the small cottage, Sadie made it clear that she'd had enough of being out of sight, out of mind. She brought a large stick over to Amelia and banged her on the knee until she bent over and tried to take it from her. That immediately turned into a tug-of-war battle with Sadie growling deep in her throat. The ferocious sound was offset by sparking eyes and a tail that wagged like she smelled bacon. When Amelia finally wrestled the stick away, Sadie sat, her tongue hanging out while she lightly panted, waiting for the throw.

Amelia realized suddenly how many years had passed since she'd stopped and simply played. She threw the stick a short distance, awkwardly, and resolved to make more time to spend with Sadie. Instantly Sadie retrieved the branch and brought it back, again banging her knee. They repeated the entire cycle a few times until Sadie sat down and didn't bother going after the thrown stick. Then they both returned inside.

Amelia rummaged around in her pile of stuff until she found the pillowcase she'd stuffed with sheets. She grabbed it and her blankets, which were a bit easier to spot, and headed upstairs to make the bed. She struggled a bit to strip the plastic wrapping off the mattress, but she finally had it off and piled it in the corner to take downstairs. Then she made the bed, relishing the chore for the first time in a long time. Already she was anticipating a good night's sleep.

That job done, she went over to shut the blind on the window, deciding to leave it slightly ajar for the breeze. Hopefully, she wouldn't be eaten alive by mosquitoes, but there was only one way to find out. It felt a little too warm to sleep upstairs without some ventilation. Sadie seemed to agree because she flopped down on the floor and appeared settled for the night. Amelia detoured to the bathroom to brush her teeth and had pulled back the covers on the bed when she realized she hadn't locked up downstairs. Grumbling, she headed down to take care of that.

Just as she was locking the front door, she saw headlights on the street pull out and the sound of a car driving away. Used to the movement in the city, it didn't register with her until she was walking back upstairs. The car hadn't been there when she'd arrived home. And all of her neighbors already had their lights out. It could mean absolutely nothing. Maybe they were visiting and their hosts locked up and turned out the lights as soon as their guests were out the door. Maybe.

Sadie let out a mighty sigh when Amelia was finally in bed and the lights went out. Amelia smiled slightly and stretched out, relishing the cushioning of the high-end mattress. Then her ears tuned in to the new environment. Was that an owl? She pulled the covers up tighter under her chin.

Chapter 15

✑

The morning dawned early and bright. Amelia sprang out of bed, delighted to not feel any aches after sleeping on a proper mattress, and pulled back the eyelet curtains at the small window in the bedroom. The sky was a pale, washed-out blue. It was still before sunrise, but a delicate tinge of pink added a blush of color to the silvery clouds. A lower bank of white in the distance suggested fog, and she couldn't help but wonder if the ocean was really that close. She hadn't mapped her new home from that perspective, but it made sense. It wasn't that big of an island, so it couldn't be that far to the sea. The air smelled fresh and damp, with just that hint of earthiness that signaled forthcoming rain.

She got dressed with her errands in the village in mind, picking out an elegant black and white silk scarf to dress up her black linen pants and blouse. She debated for a long minute whether a hat was appropriate flair or would look like she was trying too hard. With a sigh, she left her favorite hat in its box and instead fastened some vintage jade drops to her ears. That would have to do. She had unpacking to do first anyway, and too much flair might hinder her efficiency.

Sadie waited patiently in the kitchen, her eyes mournful as they bounced between the back door and the food bowl on the floor. Amelia was unclear if she wanted to go out or have breakfast, so she opened the door and left it wide while she found the can opener. Sadie stayed where she was so clearly food remained her top priority. Amelia set the full dog bowl down and Sadie came over eagerly and starting eating.

Coffee was Amelia's first personal priority. Her brain cells mostly refused to function without it, so she set up the filter and grounds mindlessly. While the coffee perked, she moved into the adjacent living room side of the open plan and eyed her pile of possessions with misgiving. It hadn't gotten any smaller, and now she was slightly intimidated as to where to start. Gently, she pulled the first few items off the top. It happened to be a few books and a painting and then looked around. The books she set on the mantle and the painting she carried around the room before leaning it against the wall of the hallway. She would have to find her hammer and the picture nails she was fairly certain were in the pile somewhere. She armed herself with a cup of coffee and moved a few more items around one-handed. It didn't take long for her to see that she was dispersing the pile, but not necessarily making progress on unpacking. She paused to go make a real breakfast, thinking that maybe food would make it easier to really commit to putting things where they belonged.

She fixed a light meal of toast and marmalade, enjoying the play of light on the kitchen floor as she ate. Her cell rang right as she was putting her dishes in the sink. Cheryl's name showed on the caller id.

"Cheryl? Good morning."

"What's it like having furniture? How'd you sleep?"

"Fabulous to both, thank the guys again for me. That was a lifesaver."

Cheryl laughed, "They're good kids, mostly. I'm also calling to invite you to the top-secret book club as promised."

"Really? When is it?"

"Unexpectedly, it's tonight. Normally it's the first Wednesday of the month which would be next week but a couple of people rang me last night to say they had a conflict and could we move it up."

"Oh! Okay. Where do I need to be and when?"

"Due to the short notice, it's at my place, like the other book club. 7 o'clock and don't bring anything this time. New people are, um, well there's something of a hazing tradition."

Amelia let that sink in. "What kind of hazing?"

"Oh, nothing too bad. And it's all book-related. I'll explain when you get here. See you then!" And Cheryl was gone before Amelia could dive into her growing list of questions.

She stared at the phone in her hand, unsure of this new information. Well, she was a grownup. If she became too uncomfortable, she would leave. The clock on her phone told her she still had over an hour before anything would be open in town, so she went back in to make a dent in the pile.

She was sliding silverware into her designated kitchen drawer when she realized the bank and the library would both now be open and it was time to switch gears. Sadie opted to come along this time, so they both got in the car. Amelia opened the sunroof, and they headed into the heart of the village, ready to get some answers. She decided on the library first.

Like her first visit, there was a small line to speak with the librarian. And like before, she didn't much care for the answer she received. "Oh, we don't have those here. I think the high-school library has a full set but with it being summer the school is shut up tight. You could try the Findlater archives, they might have some of them."

Amelia nodded, frustrated. She should have just asked Cheryl yesterday and saved the trip. But she could ask her this evening. Oh heck, why was she waiting? She needed to see them now. She left the library and sat on the blue bench at the front of the building. Sadie was already parked at one side. Hitting redial on her last received call, she waited for Cheryl to pick up. Perhaps not surprisingly, it went to voicemail, so she left a message, "Hi, it's Amelia. I'm wondering if you have the local high-school yearbooks from…" she thought furiously through the math, Donna was in her mid-fifties so she would have graduated in the mid-eighties, right? "the 1980s. The public library doesn't have them. Call me back?"

Well, that's all she could do on that front for the moment. Time for the bank. Sadie groaned as she got up as if to say they should hang out at the library some more, but her tail wagged gently as she jumped in the car, so Amelia kept to her original plan. She parked in front of Findlater Community Bank and Sadie decided to follow her out. Amelia was a little surprised when the dog also followed her into the bank. But what the heck? Everyone here knew Sadie was a law unto herself. The same woman was stationed at the front teller's counter. She was still dressed a bit like a frumpy librarian. Nobody else seemed to be in sight. Amelia sighed, already anticipating that this wasn't going to go well.

"Hi, I was in here before to speak to the bank manager?"

"Oh? Um, well, she's not available."

"I know. She's dead. Looks like she's going to be permanently unavailable. Do you know who's taking her job?"

The woman frowned, "No. Corporate hasn't said anything."

"I thought this was a local bank? I mean, Findlater Community Bank has a corporate office?"

"Oh, um, well, we are. But we're part of a consortium of small banks. I don't know if they'll send someone out or what will happen."

"Well, is there someone I can call? I really can't hold off on accessing my accounts too much longer."

The woman looked relieved, maybe because she could hand Amelia off to someone else. She wrote out a phone number on a blank deposit slip and handed it to Amelia. "You can call this number. They may be able to help you."

Suddenly she looked past Amelia and smiled widely, "Sadie! Oh, lovebug, how have you been?"

Sadie turned from looking out at the parking lot and smiled her doggie smile. Before Amelia could blink, the teller was out from behind the desk and rubbing Sadie's tummy like a pro. "Oh Sadie, I've missed you."

Sadie gave the woman a few swipes of the tongue across the face and stretched. The woman stood, and her expression was so much friendlier that Amelia blinked in shock.

But she wasn't one to let a good opportunity slip past her, "Do you happen to know where Donna was headed when she got on that ferry?"

"Hmm? Oh, she said something about going on some TV show, something like PS I Love You? I didn't really believe her though. She was always talking about how she knew lots of famous people. Never saw any of them here." She shrugged and gave Sadie one last pat before going back to her side of the counter.

"Really? How interesting." It actually was. PS I Love You, a silly name for a daytime talk show, particularly when you understood that the PS stood for Puget Sound, was the most popular locally produced daytime show. And while Amelia didn't have any connections directly at that station, she did know someone at its closest rival who was bound to have contacts. "Okay, thank you. I'll be sure to bring Sadie with me the next time I'm in."

The woman sighed and smiled wistfully at Sadie, "Thanks, I tried to convince her to live with me, but I think my ten-year-old was the deciding factor in her moving on. She's got a great soul, our Sadie."

Sadie got up smiling at the room and then headed for the door. "Guess that's my cue," Amelia waved and pulled open the glass door for both of them. She'd been wondering how to make a graceful exit.

Chapter 16

❦

While Amelia was occupied in the bank, with apparently no cell phone signal, which seemed odd now that she thought about it, Cheryl had returned her voicemail. Her response was ambiguous at best, 'I'll set aside what I have for when you get here.' It certainly didn't answer the original question, but Amelia decided it would have to do for now. If it wasn't what she needed, she might be able to pin someone down for where to look next, assuming she survived this secret book club initiation, anyway. While she still had her phone out, she looked through her contacts for Melanie's number. It wasn't there. Had it been that long since they'd talked?

Amelia had started a new contact list when she'd purchased this phone a year ago. She had figured it was one way to purge all those people that make you feel bad when you see their names, the ones you ought to talk more to but never do. Basically, the Melanies of the world. But now she needed her number and didn't have it. She sat down on the rustic plank bench in front of the bank so she could focus a little better and consider her options.

After much clicking and searching, she finally found the number buried in her email from four years ago. Odds were it was now out of date, but heck, it was worth a shot. She listened to it ring, words staged on her tongue to apologize for a wrong number. But surprisingly, on the seventh ring, Melanie answered, "Melanie Hardwick, Channel 6!" She was always perky and upbeat, but she'd moved it up a few notches.

Amelia blinked a few times in an almost fight-or-flight response to so much enthusiasm. Despite the cheerleader persona, Amelia knew Melanie was essentially a shark, constantly moving towards whatever smelled the most like blood. "Melanie? It's Amelia. Amelia Feelgood. I think I might have something for you." This was seriously the best way to grab the woman's attention. The usual prattle of 'how have you been' 'we should catch up over wine/coffee/brunch' would lead to a dial tone but a potential lead? It was fuel to Melanie's addiction.

"What do you have?" Her voice instantly switched from coy to ballsy.

"First, I need a contact at Channel 2, preferably PS I Love You, but I'll take what I can get."

"I have that, but you haven't told me why I should share."

"The woman who was found dead on the ferry."

"What about her?"

"It's something big. I don't know what yet. Her death wasn't of natural causes."

"Why isn't Channel 2 all over it then?"

"They don't know what they almost had. And I can't offer you speculation, now can I? Journalistic ethics and all that." It was a low blow because Melanie had jumped the gun on more than one story. She'd just been lucky enough not to get caught. Yet.

There was a long pause followed by, "I want the exclusive."

"First the police, then you," Amelia promised.

"Sandra Cunningham extension 512."

"Thanks, Melanie. I'll be in touch."

"You'd better."

Amelia made a quick note of the name and then got up from the bench, stretching with satisfaction. Sadie ambled over to the car, clearly ready to get on with the day.

Checking the time, Amelia considered her possible next steps. She didn't want to call Channel 2 from her car or outside; she wanted it to sound like she was in a downtown office, if possible. She needed to continue unpacking, and they needed groceries. Eyeing Sadie, who was waiting to get in the car, she decided they would get groceries and then head home for both the phone call and unpacking. Then a nice light dinner before the big book club event. She had no idea life on this remote island could get so busy. And for some reason, that made her think of Gus. Was he coming back soon? And where was he exactly, anyway? Sadie barked, finally losing patience, so Amelia unlocked the car and they headed to the small grocery store.

She still wasn't happy with the exorbitant prices they charged at the tiny market, but she gritted her teeth and put everything she needed in her cart without debating it internally. She was living here now. It was either suck it up or plan for a big shopping trip on the mainland. Of course, then she'd need a place to store the food and the minuscule cottage kitchen didn't really offer cupboards for bulk buying. Maybe Cheryl had some tips for this as well... She'd have to make a list of things to ask the woman.

As the clerk idly ran up the contents of her cart, Amelia scanned the headlines of the gossip magazines. A movie star was pregnant with an alien baby. She was sure she'd seen that headline every month since she'd been a small girl. Did anyone still want to read the details? Or maybe it was more interesting if it referenced your favorite star? Her attention was jerked back by the ceasing of the scanner beep. The clerk looked at her expectantly, and the total was over two hundred dollars. Suddenly a supply trip to the mainland started to make more economic sense. She paid with her credit card and vowed to find out how to live here like a local.

Amelia grimaced as she loaded the five bags into the back of her car. That amounted to almost fifty dollars a grocery bag — highway robbery. And now she sounded just like her father, who she tried not to think about any more than necessary. Sounding like him inside her own head was the worst part of getting older.

She was still stewing over this when she parked in front of the quaint cottage, so she almost missed the paper slipped under the door. Something about it caught her eye though and after placing the first two bags on the small counter she went back and picked it up. Someone had very carefully and very evenly folded the paper into thirds. Unfolding it revealed a message in block script. Stop asking questions. This doesn't concern you.

"Huh" was all Amelia could muster. Whoever had left her the note hadn't even bothered to cut letters out of the newspaper or a magazine. She felt cheated somehow. But then it occurred to her that this was future fodder for Melanie, who would eat it up like ice cream. She dug a manila folder out of the pile, remarkably uncreased, and slipped the note inside, then placed the entirety on the mantle.

She almost forgot to bring in the rest of the groceries, but remembered when she started to unpack the first two bags. She went back outside to grab them. While she did that, she looked up and down the street but couldn't see anything else out of the ordinary. It was remarkably quiet and serene.

Groceries dealt with, she set the timer on her phone for one hour and diligently pulled things out of the pile. When the buzzer went off, she had made significant progress. Most of her clothes were upstairs in the closet, neatly put away. They could all use a good ironing, but she'd opted to save that step in order to achieve some semblance of overall order.

She headed into the kitchen and made a calming cup of tea, taking a few sips before finding that phone number for the woman at Channel 2. It was now mid-afternoon, generally an excellent time to call she'd found. People were bored at work and didn't mind an entertaining interruption if it didn't add to the workload at the end of the day.

She input the extension and listened to it ring twice. Then a quiet female voice picked up, "Research."

"Hi, I'm looking for Sandra Cunningham?"

"This is she."

"Ms. Cunningham, My name is Amelia Feelgood. I'm with Findlater Island." She'd thought this through carefully and decided this sounded like a civic official qualification without actually being a lie. As long as Sandra Cunningham didn't ask too many questions. "I understand Donna Kline was coming into Channel 2 when she, um, was um redirected. I was wondering if you could tell me why she was coming in? It's important to me that Findlater Island continues to be the top tourist destination it is today."

"Oh um, how did you get my name?"

"One of the press corps at Channel 6 gave it to me. I understand Ms. Kline was meeting with PS I Love You. Is there any way someone else from the island can address the topic?"

"One minute." There was a long quiet pause while Amelia wondered if she'd stretched the truth just a hair too far. She breathed a quiet sigh of relief when the quiet, polite voice came back, "She was scheduled to discuss her shared high school years with Bryan Sinclair, one of the background pieces for his big book launch."

"Oh, did Mr. Sinclair arrange it then? I'm meeting with him tomorrow."

"Ummm, no. Looks like Ms. Kline approached the tip line herself."

"I see. If I can find someone else from that high school class, should I call you?"

"You can. I can pass it on but honestly, we've moved on and are now booking out for the fall hiking season and holiday gift-giving."

"Wow, well, I'll keep my ears open then and let you know. Thanks so much, Ms. Cunningham."

Amelia hung up before any awkward questions could come her way. She was positive now that Donna's murder had to be connected with that book. But clearly, Kelan James wouldn't be objecting to the publicity, would he? He'd written a pseudo-autobiographical novel of his stay on the island, so he was hardly trying to hide anything, or at least not anything he knew about. Hmm. Were there any buried secrets? She'd better find the right yearbooks and scour them. Soon.

She went back to unpacking. She was just beginning to hit a layer of kitchen equipment. The major problem now was that her condo in the city had significantly more cupboard space than the cottage here, even if the square footage had been smaller. She was going to have to get rid of things or move them into some sort of long-term storage.

Amelia had yet to investigate the entirety of the backyard, so she headed out the kitchen door to find out if there was any kind of shed beyond the large fruit trees at the back. Sadie was happy to accompany her. Amelia parted some branches of one of the trees that looked like it might be forming apples and was immediately raked across the arm by a long blackberry bramble. Looking beyond, it was clear that any shed or much of anything else was unreachable until she dealt with the blackberries, which would require double-thick leather gloves and tougher clothing than she currently owned. Now she remembered why living in the city had held such appeal. One hundred years of concrete was about all that would hold these brambles at bay.

She also hated leaving anything uninvestigated. So it was with extreme reluctance that she went back inside and repurposed a few shopping bags to hold the kitchen wares that she judged she could live without for at least a few months. She stuffed the bags into the bottom of the credenza that had come from Mariposa and called it a day on the unpacking. She wanted a bath and time to settle her nerves before driving to Cheryl's. If this book club didn't work out, she was officially done with them.

Chapter 17

Once again Amelia nervously prepared for book club. Her expectations were both high and abysmally low. She didn't think Cheryl was the type to completely misrepresent the situation, but perhaps they didn't have quite the same definition of fun. Still, she made sure her hair was perfectly straight and paired a peach embroidered t-shirt with a pair of pale blue Chinese silk pajama bottoms. A thick boho silver necklace and she felt dressed for anything that might await. She fed Sadie and refilled her water bowl before locking up the cottage. Only after she was in her car did she realize she hadn't left any lights on. It was still fairly light at the moment, but it wouldn't be when she returned. Unless it was so bad she felt it necessary to escape extremely early.

The engine running, she paused, debating whether to go back in and turn on a light or deal with it when she got back. In the end, she was too impatient and moved her foot to the gas pedal.

It was more difficult to find a parking space in front of Cheryl's apartment this time. There was no obvious reason as to why there were so many cars in front of the building. This couldn't all be for the book club, could it? Nothing was happening on the village green at the moment, so that wasn't it. And the basement Asian restaurant, the one with the bahn mi that she really needed to try again, looked almost empty. Amelia briefly considered a detour to grab a few sandwiches for later, but decided to head in. Maybe Cheryl had the yearbooks out where she could get a good look now...

There was no such luck. Cheryl had the stack of yearbooks on a side table, Amelia could clearly see them from the front door as Cheryl greeted her and bestowed a metallic cardboard crown on her head.

"Welcome back! As a new attendee, you have to wear this."

"Seriously?"

"Yes. Once everyone is here, we'll walk you through the initiation rites."

"Umm."

"Relax, it's all good fun, but we have to know how you fit in, right?"

"Sure. Right."

Cheryl turned to the ten or so people in the room. "Everyone, this is Amelia. Obviously, she's new, but you know the rules — no discussion until we've done the initiation."

Amelia waved weakly to the room. This was bringing bad flashbacks from high school. A surge of disappointment flooded her stomach. Maybe, like soul mates, there was no such thing as a good book club. And nobody had offered her a drink. People stood around with glasses and they all had name tags with weird little symbols on them. She turned to Cheryl to ask where the drinks were — a little bit of alcohol might make this whole thing more palatable, but there was a sudden influx of new people at the door.

The door closed again, and Cheryl bounced into the center of the room. Her t-shirt tonight said *Don't tell my mother I wrote that.* "Right, everybody. Let's get started so Amelia here can have a drink. She looks like she needs one."

There were giggles and laughter. Amelia stood to one side of the room, fighting the need to fidget. Five more minutes and then she'd make a decision. Then her eye caught the yearbooks. No, she needed to see this through until she could get her hands on them.

Cheryl called out, "Layla? Can you bring in the round one books?

Tom, can you grab the table from the hallway?"

Amelia turned, surprised that there was a man in this group, but actually now that she was paying attention she spotted at least three or four. Did they all read romance? Or were they here in support of significant others?

Tom turned out to be a guy in his thirties who looked like he spent a lot of time at the gym. He carried in a small table, much wider than it was deep, and set it in the middle of the room. Then a young woman came in with a stack of paperbacks that she arranged carefully in five stacks on the table.

"Right, thank you, guys. Amelia, on the table, are five stacks of romances arranged by heat level. Your first assignment is to pick your preferred stack. But be careful because this will influence several things yet to come." More giggling erupted from the group, but it was friendly for the most part.

Amelia took a minute to scan the crowd, looking to see if there was anyone here she recognized, there wasn't, and if there seemed to be any kind of cult agenda, no again. She walked slowly to the table and looked at the books from left to right. These were old paperbacks, dog-eared like they'd spent a lifetime being picked over at a thrift shop. She rolled her eyes when she saw an old Barbara Cartland in the first stack, along with an early Amish romance and a few others that she didn't recognize but could quickly tell were mild, sappy romances. She set them back on the table and moved on.

The next stack was also old but had a little more um, activity in the ones she'd already read. She was starting to get the idea here. She headed straight to the far right stack and flipped through those. She hadn't read these, and she didn't want to. There was some stifled laughter, and she set them back with a thump. Like Goldilocks, the next stack was exactly right. She'd read all but one and she was mentally making a note of the one outstanding author when Cheryl called out, "Is that your stack, Amelia?"

"I think so yes, I've read most of these. They're pretty old though."

"Yeah well, it's hard to do this with e-books so we make do. Sylvia, can you bring Amelia the appropriate drink?"

Another woman with dark hair and glasses smiled mischievously and headed into the kitchen. She came back a moment later and handed over a margarita. Amelia took a cautious sip and coughed, "Good heavens. What drink goes with that stack?" She pointed to the far right, the ones that were a little too over the top for her. "Goldschlager" someone called out. Well, that was fitting, the drink was too much for her too. "And that one?" She pointed to the ultra-clean romance. "Shirley Temple." Someone else stepped forward and pointed the rest out, "strawberry daiquiri, and then a mojito."

Huh, well once she got over the bite, it was a pretty good margarita.

"Greg, the clipboard, please."

One of the other three men left the room and came back with an old-fashioned brown clipboard. There were several sheets of paper affixed. Cheryl brought over a chair and set it in front of the table and then cleared the paperbacks off of it.

"Amelia, you might want to sit down for this part. On the clipboard is a list of books from your chosen stack heat level. Your assignment is to check off all the ones you've read and then mark with a plus any that you enjoyed and would read again." She handed Amelia a ballpoint pen. Amelia sat down cautiously, aware that everyone's focus was still on her. She looked at the list. How the heck did she know if she'd read Her Hawaiian Cowboy if she couldn't see the cover? "This would be easier with pictures," she commented.

"I know, right?" A woman called out cheerfully.

Amelia dutifully read through the list, checking things off as she went. There were about five pages in total and she'd read at least half of them, or at least she thought she had. Only a handful stood out as ones she'd thoroughly enjoyed, so those were easier to mark off as instructed.

She set the pen down and took a big swallow of her drink. "Done." She called out.

"Excellent!" Cheryl bounced over again, taking the clipboard and handing it over to a tall, thin woman with auburn hair. "Willy, would you do the calculations?" The woman nodded and took the clipboard over to a chair in the corner and took out a pencil. Amelia had a horrible feeling that she'd just taken a test without noticing. Had she passed?

Trays with nibbles started to be passed around. Amelia eagerly loaded up with crackers and cheese, she hadn't had anything to eat in a while and this was not a time to be getting tipsy. As it was, she had to remember she was driving home so she wouldn't be finishing that margarita. She was briefly sad at the thought. She glanced over at the woman named Willy. She was still busily marking and tabulating. What the heck was she doing?

Then Cheryl went over to her and they put their heads together, whispering. Cheryl stepped back with a laugh. "Okay Amelia, last part. I had no idea you were so well-read." Willy snort laughed and then called out, "Ina, looks like you're up this time."

"Excellent! I never get to do this part." A short but busty young woman came forward with several piercings in various parts of her face that Amelia hadn't been aware could be pierced. Her blue eyes were bright and friendly despite her grunge t-shirt predicting the end of the world five years ago. Maybe it was supposed to be ironic.

"Okay, Amelia, Ina here has similar taste and reading volume as you do." Amelia eyed the younger woman with new respect. "This last part is a drinking game and you can have pictures with this one. Each of you will load up a romance book you've read. If the other person hasn't read it, they take a drink. If they have you take a drink. If you hold up the same book at the same time, everyone else has to take a drink. Any questions?"

"Um, well, I did drive here."

"Sarah will drive you home. She lives about two blocks from you, okay Sarah?" Another middle-aged woman nodded with a friendly smile.

"Anything else? Can I borrow those yearbooks before I forget?"

"Yes, take them home with you. Ready?"

"I guess."

"Alright then, you have ten seconds to find a book and then I'll call out one, two, three. On three, show your phone to your opponent. If you're not ready, you forfeit the round. The winner after ten rounds gets a ten-dollar gift card."

Ina hooted, "I got this!"

Amelia wasn't sure if it was the alcohol or the friendly trash-talking, but she was starting to have fun. And she was winning after three rounds. But then Ina got the better of her with His Alien Embrace. Narrowing her eyes, she went for some of the more esoteric things she'd read in the genre, but surprisingly, Ina had read them too.

More than a little tipsy at this point, she pulled the last one up that she'd read only last week. It was about an alien dragon shifter who joined the NFL. Surely Ina hadn't read this one. When they showed their screens, they both fell back laughing. They'd both selected it. Everyone else cheerfully took a sip of their drinks. Cheryl came forward and announced, "It's officially a tie. Amelia that means as the new person you get the gift card."

"No, give it to Ina. She's earned it." Amelia knew her prize was really finding out that this book club felt like one she couldn't wait to come back to.

"Thanks!" Ina smiled, the remaining liquid splashing in her glass as she raised her hand high.

"Do you need a ride, too?" Amelia wasn't so far gone that she didn't recognize the signs in someone else.

"Naw, I live downstairs. Pretty sure I can make it." Ina's smile was broad.

The group broke up into smaller conversations then, more like a cocktail party than a club meeting. Amelia found herself the center of male attention for the first time in, well, forever. The four men that were there it turned out were all single or at least temporarily available as one or two of them alluded to the island dating rotation. Perhaps it was the alcohol, but she wasn't as curt with them as she would be normally. Sober, she'd have pointed out that they were in need of better haircuts. Tipsy Amelia asked if they'd grown up on the island. None of them had.

Chapter 18

ॐ

The next morning Amelia groggily opened her eyes to bright sunshine and the sound of a dog barking insistently nearby. She groaned and closed her eyes again. Her head was full of stuffing instead of brain cells. A wet nose poked into her palm, which with the rest of her arm was hanging over the side of the bed. "Ugh, Sadie, what is it?"

Sadie barked again sharply.

Amelia was pretty sure she knew what that meant. Carefully she rolled up into a sitting position, bracing herself gingerly. She glanced at her phone on the bedside table. Almost nine, no wonder Sadie needed to go out. "Sorry Sadie, I'm coming."

As soon as her legs hit the ground, Sadie went running down the stairs. Amelia followed slowly, shuffling and groaning, wishing there was someone present to offer some sympathy. That made her think of Gus. And that made her blush. Until, as she opened the back door for the dog, she realized that Gus was much more likely to look amused with a pinch of superiority. He wasn't the type to offer sympathy, ever. She made coffee to ward off all those feelings of inadequacy. Then she went and found the stack of yearbooks that thankfully she'd remembered to bring back with her last night. She set them on the small dining room table with a loud thump. She was going to have to figure out how to get back to retrieve her car at some point today. But for now, she could answer some of the questions that had been buzzing around in her head for the last few days.

She pulled her largest mug down from the cupboard and filled it with the extra strong coffee (French Roast, of course). She plopped down on a chair at the small table that fit neatly in the kitchen side of the open-plan space.

Amelia organized the yearbooks by date, with the oldest on top, and grabbed the first off the stack. Leafing through it, she was momentarily distracted by the crazy hair and outfits, intentionally blocking her brain from remembering what she'd worn for pictures in high school. Then she refocused on the task at hand.

She quickly eliminated the first two years as a quick check of the index showed nothing under Kline and a flip through the pages showed only a handful of Donna's that weren't the one in question. She found Donna and Laura in the next one as incoming freshmen. Donna had an eighties blowout that had Amelia sitting back in her chair with amazement. It barely fit in the two-inch school photo. Laura's photo was much more subdued, a short bob framed cheeks still chubby with baby fat. Her smile was shy but seemed genuine.

Amelia flipped through the clubs and activities pages but just like her high school most of the pages were reserved for the Seniors. The freshmen were lucky to get a background shot. She found who she thought was Laura in the Math Club. God, who would sign up for that? Donna of course was on the drill team. It was difficult to see if that was more or less prestigious than the cheerleaders at this particular school.

Their sophomore year was much the same, Laura Evans looked a little more like the woman she would grow into and Donna added dramatic makeup to go with her hairdo, which she hadn't outgrown. Still no signs of Bryan or Kelan or whatever he called himself then. The third year, though, he was practically in every shot. Amelia was sure it was him because he was using the name Kelan Alderwood and he had the same distinctive widow's peak as the modern author, Kelan James.

From that page on he, Donna and Laura were all in the drama club. In every shot, his eyes were on Laura, and Donna's eyes were on him. Could she have been blackmailing him? But he wasn't even back on the island until tomorrow, at least as far as anyone knew. It grew stranger yet. Even though the drama pictures clearly showed them rehearsing for Our Town, none of the color shots of the final production showed Laura in any of them. And why did high schools keep putting that play on? Amelia pouted, remembering that she'd been turned down yet again for a speaking part when her school had done it. Which they did every four years, and she'd known all the roles by heart because of it.

It was like Laura had dropped out, and maybe she had because there was Donna and Kelan gazing into each other's eyes front and center. Hmmm. And it got weirder still, for what should have been their mutual senior year only Donna appeared at all. Amelia was so confounded she flipped through every single page randomly taking sips of her now lukewarm coffee trying to piece together what happened. There was no photo or reference to either of the other two, not even on that ultimate of loser pages, the one for *no picture available.*

Sadie came bouncing in, her good spirits restored, and inhaled the breakfast that Amelia had remembered (barely) to set down while the coffee was brewing.

Amelia contemplated her day. The first order of business was to retrieve her car and then she needed to find out why there were rumors of Laura being poisoned when clearly she was right as rain. A little pale perhaps, but that seemed to be her normal complexion. There was something in the air that was making her feel urgent about the whole thing. Perhaps it was the book signing event. If this were a movie, that would be the big moment when everything came crashing down.

Of course, this wasn't a movie and she couldn't flip to the end of the script to find out how it ends. Unless... no, she didn't have the resources to set up a sting. And it would take too long to convince the sheriff. She would have to figure this out the old-fashioned way.

Right. Time to get dressed. She took a fresh cup of coffee upstairs with her. Selecting her favorite pair of denim overalls, she paired it with a peach linen pullover and jute sandals. In the mirror, she saw a woman of the world, dressed down for the rural environment but with inescapable flair. Anyone else looking at her would see a rather adorable woman resembling one of those ceramic figurines of a cute kid with big eyes, possibly chewing on a blade of grass.

Comfortable in her ignorance, she swished downstairs and opened the front door. It was sunny and just at that temperature that indicated it was going to be a nice day, but unlikely to get warmer than she liked. Fine, then. She would take a long walk into the village and pick up her car rather than call someone to give her a ride. Her list of available candidates for that was woefully short.

Sadie blinked at her from her new favorite spot on the upholstered loveseat placed in front of the one large window near the fireplace. Amelia grabbed her purse and locked the door behind her. She hadn't bothered with looking up the best walking route to the center of the village. She simply loosely followed the streets she'd driven the last few times. Except she got distracted when a glimpse of a yew hedge clipped in the shape of a stretching cat caught her eye. Of course, she had to go take a look. And take a picture to send to her friend Darnell (maybe this plus the ghost story would convince him to come visit.) When she turned to head back, she spotted another hedge farther up the lane, but this one was clipped like a train engine, complete with a cloud of purple clematis as the 'smoke' coming out of the funnel. How cute!

It was a whole hour longer before she found herself back on a street she recognized. Luckily, she'd been working her way closer to the center of the village without knowing it. A few minutes later and she was climbing the interior staircase to Cheryl's apartment. Amelia pursed her lips with concern that her meandering had her missing Cheryl being at home. It wasn't like she'd called ahead to let her know she was coming. She knocked briefly and was almost surprised when Cheryl opened the door. Mostly because the shorter woman was wearing normal business attire. It was then that she remembered it was a workday.

"Oh, I'm sorry. I forgot you had a real job to get to."

"Yes, not all of us are real-estate barons." Cheryl's voice was wry, but her eyes were twinkling. "Relax, I'm working from home this morning. I have a bunch of video calls with other institutions and the internet connection is better here. Come in, I've got about ten minutes before the next one."

"Right, I've really only one question. Why are rumors flying around that Laura was poisoned? I saw her recently, and she looked fine."

"She is, and she was. They pumped her stomach and warned her to be careful about what she put in her tea. Then they sent her home."

"Do you know what it was?"

"Nope. Why are you so interested?"

"I'm investigating Donna's murder."

Cheryl stepped back, her mouth hanging open. "Err, why?"

"Because I can't stop worrying about it. I've got the time, sort of."

"Maybe you should leave it alone. Let the police handle it."

"I thought you didn't want police on the island, due to your lead foot and all."

"I'd survive. I did live on the mainland without going to jail for thirty-five years."

Amelia shrugged. She liked figuring these things out. And her instincts told her it was in everyone's best interest to find the killer before they struck again. "Well, thanks for clearing that up. I'm mostly here to collect my car so I'll let you get back to your meetings."

"Okay, thank you for being a good sport last night."

"Anytime, I had fun." For once she could say that sincerely. She hoped she was now eligible to be a regular at the secret special book club. But she knew asking would look desperate and not further her cause. So she waved goodbye to Cheryl and headed back down the stairs.

Chapter 19

☙

Amelia was back in her car and buckling her seatbelt when her cell phone rang insistently. She was tempted to let it go to voicemail, but curiosity won out. She was glad she'd decided to answer when she saw the sheriff's name on the caller id.

"Hiya," she called out enthusiastically, sure he would have clues to give her.

"Must you be so chipper? You're like a sugary Hallmark movie."

"Sheriff. That's just... well, it's mean."

He chuckled in a rusty sort of way, like he didn't do it very often. "Glad I found something that puts you off. Now I found your friend and even though you didn't hear it from me, what took her to the emergency room was the same thing that killed Ms. Kline. Something called aconite poisoning."

Amelia hurriedly flipped through her purse, looking for a paper and pen. "Aconite? What's that?"

"Do I strike you as someone who does a lot of gardening? Some kind of plant. That's all I know. I'm sure your assistant Google will fill in the blanks better than I can."

"Right. Anything else?"

"Nope, you figured out who done it, yet?"

She sighed heavily, "I'm close."

He snorted, "If I had a dollar for every time I've heard that."

"You'd what? Have someone stationed here?" she inquired sweetly. She was bluffing when she said, "I'll call you later today with a name."

"And what do I get if you don't?"

"Um." She was baffled. He wasn't flirting with her, was he? She was horrified at the thought. "Uh... did you have something in mind?"

"You stop investigating things you aren't trained to and stay out of trouble."

"Oh. Well, it's not going to be an issue so okay."

Dead silence met her acquiescence. There was an odd tone to his voice when he finally said, "Poor Gus." And he hung up.

Amelia stared down at her phone, wanting so badly to call him back and demand to know what he meant. And yell at him for being so condescending. Fine, the best revenge was being right. She had work to do.

She turned her head as she reversed out of the parking space. And that was the only reason she saw them. Becky and that strange-looking young man against the brick wall of the small alley that led off the market square at one corner. Becky was against the wall and the man had his arms braced on the wall over her head while he leaned down... Oh my. That was quite the kiss. The sudden honk of someone trying to pass behind her jerked Amelia's attention back to the fact that she was still in reverse. She quickly righted things, driving forward to get around the impatient driver and wondering if she should be worried or happy for Becky. She'd check into the guy more later, just to be sure. Becky hadn't had the best luck with boyfriends, she deserved a good one.

The more she considered it, the more she realized the island was a hotbed of secrets and bubbling emotions. And that made something tickle her brain. A thought that wouldn't quite form, but had her rushing into the cottage as soon as she'd turned off the engine. She grabbed the yearbooks and headed into the garden. This time she ignored her previous targets and looked at everyone else. She flipped pages frantically, going back and forth between years. Then she shut the books and sat there with her eyes closed, going back through everyone she'd met and everything she'd observed over the last few days. It all fit.

She went back into the house to find her phone. The sheriff answered on the third ring. "Conscious got the better of you, eh?"

"No." And she gave him a name. "You need to have someone here before the book event or you'll have a bigger problem on your hands."

"You sure about this?"

She laid out her logic and was met with another sigh, "Fine. I'll have someone check out what we can and we'll have someone there for the book signing. Satisfied?"

"Only if you make an arrest."

"This isn't TV, you realize that, right? It doesn't always get wrapped up with a nice neat bow."

"It should." Amelia was never satisfied with less than completeness. People gave up entirely too easily on most everything, in her opinion.

"Please tell me you're staying away from the book thing?"

"We'll see." She wasn't going to make a promise she knew she'd be breaking. Unless of course, they made an arrest first. If that happened, she wouldn't have any reason to go hear Bryan Sinclair talk about himself. He sounded like an ass, anyway. Although now that she thought about it, how was he going to explain how he, Bryan Sinclair, looked and sounded exactly like Kelan James?

Amelia pulled up the internet search bar on her phone and felt slightly disappointed when she found that the news had already been leaked. 'Kelan James Confirms Pseudonym in an Attempt to Protect Island Locals from Fame'. Yeah, right. And she had a bridge to sell. Then it occurred to her that perhaps she did have a bridge she could sell since she still hadn't seen a complete list of all her island assets.

She wanted to tell someone how she'd solved it all and get a second opinion, but she knew that would derail everything. No, she would remain home and stay away from temptation.

But then she heard a hesitant knock at the front door. She hurried to open it, wondering what more this day could possibly dump in her lap. Becky stood on the small stoop, her shoulders hunched. Amelia looked around her to see if the young man was lurking anywhere. There was no sign of him.

"Becky? Everything okay?"

Becky smiled weakly, "Not really Ms. Feelgood. I think I need your help. I hate to ask but..."

"No problem. Come in and have some tea. Sadie is also excellent at cheering people up."

"Yeah. Okay."

Becky followed her inside the cottage, and Amelia got busy putting on the kettle. Sadie came in, her tail wagging gently, and leaned against Becky for a few seconds and then went for a sloppy drink of water. Amelia put her favorite teapot down on the table and got out her pretty teacups. Just because there was drama didn't mean you couldn't use the delicate china. Becky seemed stressed enough to not fully appreciate those niceties though. "Okay, Becky. What's going on?"

"You've seen the really good-looking guy around, right?"

"The one that was kissing you a few minutes ago? Yes."

Becky blushed charmingly, "Yes, well um. He's really nice too. His name is Ivan Olafson. We were friends years ago when he came to spend the summer with his grandfather."

"The one who panned for gold."

"Yes, that's him. Anyway, Ivan came to deal with his estate and told me a lot of stuff is missing. Things that his grandfather told him were in the bank."

"Keep going." Amelia stood up to grab a notebook and pen. This seemed important.

Becky sat, not touching her tea, twisting her fingers together.

"Well, you see... the thing is..."

Amelia cleared her throat and gave Becky a friendly glare.

"See you know about Mr. Jain and his wife's medical bills, right?"

Amelia nodded.

"What you probably don't know is my aunt has had a crush on Mr. Jain for years. She'd never act on it, of course, but she loves to love him from afar. It's been killing her that not only did his wife die but he's being buried in bills."

"Okay, but what does that have to do with the gold in the bank?"

"My aunt works at the bank. And Mr. Jain told me yesterday that a surprise donation had been made of two hundred thousand dollars, which paid off more than half his debts."

"Oh. And you're worried your aunt did something to acquire the money nefariously?"

"If that means what I think it means, then yes. But I don't know for sure. If the police get wind of it, they will cart her away without really checking into it. She's been the only person in the bank since Ms. Kline left on vacation."

"That's your aunt?"

Becky nodded miserably. "And if she did do it, then wouldn't it be better if she turned herself in, where she could make more of a case for at least not doing it for herself?"

"Um, maybe. I'm not really an expert on that kind of thing, Becky. Does Ivan have a list of what he's sure is missing?"

The younger woman nodded and pulled a folded piece of notebook paper from her back pocket.

Amelia unfolded it and scanned the contents. Mostly it was a list of very particular nuggets with names like *Claim Catcher* and *Butterfly Wing*, but there were meticulous weights and measures next to each. The old man might have been crazy, but he had excellent attention to detail.

"Right. I think this one might be best for me and Sadie to handle. Where will you be this evening?"

"I'm working at the pub tonight. I'm trying to save up enough money to move to California with Ivan. He's offered to pay for me but well, I'd prefer to be in charge of my own life."

"Good for you. I'll come find you there when I have something, okay?"

"Okay. Thanks, Ms. Feelgood."

Amelia continued to sit at the table sipping her tea. To think that the woman at the bank might have been embezzling to help her secret, unrequited love interest. And everyone had thought it was Donna. Such a mess.

"Sadie, you ready? We should take care of this before the bank closes for the weekend. Time is of the essence." Amelia didn't feel at all silly uttering this phrase. She thought it made her sound rather like an Agatha Christie heroine. The sort that would live at Mariposa and whip down the mountain in her silver roadster while wearing an elegant cloche hat.

Sadie had to bark to bring her out of this delightful fantasy. With a sigh, she headed out the front door to her silver Subaru, hatless.

The two of them waited in the bank parking lot until they were the only car left and then headed into the bank.

The same teller greeted them. "Sadie, love!" And then frowned towards Amelia, "Back so soon? I'm afraid I don't know anything new about a manager."

"That's okay. I'm not here about that. I just wanted you to know the police will be here sometime tomorrow."

The woman blanched but recovered her composure. "What does that have to do with me?"

"I'm not sure. But if you were to let them know of any, um, irregular activities at the bank first, before they find them for themselves, well, I'm sure they would appreciate the assistance." Amelia gave her a stern frown in return. "If you can help, you'll find them in the village at lunchtime."

"I don't know anything about irregularities here. And if there were any, I'm sure I'd know about it."

"Exactly." Amelia smiled and turned to leave.

"Wait. What kind of irregularities are you talking about? Is Mr. Richards complaining about his IRA taxes again?"

"I'm sure I don't know. Ask for Sheriff Harrison."

And she left her heart slightly in her throat. Of course, she'd wanted to lay the whole thing out and give a dramatic 'Ah-ha!' but it wouldn't serve. Not this time.

Chapter 20

❧

Despite the feeling of looming drama, Amelia's visit inside the bank took less than three minutes. Her adrenalin was high when she exited the old barn, but there was no viable option to burn it off. Which meant she had quite a bit of time to kill before it wouldn't be suspicious for her to be seen talking to Becky at the pub. And even though she was confident she knew the identity of Donna's killer, she decided she might as well use the sudden opening in her schedule to go do some surveillance in the bookstore.

Sheriff Harrison had not let her in on his plans as to when and where he would make an arrest or even if he would so Amelia felt obligated to check out the potential scene. If she was correct about her suspect, unchecked, the individual would be going after the annoying author sometime tomorrow.

She drove back into the center of the village and found a parking space a few blocks away from her destination. She was looking forward to a slightly less frenetic schedule, one where she could wander in and out of shops without a care in the world, including having the time to walk in from her cottage.

She checked out her surroundings as she meandered from her parking spot towards the bookstore. How had she missed that there was a European shoe store here? Everything in the window had that look of highly engineered Bohemian footwear, not much on flair but with a certain unkempt style. The price tags made her eyes water. And they certainly looked more comfortable to wear walking on cobblestones than anything she'd seen in the city. She pulled herself away from the bonanza of shoes and walked the ten paces to her intended destination.

The door of the bookstore opened with a delicate tinkle of miniature brass bells. Amelia breathed in deep and took in her surroundings. There were a handful of people sprinkled around the store, but none of them seemed particularly related to current events under investigation. The back of the main room was already set up for the book signing tomorrow. Stacks of glossy hardbacks sat on a modest table along with a small podium and a microphone. Someone had dug out the old yearbooks and enlarged several of the photos. Amelia noticed that both Donna and Laura had been cropped out of them. She supposed it would have been crass to have included Donna, given her recent demise, but why not leave Laura in? Unless everyone knew?

The small wooden tables at the ends of the book racks had been cleared to make more room for the folding chairs that were set up in a fan shape. Unfortunately, from what Amelia could see, practically every spot where someone could stand in the store would have a clear shot at whoever was presiding at the podium. Presuming, of course, that the place wasn't so crowded that people were standing in the aisles.

She strolled through the romance section, not intentionally shopping, just in case anyone was watching her. There was nothing that caught her eye, so finally, with a quick scan to confirm her original observations, she left and headed towards the pub.

The restaurant and bar area were busy, but it was still early so there were plenty of tables open. For the first time in her life, Amelia approached the antique oak bar and awkwardly sidled onto the barstool next to the blond god from California. Without turning her head, she said to him, "Hi. I'm Amelia. Becky asked me to help her with your problem."

He grunted. That made her turn towards him. He was looking

at her from the corner of his eye while stuffing his face with french fries. She glared. "I don't speak grunt. You'll have to do better."

"Don't know you. Don't want to. Mind your own business."

Just then Becky came over and placed a menu in front of Amelia. Soon enough that she must have heard that last part because she got in the guy's face. "Ivan! If you're going to be rude to people, we're done. I don't put up with that kind of attitude from anyone."

He looked chastened and his expression fell, Amelia noticed how young he really was. He turned towards her. "Sorry."

"Apology accepted. Becky? I talked to your aunt. I don't know what she's going to do, but I let her know the police will be in town tomorrow and things might go better if she initiated a conversation. I guess if she doesn't I can give the sheriff the details you gave me and he'll follow up when he gets a chance."

Becky nodded and frowned slightly. "I hope she does the right thing. It's not too late to get most of people's stuff back to them. Mr. Jain will be okay, she's got to see that."

In Amelia's experience, people rarely got that. They had too much fun getting caught up in the drama of it all. But perhaps things were different here. Anything was possible.

She decided she didn't like sitting at the bar. It was too hard to see who came in and who was talking to whom. "Becky, I'm going to move to a table. Can you bring me an extra-large fish and chips with a hard cider?"

"Of course, Ms. Feelgood. Pick any spot and I'll bring that right out."

"Thank you." She swiveled on the barstool and hopped down. It was easier getting off the darn thing. Her favorite spot in the corner behind the door was free. She hurried over there before anyone else could grab it and sank into the seat with a sigh of satisfaction. Everything was settling out the way it should. She hoped.

⁂

The fish and chips arrived at her table, hot and crispy. Amelia had to remind herself that she was not on vacation and she needed to stop eating like she was. Perhaps next week, when this little matter of Donna's murder was resolved, she could head over to the mainland and do some serious long-term grocery shopping. Buy vegetables and other not-deep fried things. Not that the cottage had very much storage space.

As she ate, she casually observed the small dramas in the pub. Over against the wall was a young couple clearly in the midst of a drawn-out fight and not willing to share it with the rest of the world. Which is why they kept glaring at each other and not speaking. In the middle of the room at a larger table, there was a passel of kids being encouraged to eat their vegetables. Amelia couldn't help but wonder if there had ever been a scientific study to find out what actually happened if you grew up without eating them. Experimenting on young children was probably frowned on.

She finished up, wiping her greasy fingers on one of the paper napkins, and went up front to pay her check. She was oddly at loose ends. Nothing to do now really except wait for tomorrow. That didn't sit well with her. She did still have quite a bit to figure out with her property business, but none of it was the sort of thing you could do on a Friday evening.

She was almost to the door when it opened sharply, like someone angry had pushed it violently. A couple stepped into the pub. It was Dana and a man Amelia hadn't met. Was this her husband? He seemed to be angry. Dana was exuding righteous indignation. Similar, but not quite the same thing. Amelia slowed her steps as she passed them, hoping for a chance to eavesdrop.

"Why did you have to do that where people could see you?" The man said between gritted teeth.

"Because we live on a frickin' island, that's why. Everyone can see everything all the time. Including when you spend the night with your so-called best friends. We all know it's not poker you're playing at."

The veins in the man's neck were standing out. If Dana's mouth got any tighter, she wouldn't be able to talk. Amelia sped up. She did not want to get caught up in this conversation. She was starting to see that island relationships existed in more of a fishbowl than on the mainland. Or at least that's how the locals perceived it and acted accordingly.

The cottage was a welcome sight when she drove up and parked in front of it. Until she went to unlock the door and discovered a second letter folded over and taped to it. This one was slightly more ominous. *Stay away from the bookstore.* Amelia frowned and slipped it into the envelope on the mantle with the other letter. That reminded her that she owed Melanie Hardwick an exclusive as soon as the police made an arrest. Even though she was sure this would be her last investigation and she didn't need to maintain that relationship, it was better to not forget. Sadie came in to see what was happening, her nails clicking lightly on the floor. Amelia fixed the dog her dinner and then sat down with a heavy sigh in the cozy living room area with her phone to try and read something light and entertaining. She was ready for tomorrow to be over with.

Chapter 21

Saturday dawned cold and rainy. Sadie kept going to the door, but as soon as Amelia opened it, she changed her mind and went back to the living room. This happened at least three times before Amelia gave up and left the door open. While it wasn't warm, the house was pretty much the same temperature as the outside, so leaving the door wide while Sadie decided when to brave the rain seemed like the easiest option. A double pot of coffee was called for in Amelia's opinion to deal with this kind of day.

The sheriff still had not called her to say when they would be arriving. Something told Amelia that he wasn't going to. But she needed to be there when everything went down. On the other hand, if she were seen hanging around too much, the murderer might get spooked and stay away. The police were so finicky about things like evidence, it would probably be better if the suspect were caught in the act of attempted murder instead of circumstantial evidence. She probably should be more concerned for the fate of Kelan James than she was, but after everything she'd heard and read, *almost* being killed seemed like what he deserved. Actually dead was taking it too far, of course.

She intentionally dressed so as not to call attention to herself. It seemed in the best interest of self-preservation not to make herself an easy target. It was hard to put on the natural linen skirt and black top without accenting it with something bright. It went against every single one of her instincts. But she gritted her teeth and even left off the jewelry. When she moved back downstairs, it was to discover that Sadie had finally braved the rain and was now curled up in the armchair in front of the unlit fireplace.

Amelia locked the house up and headed out to her car, giving it a careful inspection just to make sure nobody had left any notes or flattened one of her tires. Everything *looked* normal. She drove into the village slowly but parked several streets away so as not to get caught in something unpleasant, at least not in a way that she couldn't leave when she wanted to. As she walked towards the bookstore, she had that eerie tingling between her shoulder blades that someone was watching. She casually stopped to look in the window of one of the many knitting shops so she could check the reflection. There wasn't anyone obvious behind her. She kept walking, trying to keep one eye on her mirrored image as she passed the various shop windows.

Along the side of the village square, she noticed a hodgepodge of cars that weren't parked evenly in the marked spots. Equally unusual, a group of people were on the corner talking. One was waving her arms around rather excitedly. Amelia headed in that direction. Until she recognized the hapless bank teller and stopped. Was this the police? They looked an awful lot like tourists. Or had the bank teller gotten confused as well and was now confessing her sins to bored suburbanites?

Edging around the crowd, Amelia tried to get a better look at the strangers. The men did have awfully short haircuts, and the women were certainly more fit than most of the tourists that found their way to Findlater. She kept angling her head, trying to look at faces to see if she could spot the sheriff when one of them froze, his gaze steady on her. He said something to one of his colleagues, who began walking towards her. Oh crap.

When the man got within a few feet of her, Amelia led with a basic "Hello."

"Can I help you with something? You seemed to be, um, trying to catch someone's attention."

"Oh no, not exactly. Is the sheriff around?"

The man's eyes narrowed, "How do you know the sheriff?"

"I'm Amelia Feelgood, I met him a few weeks ago."

The man shut his eyes as if hoping she would disappear, but she calmly waited. When he opened them again, his lips stretched thin. "Ma'am, we can handle this. It would be better for all concerned if you returned home."

"Why?"

"Why what?" He seemed astonished that she would question his request.

"Why would it be better for all concerned? Do you even know who you're looking for?"

"Ma'am."

"Oh, don't ma'am me. I'm not that old. And I have a fair idea of what's about to transpire, and I don't want any of you to muck it up."

He sighed, "Well, try to stay out of the way." And he turned and went back to the group. The bank teller appeared to be running out of steam, and Amelia wondered exactly what she'd confessed to. That could wait for now, though. She sidled towards the bookstore. She wanted to get into position before the majority of people arrived.

❧

The bookstore was already more crowded than usual, but by no means packed. Amelia wandered around the sales tables at the front and then edged up towards the middle, keeping an eye out for who was here. She spotted a few familiar faces. And there stood Dana in a close conversation with whom she could only presume was Kelan James. He was shorter than she expected, and his hair was too long for someone with a crowning bald spot. But everything about him proclaimed 'author'. He wore one of those trite tweed jackets with the leather buttons and elbow patches and had expensive glasses that looked more designed to give an impression of intelligence rather than improve eyesight.

He stood in such a way that everyone could see his face and yet would be discouraged from approaching. His attention was theoretically on Dana, who was doing an excellent imitation of flirting, but Amelia noticed his gaze flicking around the room as if keeping tabs on how full the seats were. She disliked him immensely.

Taking up her pre-selected position by the end of the steamy romance aisle, she pretended to browse the paperbacks. For a brief moment, she did get distracted when she discovered a new book by an author she hadn't read in a while. Amelia took out her phone to make a note of it, and that's when the noise out on the street caught her attention.

She turned to look out the big main window and saw Laura's husband, Stan, being led away by two men in bright Hawaiian shirts. Laura trailed after Stan, wringing her hands. A fourth man in a dark t-shirt walked a few paces behind her.

Amelia's gasp seemed to draw the attention of the entire bookstore. And suddenly the front of the store was flooded with people trying to get a glimpse of what was going on outside. *Darn it*! Amelia cursed herself for limiting her own view of proceedings. She turned to head to the back of the crowd so she could go around to the exit. Kelan James stood where he'd been, his jaw hanging loose as he watched his fans disengage and abandon him. Amelia noticed his expression smoothed into haughtiness when he made eye contact with her. She looked away and hurried out to the sidewalk.

The same nameless man she's talked to earlier was holding eager bystanders at bay. Stan stood handcuffed with his hands behind his back while a man frisked him briskly. Amelia winced in sympathy because late middle age was not an ideal stage in life to experience that for the first time, and his face indicated this was definitely a new thing. Laura was still talking, pointing towards Stan and then back towards the bookstore. If she saw Amelia, she ignored her.

The woman Laura was talking to nodded and then opened the back seat of another car, gesturing for Laura to get inside. From where Amelia stood it looked like, but she couldn't be sure, that the car had one of those security dividers like a patrol vehicle. Laura continued to stand, gesturing towards Stan again, but the woman shook her head. Defeated, Laura got in the car, and the woman shut the door.

Amelia had had enough. She took out her phone and dialed.

"We've made an arrest, what do you want now?" A tired voice answered the phone.

"And hello to you too. I can see you've made an arrest. I'm standing right here. What I want to know is why didn't you wait until he tried something. I told you..."

"Funny thing, Ms. Feelgood, but confessions beat attempted crimes as evidence every single time. And that's all I'm going to say on the subject."

"Oh," she gasped, "Couldn't you...?"

"No!" He hung up on her. She stared at her phone as if it had malfunctioned, ignoring the smirk from the unnamed officer. Looking up, she scanned the crowd for anyone that might have seen more. She saw some dark corkscrew curls in between a couple of shoulders and pushed her way in that direction. She'd been right. "Cheryl!" she called out as she came upon the short woman.

"Oh my god, did you see? I seriously had no idea Stan had it in him."

"I was in the bookstore. What happened?"

"Laura dragged him over to those men and basically shoved him at them. I'm assuming those are undercover police of some sort. Guess I'd better be careful driving home." She half-smiled.

"Did you hear anything?"

"Just Laura saying he'd killed Donna and was planning on killing Kelan James. Do you suppose he's a serial killer?"

"No. That sounds much more like revenge. But that's not exactly the right word. I think he was trying to protect Laura."

"But why? I mean, I understand why he would want to protect his wife, but how was she in any danger?"

"Laura is the girl in the Endless Night."

"No! That's it, we have got to have a special book club session for this. It's too big to wait."

Amelia looked down at her new friend amused, "Which book club? One of them is running out of members."

Cheryl rolled her eyes, "Exactly. I think it's time to disband that one."

They stood on the sidewalk with the rest of the gawkers as the huddle of cars pulled away from the green and headed towards the dock.

"How are they going to get on the ferry when it's already come for the week this morning?"

"They can get the next one from San Juan to swing by. Pisses those folks off, but the cops don't care." Cheryl shrugged. "Hey, want to grab lunch?"

"Ooh, yes, let's. I'm thrilled I don't have to listen to Kelan James after all." They both glanced back towards the bookstore, which had a steady stream of people leaving. They couldn't all have been there to watch an arrest, surely?

They headed towards the pub and managed to get the last table before the line started to form in the doorway. Everyone seemed to be trying to overhear everyone else, which led to a lot of disjointed, unfocused conversations, so eventually, Amelia started talking about the new book she'd seen in the bookstore. Cheryl told her about a few more that were coming out in a few days, and they basically ignored all the prior events of the day.

Chapter 22

❧

Amelia didn't drive immediately home, she wasn't sure why but she felt restless. Perhaps because the big shocking reveal had turned into more of a fizzle. It was a letdown even if it was safer, and from what little the sheriff had said likely to work out better in court.

To rid herself of some of that excess energy, she drove through town and towards the inn. Part of her brain kept thinking about going down to the ferry dock to see if the 'extra' boat had appeared to collect its cargo. But she got distracted when she recognized one of the cars in the inn's guest lot.

She'd noticed it in the village because it had a bumper sticker declaring stupidity to be a criminal offense. It wasn't that she didn't agree with the sentiment, but it seemed unwise to put it on your car where it was likely to encourage shopping carts and other denting objects to gravitate. In any event, she was positive she'd seen it in the village just a few hours before, and now it was parked at the inn. *Not* in the line for the ferry.

She debated for a brief second before pulling into the lot and parking on the opposite side. She would just run in and have a quick chat with whoever was at the desk. Of course, that turned out to be nobody. She waited for several minutes and then considered her options. It was still early in the afternoon, so perhaps everyone was busy with housekeeping. She might just do a quick wander through and see if Becky or Mr. Jain (she really needed to find out his first name) were about.

Upstairs, she found Becky and the smirking cop in a conversation on the landing. The cop was neither smirking nor smiling at the present moment. He was frowning and rather glaring if Amelia were to attempt to describe his facial expression. Becky was wringing her fingers and looking nervous.

"Everything okay here?" Amelia inquired cheerfully.

Relief washed over Becky's face. "You tell him, Ms. Feelgood, please? That I wasn't withholding evidence?"

"I can't imagine you knew what Stan Appleton had planned. How could you?"

"No, not that. My aunt." She went back to twisting her fingers.

"What is your name, by the way? I can't keep calling you smirking cop. Well, I could, but something tells me you'll take offense."

The man did rather puff up at that. "I'm Detective Ford. That's all you really need to know." He turned back towards Becky.

"Well Detective Ford, you're on my property talking to one of my employees so no, that's not all I need to know. And FYI, Becky came to me regarding her suspicions of her aunt a few days ago. I would like to emphasize suspicions, which is not at all the same thing as evidence. I don't believe there are any laws regarding withholding speculation. In general, I find the police tend to encourage it."

He growled. Both Amelia and Becky jumped slightly, then watched as he turned and entered one of the rooms.

"He's staying here?"

"Yes, they have to do an investigation at the bank. I don't think he's happy about it." Becky bit her lip. "Do I need to get a lawyer? Are they really expensive?"

"Not yet, but remember you don't have to say anything, so don't let him intimidate you. If it gets bad, I have a friend I can call, just let me know. Actually, keep me posted on what this guy gets up to period."

"Okay, thanks Ms. Feelgood."

Becky returned to setting up the empty rooms, making sure housekeeping was complete before the afternoon rush of new guests. Amelia turned and headed back downstairs. Unless she harassed Detective Ford, which he did not seem at all amenable to, there wasn't too much more she could do here. And she still felt a little restless.

Ugh. Then she remembered she owed Melanie her exclusive. She wouldn't put it past that woman to have ties with the mob. Based on some of her leaked information, Amelia was almost sure of it. And she liked her kneecaps in their current slightly square shape.

She drove back to the cottage. She wanted to take some pictures of the notes, so she had something to offer up since the main arrest was rather a letdown. And she supposed she still had a few questions that needed answering, like how Stan had managed to poison Donna in the first place. She perked up at the thought that there was still something interesting to investigate.

❦

Back at the cottage, Amelia quickly took a couple of photos of the threatening letters and then called Melanie back.

"You're late," was how the sweetheart of Channel 6 answered the phone.

"Not really, I was talking to a detective only fifteen minutes ago." Okay, it was about something else entirely, but Melanie didn't need to know that.

"And do you have something the newswires don't have because right now I'm not smelling any kind of story."

"Yes, I do. Here I'm sending them to your email now." She attached and sent the photos and hoped this was enough to end the conversation.

"Amateur hour, save me," Melanie muttered on the other end. "Feelgood, these notes are by two different people. You know that, right?"

"Um, no? How can you tell?"

"Block letters have a handwriting style too. These are different."

"Hmm, okay. Interesting. Well, really, this is all I have. The police have taken Stan to the mainland, so there's not much else going on here."

"I'd better not catch you talking to any other reporters."

"Don't threaten me. Besides, as you said, the newswires already have it."

Melanie hung up on her without another word. Amelia slowly put the threatening letters back on the mantle, while trying to decide if that had gone well or not. It was getting late and she and Sadie should really be getting ready for bed. But something was still bothering her. She felt confident that the police had the person who had committed the crime, but there was still something keeping the entire case from folding up neatly.

On a whim, she dialed Cheryl. "Where does Laura live?" she asked as soon as the other woman picked up.

"And hello to you too," Cheryl responded cheerfully. "She lives off one of the long driveways between the village and Mariposa. The one with the yellow flower basket on top of the mailbox stand. Sorry I don't know the actual address."

"That's okay. I was just curious. Thought I might check up on her tomorrow. She must be a wreck."

"Hmm, Laura's a lot tougher than she looks."

"Really? Well, thanks. Goodnight."

And that was that. Amelia already knew she was going to drive into the woods tonight, but she tried to talk herself out of it for about five minutes while she changed her clothes and made sure her phone was fully charged. Not that she would have waited if it wasn't but she would have grabbed the charger to use in the car. Sadie shadowed her ankles, so Amelia realized she would have a partner on this trip.

They both went out the front door, Amelia remembered to leave a light on this time, and got in the car. Silence descended as she drove through the village. Sadie curled up on the passenger seat, her front paws and long nose hanging off the edge of the upholstery. The village was winding down for the evening a little later than normal, but then there had been quite a bit to talk about and hopefully overhear. But apparently, nobody was feeling like being out after dark. Except Amelia. Even though it was still dusk in the open square of the green, the overhanging trees made it fully dark when she drove into the forest. Quite frankly, it was creepy.

Out of instinct, she glanced down Gus's driveway and almost slammed on the breaks when she saw a car parked there. She avoided the embarrassment of going into the ditch (barely) but her eyes narrowed when she spied a now-familiar bumper sticker. She would stop in on her way back, she promised herself.

Amelia was starting to get worried that she wouldn't be able to see the yellow planter in the narrow beam of light provided by the car's headlights. Finally, about two miles past the Three Bears Cottage, she spotted it. The flowers looked a little limp and sad, but the marker was clear. She turned into the driveway and slowed to a crawl as she tried to see what lay ahead. It was a very long driveway. But eventually, a single story rather boring looking box of a house came into view. The flashing blue glow of a TV shown through the curtains drawn over the big front window. Good, that must mean that not only had Laura not gone to the mainland with the police, but she was still up.

A light flicked on right after Amelia parked the car. Sadie followed Amelia out the driver's door, apparently not taking any chances on being left in the car. They both walked to the front door and Amelia knocked. She heard the sound on the TV go down and then nothing. So she knocked again. Light footsteps approached, and then the door opened cautiously.

"Amelia? What on earth are you doing here?"

"I had a few questions and couldn't sleep. I thought you might be open to satisfying my curiosity."

Laura frowned, "I guess, I honestly don't have anything to hide. Do you want a cup of tea?"

"Um, no thanks." Amelia tried not to sound nasty about it, but she was not imbibing anything that came out of this house. Laura must have known what track her mind was taking because her lips quirked. "Guess I'm safe from potluck duty for a while, huh?"

Amelia followed her into the kitchen and took a seat at the round table covered with an apple decorated vinyl tablecloth. Everything in sight was clean, homey, and not terribly chic, but it all matched Laura in a rather charming way.

Laura made herself a mug of tea, adding an extremely generous splash of bourbon, and sat down opposite. "Okay, what's so hot on your mind?"

"How did Stan do it?"

"You mean Donna?" Laura sighed.

"Yes."

"He told me he only wanted to make her sick so she wouldn't do the interview. I'm not sure if that's true or if it's what he needed to tell himself. He found a list of poisonous plants on the internet and then figured out our nearest neighbor had some of them growing in her yard, so he helped himself. Then he swapped out the contents of a tea bag and dropped it in Donna's purse the last time book club met here. She was rabid about only using her brand of tea bags, which is why she always carried them with her.

I'm surprised she didn't notice the difference, but maybe she was distracted? I don't know. Obviously, she didn't consume it while she was here."

"Then how did you get sick?"

Laura grimaced. "Stan made a practice tea bag and neglected to get rid of it. Lucky for me it didn't have much contents. It's because he felt so guilty about that that I was able to convince him to confess."

"You still love him, don't you?" Amelia was perhaps more shocked by this than any of the other events.

Laura smiled tightly, taking another sip of her tea before answering, "I do. He may have been misguided, but what he did, he did to protect me, not for his own ends. Donna was a cow, always was even in high school. And as for that vicious half-brother of mine, well... the best revenge is watching his career implode, which it most certainly will after this."

"You don't think this will make everyone buy the book?"

Laura shrugged, "Don't know, don't care, but he's been exposed as the manipulative little turd that he is. The mystique is cracking."

Remembering the short, balding man left to his own devices as the crowd spilled onto the sidewalk, Amelia had to agree.

"So what now? I take it that means you're going to wait for Stan."

"Of course, I don't need to be anywhere. This island knows Stan, they won't have a problem with him coming back here when he's released. And in the meantime, I thought I'd finally read War and Peace." A small genuine smile flashed across her face and Amelia saw a glimmer of the girl from the yearbook photo, the one before Kelan James crashed into her life.

"Well, thank you. That clears a lot up."

"It does?" Laura looked surprised but didn't argue the point further.

Amelia nodded and stood, "Sadie? Wake up." The dog groaned but got to her feet and thwapped her tail gently before following Amelia to the front door.

"Good night, Laura."

"Night." Laura shut the door and Amelia watched all the lights go out as she carefully made her way over the uneven ground to her car. It was now after ten. Did she dare stop at Gus's? She decided there was no point when she saw the headlights of a car pulling out of his driveway and turn towards the village. Naturally, she followed.

It struck her as odd that Detective Ford made the turn to Schinn's Landing instead of continuing towards the inn, but she was too tired to follow him. She'd thought about asking Laura about the notes left at her place, but decided it didn't really matter. She strongly suspected that Stan had written one and Laura the other, trying to minimize the fallout of Stan's murderous inclinations.

There didn't seem to be anything else there for the police to pursue.

Chapter 23

❦

The next morning Amelia couldn't help herself and headed into the village to have breakfast at the pub. She almost always had an appetite, but what she was really going for was the gossip. And like anyone in a small town actively seeking it out, she had to wait for quite a while before anything of interest came up.

She was halfway through a very generous platter of French toast when a group just coming in the front door scanning for an open table started talking about seeing a woman being handcuffed in the bank parking lot. Amelia's ears perked up, and she looked around to see if Becky was working today. There was no sign of the younger woman. Suddenly she felt full and ready to head out, despite the ten bites or so still left on her plate. She hurried up to the counter and paid without ever having received her check, appending the tip to the total, and rushed out the door. Sadie was waiting in the passenger seat of her car. Amelia almost but not quite made the tires squeal as she reversed out of the angled parking space.

The bank parking lot looked like any other bank parking lot in the country on a Sunday morning. Empty with a few broken beer bottles left on the curb as if to bear witness to a previously higher level of excitement. The bank was dark and locked, as one would expect. Amelia wasn't surprised, but she'd felt the need to check it off. She got back in the car and headed for Ravenswood Inn.

She breathed a slight sigh of relief when she saw Detective Ford's car still in the small lot. She bustled into the lobby, Sadie at her heels, and paused with her jaw dropped at the scene. The bank teller, now forever Becky's aunt in her mind, was standing by the oak desk. Tears were streaming down onto her beige knit dress (the kind middle-aged women frequently wear to church). Her hands handcuffed in shiny steel bracelets in front of her. Becky stood behind the reception desk wringing her hands while Mr. Jain lay stretched out on the floor, apparently unconscious.

"What happened?" Amelia gasped. The aunt sobbed louder, but Becky looked relieved. "Mr. Jain fainted. He seemed... embarrassed when he learned what Aunt Penny did."

Amelia hurried over to the prostrate man and checked the pulse point on his neck with two middle fingers. She didn't really know what she was doing, but it was somehow instinctive after hundreds of hours of watching cop shows on TV. He had a pulse. She could confirm that much.

"He wasn't supposed to find out!" The aunt sobbed. "Alvin can't take any more emotional strain."

Oh, dear. His first name was Alvin? Amelia tried unsuccessfully to erase that knowledge from her brain. At least now she knew why everyone referred to him as Mr. Jain.

"Where's Detective Ford?"

"Right here." He was practically growling behind her. Amelia turned and watched him walk over to the aunt and unfasten the handcuffs.

"What on earth are you doing?" Amelia asked him with exasperation.

"Your boyfriend just called. Something's come up. Ms. Lightfingers here will have to wait for a day or two for her free trip to the mainland."

"I don't have a boyfriend." Amelia inserted indignantly. She was both mildly offended and pleased that anyone thought she did, but more than a little put out that something was going on that she didn't know about. On her island.

Detective Ford just snorted and turned towards the lobby door. "Ms. Wallace? You're to stay here at the hotel. I'll be back to pick you up as soon as possible. You are not to leave the premises. Do you understand?"

The woman just sobbed louder but nodded her head. Mr. Jain emitted a small groan from his location on the lobby carpet. Amelia looked a question at Becky who shrugged in response but finally said, "I can handle this. I'll put Aunt Penny in the room downstairs you were using."

Amelia nodded and followed Detective Ford out the door. She didn't want to let him out of her sight. Not surprisingly, despite her best efforts to tail his car as he drove into the village, he lost her in the twisty turns behind a Roman bathhouse.

Amelia had to acknowledge that he was a worthy opponent, and that she hadn't noticed that there was an Italian section, or at least she assumed it was Italian, in the village. But then Mr. Evans had said he was relocating the 'European' experience, so it made sense in an odd sort of way.

She drove slowly through the streets, trying to keep the sun at her rear until she found herself back in familiar territory. It was time to check in at Gus's place again, find out if Detective Ford had left any clues there, then she would see if what she could find out from her growing network of sources.

She wasn't completely sure who the detective had been referring to her as her boyfriend. Had he meant Gus or the Sheriff or someone else entirely? There were no signs of life, no cars, or other evidence of occupation at Gus's place. And she was reluctant to move within sight of his numerous tiny cameras without a seriously good excuse. So that meant she only paused the car in the road and rolled down the window to get a better view of his yard.

Then she had the brilliant idea to drive up to Mariposa. Cheryl's graduate students would arrive there in a day or two, but at the moment it should be empty. It annoyed her that she didn't have a key considering she owned it. But even without entering the house, there was a commanding view of much of the island from the back gardens. Perhaps she'd be able to catch a glimpse of whatever had Detective Ford in such a tizzy.

Her car barely made it up the big hill. The way it was gasping and coughing when she parked in front of the flamboyant mansion reminded her of her own lungs when she'd climbed all those stairs to the attic with Cheryl.

Amelia scooted around the side of the house to the back garden and looked down over the stone parapet. She couldn't see much from this distance, but there appeared to be ten or so people gathered on a small sheltered beach about a quarter of the way around the island clockwise from the village. Huh. She would go check it out tomorrow after breakfast when her appearance on the beach wouldn't look quite so much like stalking if anyone was still lingering from whatever this was. She could finish unpacking in the meantime, just in case she had any unexpected visitors to the cottage.

Satisfied with this plan, she got in her car, patted the dash, and headed back down the mountain.

Chapter 24

Amelia sat on her sunny front stoop, absently rubbing Sadie's ears as the dog panted slightly, a wide smile on her canine face. It was done. The arrogant and irritating Kelan James had left the island, most likely never to return. Laura had appeared in public to issue a brief statement to the media, seemingly tragically relieved by everything. Her secrets were now universal knowledge, but she had realized she was stronger for not holding them in. Or at least that's what Laura told the press. Amelia was beginning to wonder if maybe Kelan James's skill with words had a genetic component. Perhaps Laura was the next Grandma Moses of the literary world.

Meanwhile, Stan was being held without bail on the mainland but in a private psychiatric hospital. Given some of the rumors that were swirling about his diagnosis, Amelia was hoping his return to the island wasn't imminent, even if Laura did still love him.

Her phone rang and Amelia glanced down at the caller ID before sending it to voicemail. Channel 6 was harassing her again. Somewhere in there, they'd decided that the murder was not nearly as interesting as the middle-aged property mogul who solved crimes in her spare time. They wanted to do an hour-long exposé on Amelia. She'd stopped taking their calls. Two murders did not a career make, and she was planning to enjoy the rest of the summer roaming the beach and getting her business affairs cleared up.

Cheryl had called late yesterday after she got back from her brief trip to Mariposa to say that Amelia was definitely a permanent member of the secret book club. And that the not-so-secret book club was taking a hiatus for several months due to general bad feelings about Donna, Laura, and Tolstoy. Amelia was relieved she didn't have to find an excuse to avoid it. On the other hand, the new book club meeting was still three weeks away, and she needed something to occupy her time. Moving to France was getting pushed further and further out. She wasn't going to abandon a thoroughly satisfactory book club without cause.

Sadie stretched out at her feet with a groan and twisted just enough to expose her tummy for rubbing. Amelia took the hint, enjoying the sensation of soft fur sliding through her fingers. Her phone rang with an unfamiliar ring tone from the spot where she'd stashed it on the doorjamb. She leaned back to pick it up with a frown. There was no caller ID. She answered it with a hesitant, "Hello?"

"Amelia, I'm warning you, stay away from the beach for at least the next week." The call ended abruptly. Amelia stood up with a newfound urgency. The voice on phone had belonged to Gus and if he was ordering her off something that meant it was interesting and she needed to find out what was going down immediately. She paused suddenly, or was he trying to lure her to the shore so that she wouldn't encounter the real case on another part of the island? She would just have to go ask him because clearly, Gus was back.

Thank you for reading!

If you enjoyed this story, would you consider taking a few minutes to leave a review? It doesn't have to be long to be effective!

☙❧

Beth McElla writes cozy mysteries under the majestic evergreens of the Pacific Northwest.

You can find her on Facebook, Goodreads, Amazon, and Bookbub

Printed in Great Britain
by Amazon

61820504R00092